The Poetics and Politics of Tuareg Aging

T0374602

Susan J. Rasmussen

The Poetics and Politics of Tuareg Aging

Life Course and Personal Destiny in Niger

NORTHERN

ILLINOIS

UNIVERSITY

PRESS

DEKALB

2009

Published by the Northern Illinois University Press,

DeKalb, Illinois 60115

Manufactured in the United States using acid-free paper ∞

Design by Julia Fauci

First printing in paperback 2009

Library of Congress Cataloging-in-Publication Data

Rasmussen, Susan J., 1949–

The poetics and politics of Tuareg aging : life course and

personal destiny in Niger / Susan J. Rasmussen.

    p.   cm.

Includes bibliographical references and index.

ISBN 0-87580-220-6 (alk. paper)

1. Aged, Tuareg—Social conditions. 2. Aged, Tuareg—

Kinship. 3. Aged, Tuareg—Rites and ceremonies. 4.

Aging—Anthropological aspects—Niger—Agadez (Dept.) 5.

Intergenerational relations—Niger—Agadez (Dept.) 6. Rites

and ceremonies—Niger—Agadez (Dept.) 7. Agadez (Niger :

Dept.)—Social life and customs.

I. Title.

DT547.45.T83R38   1997   96-43794

305.89'3306626—dc20   CIP

Map on p. 2 was adapted from Map 6.1 in *The Berbers* by

Michael Brett and Elizabeth Fentress. Used with permission

of Blackwell Publishers.

Contents

Preface

Aging at the Crossroads of Ethnographic Knowledge

As I returned home from a late-night festival following a wedding among the Tuareg, a socially stratified, Islamic, and seminomadic people in northern Niger, I ruefully joked to Hawa, a woman friend of the smith social stratum, "I am tired, an old woman now." As I collapsed onto a mat on the sandy floor of her tent, she replied that I was not: "In order to be an old woman, you must have children, and these children must soon marry." Hawa herself had only recently attained motherhood, after five years of marriage. This was a much anticipated event, somewhat late by local standards. She and her husband, Ado, although in their twenties and apparently healthy, had remained childless for five years after their marriage. On several occasions, Hawa and other childless women had expressed anxiety about this to me, inquiring if there were medicines in America that promoted fertility. They expressed incredulity when I replied that yes, there were, but there were also medicines that prevented pregnancy, and both types were eagerly sought after by Americans. Ado inquired about "operations" he vaguely knew of that, likewise, promoted fertility: he was probably referring to artificial insemination.

Throughout the Tuareg life course, there is relatively free social interaction between men and women, and women of all ages enjoy high social prestige and economic independence. Although Islam allows up to four wives, and some men contract polygynous marriages in late life, most women oppose this, and many couples remain monogamous. Husbands do not automatically divorce their wives in cases of infertility or upon menopause. There is recognition that male sterility, as well as female infertility, may be responsible for childlessness. Although women participate in roles beyond motherhood and the domestic domain, childbearing is nonetheless important. Men and women friends often expressed concern about my own childlessness, advising me to seek religious amulets from Islamic scholars. They asked me if I was not worried about lack of assistance with livestock herds (one of several tasks rural Tuareg children perform), more general support in old age, and who would receive an inheritance from me. During my field visits after my own marriage, women who were friendliest toward me tended to occupy a social role culturally defined as similar to my own: that of a married but still childless woman. They asked me many questions about my mother, sisters, and nephews. Tuareg children are valued for household contributions not solely during childhood but also past youth and after their own marriage. In rural areas, the ideal throughout the life course is to remain near one's parents—in particular, daughters attempt to reside near mothers and sisters, even after marriage.

As individuals age and progress through the household cycle, ideally there is a place for everyone. In principle, youths defer to and care for aged persons. But there is a corollary to this: it is as in-laws that elders receive the most respect and economic security. In addition, men and women derive more respect from increasing their devotion to Islam once their children are married. These features of growing older—affinal and ritual roles—were most emphasized to me by many Tuareg friends and field assistants, during conversations concerning age.

On another occasion, as I prepared to attend a baby's nameday, I asked Tina, a recently married but childless noble woman, if she too was leaving for this event. She laughed and said, "Only old people go to morning nameday rituals. I'll go later, to the festival in the evening." Tina was probably about fifteen. Exact chronological age is uncertain in rural areas due to lack of hospital birth records, but it is possible to estimate relative age in many cases, since most girls of noble origin tend to marry shortly before or after menarche. This pattern is encouraged by efforts to preserve precolonial concepts of noble purity of descent and to preserve a cultural autonomy that is threatened by ecological disaster, economic uncertainty, and political conflict.[1] Life is precarious and highly valued. Formerly, mothers attempted to hasten daughters' puberty and fertility through such means as ritual force-feeding. Today, the birth of the first child remains a very special occasion, its nameday more elaborate than that held for subsequent children. The maternal grandmother and other older female relatives play key roles in certain phases of this ritual: at sundown on the sixth evening after the child's birth and before the official Islamic nameday early in the morning on the seventh day after the child's birth. Youths, for their part, are encouraged to attend later, in the afternoon and evening when dances and songs are held. While older persons are not technically forbidden to attend these latter events, they gradually withdraw from them with increasing age and as more and more children marry.

In many respects, Tuareg cultural elaborations of age conform to observations about power, personal destiny, notions of personal agency, and reproductive symbolism over the life course that are widespread in African rituals and cosmologies (Fortes 1959, 1987; Bird and Karp 1987; Arens and Karp 1989; Herbert 1993). On the surface, they also suggest ideas of linear progression from youth to death, in which the aged occupy intermediary status (Fortes 1959, 1987) and appear to confirm standard "disengagement" theories of retreat from some areas of activity and participation in others (Cumming and Henry 1961), with the related concept of gender role inversions in late life

(Myerhoff 1978, 1992; Gutmann 1987:97). But rigid, dichotomous theories
of disengagement and activity, as well as Western essentialist and linear perspectives, become problematic when applied to the Tuareg.[2]

In the present analysis, I follow a number of anthropologists who raise
questions about conventional approaches to aging, the life course, and the
ethnographic representation of culture and who recognize that in cross-cultural perspectives of the life course, "age," "aging," and other related terms
require quotation marks (LeVine 1978, 1980a, 1980b; Keith and Kertzer
1984; Rubinstein 1990; Spencer 1990). I benefit from, and hopefully contribute to, efforts toward deconstructing standard age-related categories and
toward exploring the relationship of age to other crosscutting influences, such
as gender, social stratum, and kinship (Gutmann 1987; Di Leonardo 1990;
Katz and Monk 1993).

In this book, I explore processes of growing older among the Kel Ewey confederation of Tuareg in Niger, as a system of local meanings and as a critical
reflection on encounters with the outside world. I focus upon the connection
between the public and personal sides of experience, notably the way pub-
lic/collective boundaries and categories articulate changing personal/private
identity and relationships, not solely in "old age," but throughout the life
course. Specifically, I examine public participation in performance and ritual,
private power and agency, and transformation of self over time in Kel Ewey
society. I analyze these ethnographic processes through the lens of wider theories on poetics in social life (Bachelard 1964; Aristotle ed. D. W. Lukes 1968;
Herzfeld 1985; Cowan 1990) and problems of expression and representation
in ethnography (Rabinow 1977; Clifford and Marcus 1986; Rosaldo 1989;
Blacking 1990; Myerhoff 1992; Crapanzano 1992). I utilize this framework in
order to detach aging from essentialist, literal, and linear portrayals prevalent
in some conventional Western popular and academic formulations. I connect
this framework to broader concerns in the current anthropological literature:
namely, finding an alternative to circular arguments over essentialist and
deconstructionist approaches to culturally contingent categories and finding
an experience in the researcher's own life in order to understand local associations. The researcher arrives at his/her own position in the field by combining
the past and present of his/her own life with the social life of the field (Rosaldo
1989:4–8; Blacking 1990:121–30). In routine interpretive procedure, according to the methodology of hermeneutics, ethnographers reposition themselves
as they go about understanding other cultures.

This key concept, that of the "positioned (and repositioned) subject," raises
important issues for life course research. At no point can people say they have
completed their learning or their life experience. In portraying the Tuareg life
course, where does the experience of the anthropologist leave off and that of
local residents begin? When and where exactly does that time and space

encompassed by "the field" end, if ever? Indeed, the making of the story, rather than the story itself as a finished product, appears particularly apt in long-term ethnographic field research.[3] My work in a community over a lengthy time period (1974–1979, 1983–1984, 1991, and 1995) entails special problems but also opens up new perspectives in this respect. In recognizing all interpretations as provisional, made by positioned subjects prepared to know certain things and not others, life course studies test and offer excellent insights into this problem of the limits of ethnography. It is therefore true that analyses are always incomplete. But in my view this predicament offers insights rather than limitations. There is continual reformulation of experience and reinterpretation of this experience during each encounter in the field, not solely by the researcher but also by local residents. These mutual reformulations, questionings, and efforts to locate and classify each other come into particularly sharp focus in long-term field research on the life course and open up new perspectives in ethnography as well as the study of age. Researcher and local residents in effect continually reposition each other, and conduct an ongoing ethnography of each other over the long term.

Thus two alternating strands of analysis form the underpinnings of the experiences I examine. I focus upon youth and age in jural transition, as well as upon festivals and rituals as modes of expressing these transitions in terms of cultural and sociopolitical constructions of the aging process. I also analyze ways these are juxtaposed against long-term relationships between residents and ethnographer.

What is particularly interesting about the Tuareg life course are cultural values that permit and discourage certain kinds of public expression by persons of specific ages. Local adults were acutely aware of, and many spoke explicitly about, these values. They not only referred to them in formal exegesis elicited by myself but also used these terms to frame their entire way of relating to me, as friend and participant-observer in their community and more broadly in the life course. Ways of growing older are connected to power relations within the local social organization and between local residents and the outside world. Thus it is useful to analyze aging as relational and processual in terms of its meanings for local residents, and in terms of how these meanings shape local views of the aging anthropologist, rather than representing it as a set of fixed essential meanings. Here I take a position similar to Di Leonardo's insights on gender (1991:30), that aging and the life course are "embedded, both as a material social institution/process and as a set of ideologies." Societal categories are culturally contingent constructions. Consequently, there is need to attend to and investigate actively the multiple layers of context through which particular cultural realities of the life course are perceived. I also follow Keith (1980, 1985) in the view that age is a salient social category but cannot be adequately studied in isolation.

The setting of this study is a rural community of Kel Ewey, a confederation of Tuareg in the Saharan Aïr Mountains of northeastern Niger near Agadez, a town historically important for Islamic scholarship and trade. Until the recent (1991–1995) rebellion against the central government by Tuareg nationalist/separatist forces, the Aïr region was also a center of thriving tourism. In rural Aïr, Kel Ewey society is characterized by official adherence to Islam; semisedentarism and mixed subsistence patterns of livestock herding, oasis gardening, and caravan trade; bilateral descent and inheritance, with strong elements of ancient matriliny; stratified, endogamous occupational groups of nobles, smiths, and former slaves, based upon descent; and high social prestige of women, who inherit livestock, own the tent, and may initiate divorce. Social interaction between the sexes occurs in casual visiting (even married women need not ask husbands' permission) and more formalized courtship during festivals.

Music and poetry are important in courtship and as a means to social mobility. Much courtship between young people takes place at mixed-sex, mixed-class festivals held late in the evening, lasting well past midnight. Elders, in particular "older" women (defined as those having children of marriageable age), are not supposed to attend these festivals. As women grow older, they acquire additional prestige from their roles as mothers-in-law and as prominent participants in rites of passage. Some older women become herbalists or diviners. As men grow older, many become specialists in professional Koranic scholarship, combining legal functions, psychiatric counseling, and other curing in rural areas. Both sexes cite devotion to religion as important in later life. One elderly woman of servile origins, a mother of two grown sons, prosperous in livestock herds, and married to a retired caravanner and tour guide, insisted that she did not miss her former renown as a player of the *anzad,* a one-stringed, bowed lute: "What use is the *anzad* to me now? As a young girl, I played it by watching the hands of other players, I practiced. But now the *anzad* is worthless to me. It is prayer that is my 'good route.' Prayer is better for an old woman. Here you will find me, at home, lying down, praying."

My interest was first drawn to the Tuareg life course, concepts of personal destiny, and aging during earlier research on female spirit possession. At that time I met a large number of individuals who indicated that they no longer attended evening festivals or musical possession exorcism rites as audience members and no longer danced, sang, or performed music because they were "now old." They asserted that they now devoted themselves to Islam. A few years later, they critically questioned from their own cultural perspective my own continuing interest in such performances as spirit possession, which they classified as a more secular event for youths, as well as my travel far from family obligations, my singleness, and later, my lack of children. In order to understand these responses, I argue that aging must be detached from its literal notion of "the aged," thereby opening up additional perspectives on the life course in different cultures, as well as the dialogical relationship between long-term anthropological field researchers and local subjects.

The subject of age has appeared in ethnographies and theoretical works, but anthropologists have only recently concentrated upon formulating a theory of aging in its own right. Most early work was done in societies where physical aging was defined in formal systems of age grade/sets; other studies were conducted in clinical, institutionalized settings. At first, many studies' primary focus tended to be epidemiological or functionalist. Many pioneering as well as more recent works (Fortes 1959, 1987; Goody 1958; Stenning 1958; Riesman 1986; Myerhoff 1978, 1992; Keith 1980, 1985; Foner 1984; Sokolovsky 1989; Spencer 1990) have made a valuable contribution by devoting greater attention to local cultural constructions of personal destiny over the life course. This makes it possible to examine aging more processually rather than as a static category with discrete boundaries.

I follow approaches to aging and the life course that emphasize, not solely the position and treatment of the aged based on positivist "behavioral facts," but the experience of age through such methods as narrative and meaning (Smelser and Erikson 1980; Manheimer 1989; Spencer 1990; Cole 1992). Also beneficial are approaches that have broadened to the advantage of the life course perspective (Keith and Kertzer 1984; LeVine 1978, 1980a, 1980b; Riesman 1986). Unclear boundaries of the life course can open up new perspectives. In this respect, the tug-of-war over paradigm and framework in age theory recalls battles in the anthropology of gender. Some scholars, for example, have argued that age is best understood subsumed beneath an umbrella of social differentiation. For example, Maybury-Lewis argues that a theory of age is "impossible except as part of a theory of society." Others have displayed concern with age in relation to structuralist "nature/culture" boundaries (Maybury-Lewis 1984). Aging studies stand, to use Di Leonardo's phrase regarding gender studies, at a "crossroads of knowledge." Thus the avenue I pursue is the interface between aging, positioned subject in ethnography and poetics in social life.

I alternate between focus upon "doing" (Herzfeld 1985)—the making of persons (including myself) of one or another age group—and conventional ethnographic methods of eliciting symbols and meaning (in particular, those surrounding procreation, fertility, marriage, and death), as well as analyzing whose interests these serve and how they come to be accepted by diverse interest groups. I resided near Mount Bagzan in the Aïr Mountains, in the nearby Saharan town of Agadez, and in the capital, Niamey, for nearly seven years between 1974 and 1995.[4] Here I emphasize data I collected in the rural Aïr communities, where I conducted most of my research. Specific techniques included participant observation, oral art collection, retaking and updating of previous household censuses, and longitudinal follow-up of earlier life histories and case studies, as well as the collection of new cases. I conducted structured and informal interviews, as well as guided conversations, with men and women in order to elicit beliefs regarding crucial life transitions and gender and class differences in experiencing these transitions. I photographed, taperecorded, translated, and transcribed rites of passage, in particular, namedays and weddings, and collected songs and tales. I studied mortuary beliefs and practices, elicited from men their experiences of face-veil wrapping and circumcision, and elicited from women their experiences of menstruation, childbirth, and post-childbearing years. I gathered case studies focusing upon property transfer and residential changes over time.

Throughout my research, I also recorded residents' attempts to locate me in their social space, expressing as much interest in my own life course as I did in theirs. Early in my residence, friends asked me why I was not married and elaborated on themes of marriage; later, upon my return as a married woman, they asked me why I did not have children and discussed parenthood. Their questions and repositioning of me highlighted the dilemma of gathering more and more knowledge but at a cost of continually outgrowing one's former status in local eyes. Hence the paradox: the more one pursues research on the meaning of the life course according to Western academic cultural anthropological standards, the more one becomes alienated from local standards of a meaningful life. In this respect, my account, while primarily an ethnography of aging and the life course for anthropologists, African Studies scholars, and graduate and advanced undergraduate students, also belongs to the broader tradition of works in ethnographic criticism that emphasize the mutuality of knowledge in the field encounter (Stoller and Olkes 1987; Gottlieb and Graham 1993) and authority (Rosaldo 1989). This is how my account is the product of residents' voices as much as my own: in their repositioning as they went about understanding me.

Relevant here are relationships over time between Kel Ewey Tuareg men and women of diverse social strata, and between local residents and myself, in the broader sense of "politics" and hegemonic perspectives. Residents express their perspectives of the waxing and waning of alternative powers through these relationships. These powers are asserted both within local society and, protectively, against threatening outside forces. Many Kel Ewey are explicit about local categories of different ritual and jural powers over the life course: they use contrasting terms, *amghar* and *wa wachere,* alternately to connote leadership, householding, and decrepitude. But these terms reflect not solely physical strength or material productivity but also alternative sources of available power (ritual as well as property based).

I argue that, although local residents articulate life course transformations in terms of kin roles and religious specialisms over time, they are based on efforts to consolidate wider social distinctions and to preserve local political autonomy—indeed, physical as well as cultural survival. For example, throughout cultural imagery there is a parent/child noble/former slave analogy. The body is not merely a natural object but a socially constructed one. Thus while this study elicits symbols and meaning surrounding procreation, fertility, marriage, and death, I also analyze whose interests these serve and how they come to be accepted by diverse interest groups. Yet in the aging process, there is a tension between natural and social forces that cannot be ignored, and many local cultural constructions address this tension. I ask who directs the performance of aging, in terms of agency and power. One set of data I analyze are activities at specified points in life that feature inversion of social convention. In rural communities, for example, smiths and former slaves in their youth are expected to lack reserve, an ideal noble attribute, but in later life they may become Islamic scholars and practice increased reserve. Men and women sometimes invert roles in certain ritual contexts. Thus there are opportunities for flexibility and transformations in this traditionally stratified system. Upon one's children's marriage, women as mothers-in-law become "like men" in their authority over daughters' new husbands during initial uxorilocal residence. Young smith and former slave women are less observant of age, gender, and class-based taboos: for example, they are more lax about observing menstrual taboos than young noblewomen. I argue that these processes do not imply rigid, overgeneralized role reversal, androgyny, or instrumental/expressive reversals in a simple fashion (Gutmann 1987; Myerhoff 1978, 1992). Rather, these processes express a gradual convergence (though not "blurring") of roles and a complementarity of interests for specific persons upon aging. They also express, in microcosm, efforts to maintain a balance between hierarchical, competing power bases and complementary, interdependent powers, both within and beyond the household. I show how, throughout the life course, gender and social stratum roles are alternately negotiated, inverted, and reinforced through symbolic condensation in age imagery, during performance contexts of rites of passage and their associated festivals, and how they parallel jural/economic/political interests. Older persons of all social strata play key roles as facilitators, thereby making these internal class and gender roles more palatable and also guarding the borders of Tuareg culture. I also show how elders and nobles as parent figures deploy younger and lower-status persons (e.g., smiths, ex-slaves, children) as buffers and mediators against the outside world (past colonialism, current central government, researchers, travelers), which is perceived as threatening, from local historical experience of Tubu raids, French and (more recent) control schemes and massacres, and current economic crises. Dialogues between the different age groups therefore also inform broader problems of identity and power in studying others. Local concepts of personal creativity and public performance at different ages reflect these processes.

Although Tuareg have no formal age set/grades or elaborate ancestor cults, the life course is marked by ritual and jural processes, in which public performance is explicitly linked to private forms of power. Access to property has to do with intergenerational as well as social stratum relationships. Kel Ewey display specified modes of conduct toward aged persons of all social strata and either sex in everyday sociability and rites of passage. There are clearly articulated beliefs about aging and proper conduct surrounding it. Many of them pertain to verbal and musical skill and performance, as well as occupational practices. Different age groups are encouraged to participate in some rituals and performances and are discouraged from participating in others. Young men and women of all social origins are encouraged to attend evening festivals following daytime rites of passage, to enjoy music on two instruments (the *tende* mortar drum and the *anzad* bowed, one-stringed lute), and to perform sung poetry and stories called *imayen* or folktales. Later in life, individuals are discouraged from pursuing these activities and are encouraged to devote themselves to religious fasting and prayer. They are to withdraw from secular music and dancing festivals where courtship takes place and to perform only Islamic liturgical music and tell legends called "history" *(idaman iru)*, which are taken more seriously than folktales. Tuareg youths are supposed to refrain from pronouncing the names of elders and deceased ancestors, particularly on the paternal side. Young persons should also refrain from asking elders questions and postpone taking up ritual/occupational roles of Koranic scholarship, herbalism, or smithing independently until they are considered to have attained aged status (i.e., their children reach marriageable age).

Thus changing styles in performance of verbal art and music, as well as contrasting ritual, political, and economic roles, characterize Kel Ewey Tuareg transitions over the life course. There is a dichotomy here, depending upon age, between ritual and festival frames of expression for individuals. This necessitates a focus on the "sacred" (Parkin 1991) as well as the "secular" and also breaks down the Western cultural opposition between the two. Rites of passage, for example, are usually held in the morning, when elders and Koranic scholars (called *marabouts*) preside over them, whereas secular festivals celebrating them follow after sundown. Young people attend these latter, which are organized to encourage free courtship and are presided over by smiths. Yet smiths, and some elders, also bridge these domains in arranging marriages and participating in both the official and unofficial shaping of personal destiny such as naming. These opposed yet intertwined domains—sacred ritual and secular festival, official descent and unofficial courtship—provide the backdrop throughout this book for exploring Tuareg aging, not in terms of linear, chronological time, but rather in terms of social space. Across this social space extend beliefs and symbolism concerning personal destiny, in the sense analyzed by Fortes (1959, 1987): the fate of the self, its jural/economic bases, and sociopolitical boundaries.

Some previous studies of aging and the life course tended to treat the economic/jural and the expressive as separate domains of experience (Fry 1981; Keith and Kertzer 1984; Foner 1984). As Keith and Kertzer observe, until recently a "mythologized" view of age was presented, in which age was superseded by more complex variables such as kinship (1984:21). The position I take in this is inspired by Fortes but with the added poststructural concerns of ethnographic reflexivity, authority, and representation: I focus upon both age and kinship, for these intersect in constructing personal destiny through time. The goal is to integrate ritual and jural domains of aging experience, as well as its structural and practical aspects. Works I draw upon to construct my own perspective include some that are not explicitly classified as "anthropology of aging" works (Fortes 1959, 1987; Goody 1958, 1962; Stenning 1958; Kopytoff 1970; Brain 1973; Jackson and Karp 1987), while others do fall into this category (Myerhoff 1978, 1992; LeVine 1978, 1980a, 1980b; Riesman 1986; Gutmann 1987; Sokolovsky 1989; Blacking 1990 in Spencer). All these works offer a mosaic of insights (intergenerational and class conflicts, domestic cycles, female/male aging, ancestor beliefs). Their common thread, changing concepts of personal agency and fate over time, provides a framework for bridging a number of domains of experience that are traditionally opposed, or at least compartmentalized, in anthropology: living elder/deceased ancestor, rite of passage/property transfer, domestic cycle/life course, and gender roles/class roles. Their approaches provide a useful lens through which to examine the Kel Ewey Tuareg life course, where personal destiny upon aging is complicated by crosscutting influences of gender, social stratum, and seminomadism, all of which, furthermore, impinge upon long-term relations in the field between an aging anthropologist and residents. This encourages, indeed requires, balanced humanities and social science approaches. Age relations also need to be analyzed as a variable distinct from one's position in other networks, for example, the domestic group, but nonetheless a part of it. Kel Ewey Tuareg society provides a unique backdrop for this task, for individuals alternately retreat from and participate in wider roles, based upon social stratum affiliation in a rural client-patron system still vital in some contexts, albeit with modifications from recent political and economic changes. There is much free social interaction between the sexes, though this freedom occurs within each age group and between men and women in specified kinship relationships rather than generally between all men and women. Standard ethnographic portrayals tend to mention Tuareg aging only in piecemeal fashion. Nicolaisen (1963), Keenan (1976), Bernus (1981), Casajus (1987), Dayak (1992), Claudot-Hawad (1993), and Spittler (1993) focus primarily upon ecology, religion, kinship, descent, and politics, giving only passing mention to the life course in asides and afterthoughts.[5] Hopefully, this book fills a need to forge a link between Tuareg ethnography, aging theory, and reflexivity in anthropology.

Preparation, Background, and Techniques of the Study

My methodology for this study reflected the dual focus of this book. In order to illuminate the poetics dimensions of the life course, I concentrated upon ritual and symbolic analysis, the collection and transcription of oral art forms (in particular, songs, folktales, and historical legends), and the gathering of life histories and narratives. In order to illuminate more political aspects of the life course, in terms of power struggles within Kel Ewey society and conflict between the Kel Ewey and outsiders, I concentrated upon local notions of personal dependency and independence as these change over time and vary across context (in particular, the interweaving of age typifications with those of social stratum and gender) and also upon cultural encounters with external forces of domination. These latter are relevant here, I argue, because the cultural elaboration of age plays an important role in confrontation with the outside world beyond the household and even the community. I collected data on property transfer from census and genealogical data. I utilized a variety of field methods over several intervals of my field research. I kept a diary reflecting upon residents' perceptions of my own role, including specific questions and comments they directed to me. Preliminary informal research, including study of Tamacheq and Hausa languages, was carried out in 1976–1978 in Agadez and the Aïr Mountains during my residence as a Peace Corps volunteer and later in Niamey as a local contractor for the Ministry of Education, when I taught English. Later phases of residence involved more structured anthropological research. I focused intensively upon female spirit possession in 1983, the life course in 1991, and most recently upon female herbalist and diviner specialists and health care in 1995. For assistance in these endeavors, I am grateful to the following sources: Wenner-Gren Anthropological Foundation, Social Science Research Council, National Geographic Society, Fulbright Hays, Indiana University, and University of Houston. Throughout these projects, some of my techniques were continuations of longitudinal research based upon my 1983–1984 study of female spirit possession and upon my earlier preliminary residence.

Significantly, in all these projects I encountered local concepts of aging and the life course regardless of my official purpose there. In fact, rather than my seeking and collecting aging data, these data in effect came to me; for in Niger, residents continually related to me on the basis of my status, in their eyes, resulting from age-related factors: single/married and childlessness/motherhood were the most salient markers. This pattern provided insights into the practice of life course research as well as the topic itself, for this topic is perhaps more important to local residents than to outside visitors from the West, many of whom disparage age, considering it to be a "depressing" topic (Myerhoff 1978). In this respect, aging and the life course offer ways to circumvent the problem of what is termed the "panopticon" (Said 1979a, 1979b; Foucault 1980) in the anthropological gaze and to develop more fully the mutuality of the field encounter (Stoller and Olkes 1987; Gottlieb and Graham 1993).

It would be impossible in this space to thank all those local residents, friends, and assistants who made this study possible, in particular recently, under extremely arduous economic and political conditions: a drought in the early 1980s just following my field research on female spirit possession; an epidemic just before my most recent (1995) visit; the recent armed conflict, beginning in the early 1990s between Tuareg separatists in parts of the North and the central state government; and current uncertainties since the 1995 pact between rebels and government. Here I wish to express my gratitude for the kind assistance, hospitality, and suggestions of a number of persons in Niger: Monsieur le Directeur de l'IRSH (l'Institut des recherches en sciences humaines) and Alitinine ag Arias, transcriber and language instructor at the Centre de la Tradition Orale in Niamey; Saidi Umba, smith/artisan in Agadez; and many others in oases and camps of the rural Aïr region, including Ibrahim Ihossey; Mme. Salma; Mohammed Akhmoudou; his wife Awa; Mme. Chabo Dila; her parents, her sisters, and her husband Ama; Malam Mounkaila; and many others who offered valuable encouragement. In France, I also received valuable suggestions from Professors André Bourgeot and Dominique Casajus. In the United States, I am grateful for the intellectual inspiration and encouragement from Dr. Michael Herzfeld during the 1990 National Endowment for the Humanities Summer Seminar and from Dr. Ivan Karp and Dr. Mary Jo Arnoldi at the Smithsonian Institution.

In organization, the book alternates between two interrelated and complementary perspectives: (1) so-called objective data and the forms of knowledge this yielded; and (2) local residents' assessments and repositioning of myself relative to the time period of our encounter as this coincided with different phases of our life course. Since I wish to avoid imposing Western cultural notions of literal, linear, and chronological age upon local notions, I do not organize the book in these terms. For example, I intentionally avoid ordering chapters in linear, "birth/marriage/death" sequence; rather, they are organized topically and conceptually. I also alternate back and forth between more conventional data analysis (of ritual, symbolism, inheritance, and other relevant processes) and intersubjective, reflexive passages. Key "informants," assistants, and their narratives are presented approximately in order of their openness and familiarity to me, on the basis of when we established mutual trust. All personal names are pseudonyms, in order to protect privacy.

First, between this section and the main body of the book, is an interlude consisting of a brief ethnographic introduction. Here I provide general historical, social, economic, and political background on the Kel Ewey Tuareg in order to orient the reader. This section neither replaces nor duplicates the ethnographic material expanded and elaborated upon in various relevant discussions in the text following it, for the latter are interesting in that their enlightenment occurs in patches, just as it does in the field. The idea here is that, combined with the cases, vignettes, and commentary on actual experiences in the field interwoven throughout the book, they help make the reader also the fieldworker. Following the brief background section is part one. In part one, through two narratives, I begin to explore cultural notions of aging through performance, ritual (in particular, marriage, the most central focus of the life course among Tuareg), and symbolism, as these are connected to the developmental cycle of domestic groups. In part two, I continue this analysis but focus more intently upon the interplay between poetics and politics: symbolism and power, including the idea of discourse about aging as an idiom for resistance and autonomy and as a marker for boundaries of self and other in Kel Ewey Tuareg society.

In part three, I explore local notions of personal destiny, that is, concepts of fate in regard to the self as this is connected to others: in particular, parent-child and youth-elder-ancestor relationships, in terms of local authority roles and their implications for ethnographic authority. I include here additional cases and narratives. This leads into the conclusion, in which I discuss the implications of my different types of data and emphases for issues in the construction of the knowledge about age and ethnographic authority.

Throughout my field research, I collected oral traditions on local history from elders who were willing to relate them (Rasmussen 1993, 1996). Initially, these were a means to other goals: studying female spirit possession, aging, the life course, and herbalist/diviner healing specialists. But early in my residence, I was faced with a problem: the cultural patterning of aging that makes speech about certain topics inappropriate with youths and discourages younger persons from asking direct questions of elders. Thus I became interested in methodology and reflexivity, collecting data on public performances of life course rituals (the poetics or ritual/symbolic aspects of aging), life stories, and other oral data, in terms of my own intersubjective encounters as an outsider—but also student and friend—in the mutuality of the field encounter. Collecting oral traditions on local history and origins underlined the need not solely to present and analyze how Tuareg men and women live and experience their lives, given the conditions that differentiate their situations from ours, but also to include their reactions to me at different stages of my life and their attempts to make sense of me in their own terms. Studying Tuareg ethnography and ethnohistory therefore led me to include myself in my ethnography as a kind of anomaly whom local residents seek to decipher, but not as a form of narcissistic anthropology or "navel gazing." Rather, I hope that from this perspective, a deeper understanding is gained of sources of pride and shame for Tuareg men and women over their life course, of how they cope with physical decline and economic uncertainty, and of how conditions varying from one person to another (as well as from one social stratum to another) tend to diversify this experience and give some meaning to metaphors used to conceptualize aging. In this account, therefore, the anthropologist is and is not a part of the society where she works. She is part of society in the sense that she establishes many friendships, and, moreover, she is part of the phenomenon being studied: the universal process of aging and the life course. She is an outsider in the sense that she is, by local standards, unconventional for her age. Thus my predicament, in delving into the ethnographic background of the Kel Ewey Tuareg, encouraged more critical reflexivity on subjects' and anthropologist's experiences as part of knowledge production.

The Poetics and
Politics of
Tuareg Aging

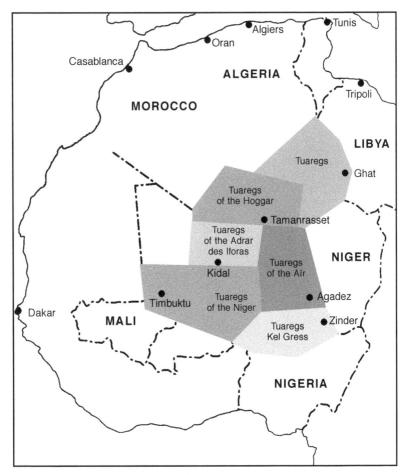

Principal Tuareg Groups

Introduction
The Kel Ewey Tuareg Ethnographic Background

Tuareg, who speak a Berber language, Tamacheq, and its regional dialects, live in the contemporary nation-states of Niger, Mali, Algeria, Libya, and Burkina Faso. They are Islamic, and their social organization is characterized by stratified noble, tributary, smith, and formerly servile groups. Many Tuareg confederations (precolonial political categories with traditional leaders) have practiced intensive pastoral nomadism. Most people in the Kel Ewey confederation tend to be seminomadic, living in small hamlet-villages and practicing mixed subsistence patterns of livestock herding, oasis gardening, and caravan trading.

The Kel Ewey Tuareg predominate in and around the Bagzan Massif of the Department of Aïr, named for the major mountain range in this region, of northeastern Niger Republic. Their stratified, officially endogamous occupational groups remain significant in local ideology, although slavery has been abolished and client-patron relationships are breaking down. There is now less coincidence between prestigious descent and socioeconomic status. Some intermarriage occurs between persons of noble origin *(imajeghen)* and descendants of slaves. (These latter are popularly called "Buzu" throughout contemporary Niger. Local terms once expressed finer distinctions: *iklan* denoted livestock herding and domestic slaves, and *ighawalen* denoted tenant gardeners.) Smiths *(inaden)* remain the most closely endogamous of the social categories. In recent years, particularly in the towns, there has been increasing identification from broader bases, beyond kin and class affiliation. For example, leaders of Berber nationalist and Tuareg cultural revitalization movements appeal for unity on the basis of the Tamacheq language and tend to deemphasize precolonial social stratum differences. Since the 1984 drought and the 1991–1995 rebellion, followed by the peace pact in April 1995, there have proliferated organizations devoted to teaching Tifinagh, the Tamacheq script, and to refining and reformulating Tuareg cultural identity and autonomy. These include Temoust ("identity"), Timidrayat (an association of former Tuareg slaves), and Amana (a political party denoting "trust"). Confederations are acquiring new importance as political fronts in current nationalism. As of this writing, it is difficult to predict future trends, particularly since the military coup d'etat in January 1996.

These broader bases of identity have not, however, replaced precolonial kinship and social stratum identities; rather, they provide an additional over-lay or leitmotif for them. Although descent tends to become subsumed beneath broader concerns of cultural autonomy in urban areas, by contrast, in the countryside, the primary setting of this study, descent remains salient. Individuals appeal to this for prestige purposes, for example, in evaluating moral values and personal conduct.

Most Kel Ewey combine subsistence patterns. In rural areas, men conduct caravan trading expeditions east to Bilma to obtain salt and dates, and south to Nigeria to trade these for millet, household items, and other consumer goods. Many men also practice oasis irrigation gardening, as well as camel and goat herding, and (nowadays) migrant labor in Nigeria, Algeria, Libya, and occasionally, France. Some are refugees and exiles who have fled recent drought, famines, and massacres.[1] But caravanning, gardening, and herding persist despite the recent turbulence in the region. Both sexes and all social strata inherit, own, and raise livestock, but noble men tend to own and herd more camels, and women in general tend to own and herd more goats, sheep, and donkeys. Smiths remain more specialized in their work. In the country-side, they continue to manufacture jewelry, household tools, and weapons; sing praise-songs at noble weddings; recite genealogies and oral history; and serve as ritual specialists and political go-betweens for their noble patron fam-ilies.[2] In the towns, smiths are active in the tourist trade.

The Kel Ewey descent and inheritance system, like other Aïr confedera-tions, is predominantly bilateral, with its ancient vestiges of matriliny sub-sumed beneath patriliny introduced by Islam.[3] Yet Tuareg women's generally high social prestige and economic independence is subject to some variation and change among the different confederations, in nomadic and sedentarized communities, and in groups where Islamic scholars exert strong influence.[4]

Islam entered Tuareg culture from the west and spread into Aïr with the migration of Sufi mystics in the seventh century; various traditions credit Sidi Okba, Ibn Yacin, and an Almoravid marabout as proselytizers (Norris 1972, 1975). The local belief system, with its own cosmology and ritual, interweaves and overlaps with official Islam rather than standing in opposition to it. Tuareg initially resisted Islam and earned a reputation among North African Arabs for being lax about Islamic practices. In the Middle Ages, the Arab Moslem trav-elers Ibn Battuta (1843) and al-Idrisi (cited in Norris 1975:33) criticized Tuareg for not washing, not praying regularly, not giving alms, and above all, not properly restricting women. Moreover, local tradition did not require female chastity before marriage. Kel Ewey tend to practice official Islam more devoutly than some other Tuareg groups. In the Bagzan region, there are numerous maraboutique or *ineslemen* clans of Islamic scholars who treat cases of mental illness, supervise inheritance and, with elders on village councils, rule in local divorces and other legal cases. Despite considerable freedom of social interaction between the sexes among Kel Ewey, female chastity is becoming more important, in particular among marabout families and in clans who claim descent from the Prophet. However, women are not secluded or veiled; in fact, among Tuareg, men wear the face-veil. In Tuareg Islamic observances, men are more consistent about saying all the prescribed prayers. Men also employ more Arabic loan words, where women tend to use Tamacheq terms. Women increase their participation in official Islamic, as well as pre-Islamic, rituals upon attaining a status culturally defined as aged or elderly. Although women of childbearing age are not technically forbidden to become marabouts, they tend to cease studying the Koran after they marry. Yet religious activity and professional specialization are more dependent upon age than gender. For example, younger men also observe certain restrictions: they likewise are discouraged from the professional practice of Islamic scholarship and marabout healing until they are older. Furthermore, healing careers that many older women pursue combine Koranic and non-Koranic methods in herbalism and divination. Thus both men and women tend to excel in healing careers—men as marabouts, women as herbalists—in later life. This is part of the more generalized increase in religious devotion upon reaching the status culturally defined as elderly, thereby breaking down rigid gender dichotomies, including theories of generalized role reversal, even in aging. These practices, as shown, were what initially drew my attention to the topic of the life course and aging among the Kel Ewey Tuareg.

Due to culturally patterned restrictions of verbal expression based upon age, Kel Ewey Tuareg oral traditions were revealed to me only gradually over the course of many return visits and residences. Oral and written sources on the Aïr Tuareg have been analyzed by Rodd (1926), Nicolaisen (1963), and Bernus (1981), but not reflexively in terms of interaction between the researcher and the tellers of the histories. Thus these authors report that information about early migrations is "scanty," consisting primarily of rock inscriptions, and later, records in Arabic, often designed to establish the noble origin of various clans. However, these authors account for the paucity of sources, not by reference to Tuareg cultural values constraining communication between the different age groups and social strata, but rather by reference to historical events. Many of these materials were lost when the area north of the central Aïr massifs was plundered by French patrols after the 1917 Tuareg Senoussi Revolt led by Kaousan.[5] The policy of the French administrators was to remove the population from Aïr and resettle them in the lands to the south (then known as Damagarem and Sudan, Hausa regions around Zinder, Sokoto, Kano, and Katsina). Depopulation of the Aïr region caused the desert to encroach: wells fell in, oasis gardens receded, and livestock herds were decimated, making it more difficult to reopen the caravan trade routes. Many older people living near Mount Bagzan during my earlier 1983 field residence had been born on Mount Bagzan, had spent their youth in Hausaland, and had returned to the region of their birth. Many settled in caravanning and oasis villages at the base of Mount Bagzan as young adults, when the region began to be repopulated and caravan trade, wells, and gardens again revived. Many of their memories of these events evoked painful experiences. Therefore a combination of factors—historical events, cultural values, and intersubjective positioning of outside researcher(s) and local residents—are involved in reconstructing ethnographic/ethnohistorical knowledge of this area.

It is primarily oral histories and the Agadez Chronicle, various Arabic manuscripts in the care of the Sultan of Aïr in Agadez, that survive. Details of early Tuareg migrations are beyond the scope of this book. I shall summarize here briefly only those features of history and traditional political organization that give a notion of contemporary characteristics that are widespread in the region and specific to Kel Ewey. For further discussion, I refer the reader to Barth (1857), Jean (1909), Rodd (1926), Norris (1972, 1975), and Bernus (1981). Most source materials, despite conflicting views of early origins and migrations of the Kel Ewey and their relationship to other Aïr groups, agree on the existence, at an early date, of a people called the Goberawa, an aristocratic division of Hausa-speaking people throughout North Africa, and a people called Sanhaja in the west. Both these groups were in the region now called Aïr before the arrival of the first Tuareg groups. Barth and Rodd maintain that the Goberawa were later either driven back into the Sudan or became servile groups of the invaders, incorporated into Aïr Tuareg groups as tributary *(imghad)* groups.[6]

Nicolaisen (1963:411) suggests that the first Tuareg to come to Aïr were caravan traders attracted by the region's grazing grounds. Tuareg are believed to have entered the Aïr region in three successive waves (Rodd 1926:373–380). The first was an invasion of Aïr taking place from the southeast, around Lake Chad, from Kanem and Bornu at the end of the eleventh century; these invaders had cultural ties to the Fezzan. The second wave was that of the Kel Geres from the north. The third wave was that of the Kel Ewey, between the latter half of the sixteenth and the first half of the seventeenth centuries. Expulsion of the Kel Geres by the Kel Ewey suggests a numerical superiority and a firm hold over the trading route to the north.

The dominant position, separate political organization, and other distinctive characteristics of the Kel Ewey suggest that they arrived in considerable numbers. Kel Ewey mixed extensively with the sedentarized Sudanic oasis populations, also known today as Kel Ewey. The social category of tributaries *(imghad),* important in other Tuareg groups, did not exist among Kel Ewey. Also, instead of allegiance to the Sultan of Aïr in Agadez, Kel Ewey owed allegiance to the *Anastafidet,* their own traditional leader.[7]

Nicolaisen lists seven original clans (sing. *tawsit*) of the Kel Ewey, and five of them still exist. These groups claim descent from a common ancestress.[8]

Women belonging to clans of the Kel Igurmaden descent group around Mount Bagzan identified to me a woman called Tagurmat as an important female ancestress. According to Rodd (1926:306), the Igurmaden Kel Ewey are the parent stock of the Kel Tafidet, who became a prominent division within the confederation, whence came the Anastafidet. But there are competing traditions concerning origins: older men and Islamic scholars tend to downplay the figure of Tagurmat and instead emphasize early (male) marabout and warrior heroes, while women and youths emphasize this ancestress. Despite challenges to these matrilineal traditions, however, alternative forms of inheritance persist today that protect women by counterbalancing Koranic forms that favor men.[9]

From these reconstructions of Aïr history, many authors (Rodd 1926; Nicolaisen 1963; Bernus 1981; Spittler 1993) emphasize the traditionally compact political organization and definite cultural division existing between Kel Ewey and other groups in Aïr and identify two principal influences upon Kel Ewey culture: the Hausa South (in language, Hausa is the second language, a lingua franca in trade, and a frequently heard conversational language of men, particularly caravanners; and in tools and household items imported from Zinder and Kano) and North Africa (in religion, Islamic study lodges, and retreats to saints' and marabouts' tombs). Men in many Bagzan region families are affiliated with the marabout *(ineslemen)* clans of Islamic scholars, although this specialty may also be learned through apprenticeship. The clans who claim descent from the Prophet are known as *icherifan* and are believed to possess mystical *(al baraka)* powers that bless and heal.

Semisedentized compound of rural Kel Ewey Tuareg household.

Semisedentized rural compound, with kitchen and traditional nomadic tent in foreground.

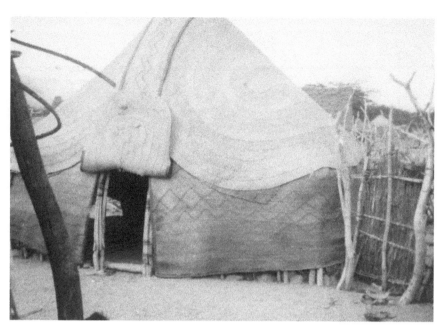

Married women's tent, traditional nomadic style *(ehan)*.

Women and children constructing conical grass tent.

Mother and child in dried riverbed, gathering clean sand for tent floor.

Traditional method of oasis garden irrigation.

Part One
Public Performance and Personal Identity

Phases of the Life Course and Household Cycles

A Kel Ewey Tuareg riddle poses the following question: "What is this: something very full (i.e., contagious)?" The answer is "The elder who goes courting in the evening. . . . He coughs, he goes around the household (i.e. he is full of sickness and transmits this)."

This riddle, a rhymed couplet usually told by pairs of young women and called *mislan mislan*, or "What is this," points to some seemingly contradictory elements in Tuareg conceptions of the life course. On the one hand, there is a consciousness of decreasing physical strength. On the other, local notions of aging are distinctly nonlinear and have additional referents beyond biological states and chronological processes. Furthermore, while most residents are aware of clearly defined role expectations throughout the life course, these cannot always be explicitly stated by everyone, for several reasons. Youths are not supposed to ask elders questions directly, nor pronounce names of living elders or deceased ancestors. Nobles of all ages, but particularly elders, pride themselves on two valued qualities: reserve *(takarakit)* and speech by allusion or "shadowy speech" *(tangal)*. Many older persons, for example, hesitate to relate folktales that are viewed as anti-Islamic. Some elders, despite their knowledge of historical legends, are reticent about offering any direct narrative on these or any other subjects. Thus it is difficult to elicit direct impressions of aging by those who most immediately experience, and are affected by, it.

Additional values further define public expression and performance over time. Prominent in Tuareg cultural ideology is an association of youth and age with two opposed domains: courtship and secularism versus prayer, on the one hand, and music and noise versus calm, on the other. These oppositions, while not a rigid structural dichotomy, are nonetheless salient socially and jurally, as well as symbolically, for they entail distinct changes in conduct that evoke underlying power relationships: specifically, modes of personal expression and appearance, ritual and jural participation, and styles of verbal art performance. Once individuals grow "old" (culturally defined as having children of marriageable age), their ritual status changes. They should not attend evening festivals with secular music, songs, and dancing at which courtship takes place since they may encounter potential affines at these events. They should not relate certain non-Koranic folktales or gesticulate with the hands too vividly, nor should their children or children-in-law perform these verbal arts in their presence without their express permission. On the other hand, only very elderly persons should speak of the ancestors or origins of the community. Although divorced or widowed men and women may remarry later in life, once children are grown, the wedding of such an older person is referred to as a "wedding of calm"; this takes place only at the mosque and omits the evening musical festivals and loud drumming customarily held following the "wedding of noise" for a young couple "in order to open their ears."

Over the life course, there are also marked changes in dress: increased covering of the head, particularly the facial area, for both men and women. One woman of noble origins, a close friend of mine, formerly a famous singer whose fifteen-year-old daughter had recently married, covered her mouth with her headscarf during her singing at a holiday camel race. She indicated that, although she still sang at holidays, festivals, and the festival-like spirit possession rituals, all of which feature a youthful female chorus and drummer, she now had to begin covering her mouth on such occasions because it was "shameful" to expose her mouth while her son-in-law was present. She also teased me, asking me laughingly and somewhat incredulously if, after all this time, I was still interested in spirit possession, my previous research topic. When I expressed a wish to continue attending these rituals, she indicated that she herself felt hesitant about going, for she was now becoming "too old" to attend spirit possession rituals as a singer or part of the audience. This is because Kel Ewey view possession rituals and other musical festivals, which feature performance of non-Koranic singing, dancing, and accompanying audience courtship, as frivolous, anti-Islamic, and threatening to officially endogamous marriage. These activities are therefore appropriate for youthful audiences, who may engage in temporary flirting during those events. Only the possessed, for whom these rites are held for the purpose of exorcism, may sometimes be an elderly woman (Rasmussen 1995). Another woman, a blacksmith whose daughter had been married for several years, expressed a similar view of these changing roles when she told me that, since having a son-in-law, she no longer attended evening festivals at all. Elderly women also often wear the headscarf drawn up over the mouth, closely resembling the men's face-veil. (In Tuareg society, men, not women, veil the face, and noble men are strictest in observing this practice; see Murphy 1967; Casajus 1987; Rasmussen 1991b).

These patterns of conduct—of gradually increasing reserve, indirect expression, and religious devotion—do not imply disengagement or withdrawal from social life (Cumming and Henry 1961) but nonetheless convey transformations in activity and personhood. The Tuareg data indicate much more complex processes are occurring here than disengagement or activity in an "either/or" sense, simple gender role reversal (Myerhoff 1978; Gutmann 1987), or simple inversion of class roles. These patterns are, however, most stringently observed by persons of noble descent and by males, who display the most reserve *(takarakit)* in Tuareg cultural values. These patterns tend to be less stringently observed by women, smiths, and former slaves, who display less reserve. Yet despite varying degree of strictness, all persons ultimately express ideological adherence to these values: men and women, nobles, smiths, and former slaves differ only in degree in their observance of *takarakit.* For example, a woman attending a festival should get up and leave abruptly if her father or older brother approaches. In principle, all men with daughters-in-law do not dance at evening festivals, though they sometimes attend discreetly as audience. But men too should gradually curb their attendance, for this becomes, over time, more and more shameful. Kel Ewey say, "prayer is better than song" as one grows older. These transformations reflect changing configurations of kinship ties and relationships to property within the household as well as ways of relating to the outside world of stratified yet negotiable class distinctions and beyond. Men and women from diverse social strata elaborated on these themes informally, though at times indirectly, in daily interaction with me as well as in more structured accounts of lifetime events.

These restraints on expressiveness and changes in participation took on significance over the long term in my research. Some older persons who were less restrained in expressing their sentiments—for example, lower-status persons such as smiths and former slaves, said to lack reserve—became excellent informants, but paradoxically, they also contradicted the dominant norms of growing older in Tuareg culture. Furthermore, on each successive visit to local communities, my social status changed with my own aging, in ways that complicated my methods of research. At times, local residents' and my own life course transitions came into conflict with Tuareg expectations about the change over time in social roles. Aging challenged the ideally open and dialogical communication in the field research situation. As a youthful, unmarried female, I was not necessarily maligned or disrespected, for single women in the countryside are not stigmatized or assumed to be prostitutes. Yet as a woman residing alone, far from her own kin, and later as a married but childless woman, I was looked upon somewhat ambivalently. Most elderly persons, particularly those of noble descent, were courteous toward me but tended to treat me with aloofness. Although they dropped by to greet me and visited frequently, many elderly women gently but firmly refused to drink tea with me, often remaining seated at my tent doorway. Whenever I approached, many elderly noble men in my host family would remain seated with their backs toward me, hastily raising their veils, even after I had resided there more than a year. Whenever such men referred to me, or more rarely, addressed me, they would use the formal term *tamagart,* denoting a guest, stranger, or foreigner. By contrast, other people either used my personal name or, in cases of friendship and respect, called me *taneslem,* denoting literally a female Islamic scholar, an approximate equivalent to "teacher" in rural Aïr communities. Occasionally, a few individuals expressed ambivalence or hostility by referring to me as *takafirt,* denoting "infidel" (non-Muslim or unbeliever). Because this latter term is considered pejorative, adults who used it tended to do so away from my presence. I only discovered its use when young toddlers occasionally blurted it out, causing acute embarrassment among older persons, who were almost without exception outwardly courteous. Some older female residents referred to me as the "daughter" of Mariama, in reference to my fictive kinship relationship with the woman whose household I resided in for a year, but they nonetheless remained distant from me until after a long association in friendship and many visits. Others disapprovingly asked me how I could "abandon" my own family for so long a time.

Thus the case of Adoum, a former slave man between 80 and 90 years old who related his life history to me spontaneously and without any prompting by myself, was decidedly atypical of older persons. Nonetheless, it provides insights into aging among Tuareg in two respects: as a kind of "foil" to noble ideals of aging, and as an illustration of metaphorical extensions of precolonial social stratum identity into contemporary age identity. Adoum was born around the turn of the century in the region to the west of the Saharan town of Agadez. Despite the lack of birth records, it is possible to calculate residents' approximate age, based on reference to historical events and intergenerational relationships. Adoum, like many elderly residents of the Aïr region, calculated his age by using the Tuareg Senoussi Revolt against the French (1917) and the exploits of its leader, Kaousan, as a reference point. Many elders of his generation state they were born "around the time of Kaousan's war against the whites (i.e., Europeans)," during a famine following it, or several years before it. Other reference points facilitating age calculation were these persons' position in the domestic cycle, for example, the number of coexisting generations, the presence of grandchildren, and so forth. But my major concern here is not chronological age but relational life course processes. Indeed, Adoum's exact age is probably not possible to specify, but there is no doubt about his social and ritual status as an elderly man.

Adoum resided with Saidi and his wife Tima in a seminomadic camp near my base village of research. Saidi is the son of the people whom Adoum once served, or, in Tuareg terminology, who "raised" Adoum. This terminology is significant, for it conveys the stratified yet negotiable and flexible quality of past servitude. Nobles and their slaves were defined as standing in a fictive kinship relationship. This had important consequences during emancipation. Although many slaves were manumitted after the French invasion of Aïr in 1917, some continued to perform herding, caravanning, and domestic labor in many rural areas up to the mid-twentieth century. Slaves were traditionally absorbed into the Tuareg social system on a kinship model: nobles were said to be "like fathers" to slaves and the latter were "like children" to nobles. Thus

Adoum in some respects was still considered a "child" despite his advanced age. This led him to didactic, self-conscious commentary on aging (but also subtle critical commentary on local history and relations of domination) in my presence. Adoum had been attached to the same household since his childhood, when he was first taken as a captive and then treated, in local cultural conceptualization, as an adopted son while he fulfilled obligations of a client-patron relationship, working for the same family over many years. The family whose slave he had once been was that of Anko (pseudonym), whose other son, El Hadji Bado (pseudonym), is the current chief of a descent group or section within the group of Kel Ewey around Mount Bagzan. Adoum still regularly visited the household of a local chief in the village at the time of my research. Although Adoum was generally treated with respect, people nonetheless felt freer to joke with him due to his status as a former slave and jural minor who was still supported by his former masters. Adoum complained ruefully, "People are always trying to trick me—they claim to be magicians and make fun of me!" Therefore, perhaps due to his awareness of his marginal and ambiguous position, his relative freedom from values of reserve, and his joking relationship to nobles, Adoum didactically explained and commented upon local culture. Indeed, he exaggerated the norms of an elderly Tuareg male in his personal conduct and appearance with me, thereby providing a particularly vivid foil in appearance and commentary on the life course. He also provided direct commentary on other aspects of social difference among the Tuareg. Like noble men, Adoum wore a style of the men's face-veil commonly seen among many elderly men, called *barkawen* or *tamajergh*. This style is similar to that of the younger men's face-veil in its covering of the mouth, but it differs in extending further, hoodlike, down over the forehead.

My first meeting with Adoum occurred one morning during breakfast when he came by the household of my hosts, a family related to the chiefly families, and began to relate events from his life spontaneously. He remained seated on a mat in the compound separated from the noble family, but they offered him tea, which he accepted. I offered him more tea and sugar to take home. This was in keeping with local patterns of interaction between the social strata: while nobles nowadays socialize with lower-status smiths, ex-slaves, and descendants of peoples of varying degrees of servitude, in rural areas some notions of pollution persist, which take the form of taboos against eating and drinking from the same containers and sitting on the same mat.

Adoum, in contrast to many older nobles, confided his sentiments as well as the events of his life early in our relationship. He did not, moreover, appear to find my own travel so far away from my family to be unusual. His attitudes seemed partly due to his life experience of early uprootedness from immediate kin and partly due to his social origins: because ex-slaves and blacksmiths are believed to "have less reserve" than nobles, they often serve as confidants of noble women and go-betweens of noble men. When outsiders first approach Tuareg communities, it is low-status persons—smiths, ex-slaves, and school-children of all social strata—who are initially friendly. In keeping with these local formulations, therefore, I begin by examining closely the cases of several persons of servile descent, since they were the first in their communities to discuss the life course explicitly. I then expand my scope of analysis to include portraits that gradually emerged of persons from diverse backgrounds, who, while also offering me hospitality, friendship, and insights, tended to do so more gradually. The case of Adoum, furthermore, is also of interest because it clearly encapsulates local notions of age as a relational entity, crosscut by gender and social stratum. In the situation of an elderly, formerly servile person, diverse trajectories of Tuareg personhood converge: parent/child, dominance/dependency, patron/client, insider/outsider. In these narratives, issues coalesce that are of great significance to all Tuareg throughout their life course.

Adoum was still attached to the family of a local chief, but because he was now too fragile to perform heavy work, he enjoyed the benefits of this family's "social security"–like support with no further obligations to herd, garden, or conduct caravan trade for them. Like many divorced men of all social strata, he lacked a tent of his own, for Tuareg women own the tent, which they receive upon marriage as a dowry, and have the right to eject the husband upon divorce. He frequently came by and joked with my noble host family. Between nobles and former slaves, as well as between nobles and smiths, *adelen* relationships are practiced: behavior characterized by a great deal of horse-play, mutual insults, and general familiarity. Much of Adoum's joking addressed the topic of his age. Yet throughout his narrative, he nonetheless kept his veil in place over his mouth, as noble men do. The only time when he diverged from this pattern was in lowering it briefly and smiling broadly for a photograph. Such an act would be unheard of for a noble, and even Adoum quickly readjusted his face-veil following this brief lapse. When I questioned him about face-veiling and aging, he replied:

> In the past and now, it is not the same. The style of the face-veil that I used to wear, people asked me to do it. He who knows that has only to style it, for example, in the style called "rabbit's ears" worn at festivals. Another style was the "rooster's or cock's comb," a veil style with the cloth above the forehead. One other is called the "goat's horn," a style rising up high, turban-like. Today, there must be a special ritual for me to do that style. I can no longer do it because I am old, due to reserve. Young people can wear these styles even without a ceremonial occasion.

These are all traditional styles of the face-veil Adoum indicated he no longer wraps or wears himself, as they are either inappropriate for elders to wear or are difficult to wrap. He continued:

Formerly in the oasis where I lived, I did a style and my divorced wife said, "Are you going to return to me?" [This style was so attractive that she wanted to remarry.] I said, "Yes, sure, I'll come back here." I was at Fatima's [friend's] home, and women came out and I went to the well. Fatima said, "Such a person is much loved by women. Please, Adoum, you must lessen [the veil's attractiveness]; the women cannot work, you are distracting the women." *Barkawen,* the style that hides a little of the face people really look at me [i.e., this is a style he prefers, but is difficult to do]. I veil my face, but the way I veil since I have been ill, I do not do fancy styles anymore. I simply cover my head with my cloth. When I go see people I do it this way [indicating the hoodlike style]. But I like the old styles I used to wear, although they are not for me now. There are people who say, "Adoum, if you do the traditional styles, other men are going to get divorced!"

The men's face-veil, although traditionally most strictly practiced by noble men and dropped by some youths in large towns, is a pervasive symbol worn by nearly all Tuareg men in rural areas. There are slightly different styles of wrapping according to social stratum and age. Nobles in rural areas tend to wear it highest, covering the nose and mouth. It is associated with male gender role identity and has complex referents. On the one hand, it signifies modesty, a manifestation of the cultural value of reserve, particularly important in the presence of affines (Murphy 1967; Casajus 1987). On the other hand, it is believed to protect against evil spirits entering through the orifices, in particular the mouth. In addition, I observed that the veil also can be used flirtatiously; it is, in effect, analogous to a hairstyle for men. Adoum's attitude here is not atypical. It highlights personal vanity, an important dimension of male veiling. Men indicate that they "feel more attractive" with the face-veil (Rasmussen 1991b).[1]

Adoum did not object to my tape-recording his stories. Kel Ewey individuals vary in attitudes about this. Some, though not all, elderly noble persons hesitated to allow me to record them because they did not wish their voices to be heard by their descendants. Elders speak for ancestors. Respect and reserve values require youths to refrain from verbally referring to living elders or deceased ancestors. In particular, they should not pronounce their names, in reference or address; this is also the reason why youths should not ask questions of elders. In this regard, my own status was ambiguous, somewhere in between youth and old age. Obviously I was biologically an adult, but since I was childless (albeit married), I was still classified as "younger" than an elder. Deceased ancestors are seen as the sole legitimate purveyors of sacred (Islamic) legends and songs, authored by God, whose words were spoken to the Prophet and recorded in the Koran. Nobles, in particular, hesitate to speak to and for elders, ancestors, and religious authorities. Another reason for reticence on the part of and toward elderly nobles is the reserve expected toward various kinspersons. One woman from a noble maraboutique family, whom I'll call Fatouma, was about to record genealogical information about her family as a favor to me when her son-in-law, with whom she practiced an extreme reserve relationship, approached. She suddenly hid her face in her headscarf, insisting she "knew nothing," and declined to continue, indicating she preferred to discuss this on some future occasion at the home of her female cousin.

Adoum felt less constrained by these noble values, and he expressed this in his life story:

> Listen . . . I did the work of herding first. I was young at that time. I herded livestock for seven years. The people who took me were *imghad* [tributary people from West of Agadez]. We call [them] "red" [a reference to their reddish complexion tone, seen locally as lighter than that of some other Tuareg]. Before Kaousan's Senoussi Revolt against the French, the tributaries took animals and made the animals' owners slaves *(iklan)*.[2] When my parents learned that, they took flight to save themselves. When my parents fled they left camp, since they (the *imghad*) were uprooting us, and we went looking for cows. We walked and walked, until we arrived at a place and proceeded, step by step. And then they were taken, one by one. I escaped [and] was left alone again for three days, until I reached a well at Tadalanfaye near Agadez. At that time, I was an adolescent. I was not really an adult but was tall for an adolescent. When I came to the well, I found other escaped women. At first, then, when taken [captured] by the *imghad*, I was with those women.
>
> When they saw us from far away, they galloped toward us on their camels. The person who [initially] captured me exchanged me for a woman. They first took me as a slave and then raised me as an adopted child. They told me to climb onto the camel. When I climbed up, we left. As soon as we looked, we saw Anko, one of the cameliers, father of El Hadji Bado and Saidi, with a woman he had taken captive. I was with his brother. His brother said, "I'll give you him for her." He said, "Here is the boy, for you." So thereafter, I was at the home of the elder (Anko), the father of (now living) El Hadji Bado, chief of our descent group today.
>
> The time came for us to go to Hausa country in the South on caravan trade. A man called Haidara, the older brother of a certain Boubacar, had a camel called Egade. The father of El Hadji Bado liked to ride Egade, this camel, all the time. That camel was a racing camel. Anko, father of El Hadji Bado, said to Haidara, owner of the camel, "You want this child, then you must give me the camel." I did not know about these plans to trade me for a camel. Anko said to me, "OK, we're going to Hausa country." But the old mother in the household, who knew of these plans, warned me, "If you leave, you will never return." And I told Anko, "Well, I'm not going." The reason for my not returning were these plans to trade me for the camel. As soon as I was informed about that, I refused! My boss said to me, "There are two female camels. You must go catch one." And the boss left with one of the two camels. I told him, "Go ahead, catch the other also, I don't care." They were trying to trick me! The first one that Anko caught

eventually died on the road. As a person, even for one single day, I am worth more than a camel! Especially Adoum, who is not lazy, nor are the people where he came from! Anko became angry; but I refused and was not exchanged for a camel, after all.

So that year, I did not go to Hausa country. I led herds of sheep, which were taken from me by the whites [French] later with the coming of Kaousan. The sheep were Anko's and were entrusted to me but were taken by the whites. Then [later on] the whites [French] gave herds to Anko to watch. They had entrusted raided herds for safekeeping, and I drove herds, as they asked me. I was often behind them. I could not see their beginning, they were so numerous! If I shouted, all the animals knew me. They made a half turn in their tracks and came back to me. They were there until I told Anko, "I am tired of watching the herds." I do not know where they led those herds after that.

When I left this work of herding [sheep] I began to lead Anko's camels. I went through Hausa country always, back and forth between Aïr and Damagerem.[3] When I came back from Hausa country, I went to the pastures, for a long time. Then Anko told me, "You are going to work in the gardens now." When I left the gardens, [later], I began once again to go to Hausa country [on caravans]. Now I left for Hausa country with Boubacar [a relative of Anko, now deceased]. And then [later] I began to go with El Hadji Bado, son of Anko, chief of the Kel Nabarro today. From then onward, I was always with Bado until my illness, which I caught in old age. Since then I have ceased to go to Hausa country on caravans. I have not moved. I am settled here and I find it best. I do not go South anymore.

I used to be with my wife in an oasis north of Agadez. And over there I said to her and my in-laws, "It is better to take me where I find my stomach" [*cibi* in Hausa, or *tedis* in Tamacheq, which denotes the original center of his dispersed matri-kin; attachment]. And so they brought me here, where I now live. My wife was in the oasis. My wife and I divorced. At first, she came here. She came over to her friends, Tamo and Bilcha. She told them, "I want a serious husband." And her friends answered, "There is no one worth more than Adoum." They told me that, and I told them, "You know me." And the woman from the oasis said, "Well, you came in search of a spouse?" And I said, "Is it true you want an eligible, hard-working man? Why is it that you have left your own village without finding one?" I then told her, "If [we marry, and] you are not serious, I shall divorce you." El Hadji Bado told me, "Is this news I heard true?" "It's true." So he helped arrange the marriage for me. I was ready for this marriage. And during the wedding, people from the oasis gave 1,000 CFA [about $4]. The family of the girl today gives about 3,000 CFA to the marabout, for the mosque upkeep. Then I gave them 20,000 CFA for the bridewealth. But I did not pay that all at once. [The family of the groom gives the bridewealth; however, in the past, nobles paid bridewealth for their slaves' marriage, as fathers would for sons. From this account, it appears that with assistance from El Hadji, in his role as a fictive father, Adoum paid the bridewealth in gradual installments.]

With that woman, I settled in the oasis and stayed there until she became a "loose" woman (i.e., unfaithful) during the night. In the middle of the night she returned home. She grew apart from me, and she slept elsewhere. One day I pulled her skirt and she raised her head. When she got up, I did the opposite. I no longer spoke to her from evening until morning. I said, "I am not happy." And I left. I said, "That's all, I shall not return anymore. [I am] the [person] whom you used to love, whom you do not love anymore." That was my motive for divorcing her. I remarried in the oasis and the third wife returned with me to the caravanning village where I am now. I returned her to her family, and I came back [again] to this village.

My daughter who lives in this village, she [later] moved here with me and my [second, also divorced] wife. She helped me get established in the *tettrem* [conical grass building] next door to her. But I [soon] noticed that things were not working out. Because even if someone invited me to visit, she would ask me "Why?" I got angry. Once there was a distribution of free [relief] food, brought by our chief, and they told me to come get my portion. I went over there [to a neighboring village]. They gave me some alms, and I returned. They gave me two measures of cereal, and I took it back to my *tettrem*. When I gave some to my daughter, she said, "What is that?" I told her, "Take the cereal, give me the container." The girl said, "Who told you to go over there? Did they call you over there?" I said "Shut your mouth." I thought that if I left to go somewhere to get something, she would not say anything to me about it. I did not know my contentment was becoming bad [i.e., things were going sour]. So, from my daughter's, I moved again, over to the granddaughter of Anko, the former master who "raised" me. I took all my belongings. I told my daughter, "If I had known this, I would not have come here." She told me, "So, you must go back to the oasis." I said, "Shut your mouth." I left to live at Tima's, Anko's granddaughter. My daughter and her mother do not greet me; even if they greet me, I do not look at them. [Among Kel Ewey, household compounds are traditionally identified by the name of the woman tent-owner, though the husband, if prosperous, may own a mud house inside.][4] I am in the household of Tima. That's where I am installed with my cushions. I do not set foot over there [at his ex-wife and daughter's home]. She [the ex-wife] came to tell me, "From this day onward, you must not come to our home." I told her, "Your home, I swear on God I would never touch it. What is there in your home, what riches are there inside that you have over there? You do not even make me pants, not even a shirt. May God leave those [you] people! Me, even the Hausa respect me more!"

A number of themes emerge in this account. The first concerns his residences: Adoum, as observed, was without a tent. In this respect, his situation is not atypical and stems from his status as an elderly divorced male, as well as from his poverty (though not all ex-slaves are poor).[5] Such persons can often rely upon matrilineal kin in later life, but Adoum's situation as a former captive from raids compels him to turn in other directions. This underlines his dependency upon others along three dimensions—as elder, divorced male, and ex-slave. In this case, since his falling out with his nearest kin, he has been dependent upon the chiefly family who previously owned him and metaphorically "reared" him, according to noble ideology, in a fictive kinship relation. In Tuareg society the classic nomadic tent or *ehan,* important jurally and symbolically throughout the life course, was traditionally the property of the married, noble woman. Nowadays, women of all social strata acquire this from their mothers as a dowry upon marriage. It is built by elderly female relatives gradually over the eight-day wedding ceremony. This tent is a central feature of most compounds throughout married life.

In the seminomadic villages around Mount Bagzan in Aïr, the number, type, and arrangement of dwelling structures within individual compounds are consistently patterned. This spatial ordering reflects changes in household structure that are linked to phases of the life course of all Kel Ewey. Built form and spatial arrangement of compounds reflect concepts of person and destiny as well as jural changes and alterations in household composition and organization over time. Although there is a classic pattern traditionally characteristic of noble domestic cycles, nowadays it is also applicable to non-nobles. Several types of residence are prominent. Their patterning corresponds to the developmental cycle of domestic groupings from marriage, through parenthood, into affinal relationships, and later, into physical decline and death. During the first two to three years of marriage, the couple's compound features a single nomadic tent, located about fifty feet from the first type of compound. It lacks a fence enclosure and also usually lacks a full kitchen. The newly married couple are essentially jural minors until the marriage is deemed stable, a decision made by the mother-in-law. This decision depends upon a strict respect relationship between groom and parents-in-law, which entails name teknonymy, refraining from eating in each other's presence, and strict face-veiling of the male affines. Parents-in-law and son-in-law must observe this custom fastidiously. During this time, the new groom completes bridewealth payments, contributes grain and other household items from caravan trading expeditions to his parents-in-law's storehouse, and performs herding and gardening for them. Soon, if all goes well, the single nomadic tent, the mere kernel of a household, acquires a kitchen, and later, it includes one or two conical grass buildings as sleeping rooms for unmarried children or guests.

Another household type consists of several structures enclosed by a fence. It includes the classic nomadic tent (*ehan* or *edew,* as this is called in the wedding ritual where it is first constructed as a nuptial tent) made of finely woven mats stretched over a frame of wood. In addition, there are a few adjacent grass, conical structures *(tettrem);* a square grass or mud structure with a log roof serving as a kitchen, or, in its more abbreviated form, a simple canopy serving as shelter; one or two shelters or windscreens in the inner courtyard of the compound; and sometimes, depending upon the economic means of the family but increasingly common among more prosperous gardeners and Islamic scholars (called marabouts), a mud house *(taghajemt).* This latter is built and owned by men. All structures are enclosed by either a circular wooden fence of tree branches, with a gate of one branch that can be opened and closed, or, in more sedentized compounds, a mud wall that occasionally has a corrugated tin door. As one climbs up the socioeconomic ladder, increasingly these doors are fitted with locks. Such a compound represents the jural adult/parenthood phase in life, ideally characterized by a married couple with independent tent, kitchen, and herds, with bridewealth payments completed and, usually, a few children. At this stage, after the husband has "pleased" his parents-in-law, in particular the mother-in-law, the married couple may choose to move away or remain nearby, adjacent to the bride's mother's compound. Many men attempt to move their household to areas near their own patrilineal kin. If they succeed, the husband owns the land beneath residential structures; if not, the wife may own it as well as her tent. At this stage, also, the married woman is permitted by her mother to disengage her livestock from her mother's herds, set up her own kitchen, and establish herself as a "woman within the tent." The husband, though still under obligations to show respect toward and periodically contribute grain (from gardens or trade) to the household of his wife's parents, now enjoys greater independence than previously during his initial two-to-three–year phase of marriage that featured obligatory uxorilocal residence and groomservice.

Thus there is a struggle throughout married life between forces pulling the husband and wife in opposite directions, toward living near his or her kinspersons for purposes of property ownership and security. Women, on their part, prefer to remain close to mothers and sisters and often refuse to follow husbands upon their departure. Men's relocation to start gardens or other work near their own kin is a common cause of divorce. Thus physical variation in residence, as well as attributes of conduct and appearance, are connected in sequence to processes over time. Friends expressed amazement that I could reside, even temporarily, so far from my mother and sisters, whereas husbands and wives are often separated by travel. Women, in particular, benefit from remaining near their mothers. In wedding praise-songs, blacksmiths advise the girl to "stay close to her mother's cushion" if she wishes a good bridewealth and a happy marriage.

Before a fence and kitchen are added to the newly married woman's compound, the young bride cooks meals in her mother's kitchen. For a smooth transition to take place, the groom must be polite to his parents-in-law. He must generously give gifts, in particular millet, to the bride and her household, but he must never look into their storehouse.

In this respect, Adoum's situation was double-edged. On the one hand, he had very little private property; one camel had been given to him by his owner-family, but it died. On the other hand, his noble/chiefly family's obligations to support him provided him with significant assistance, as in El Hadji Bado's help with the wedding expenses and bridewealth. Since slaves taken as captives were effectively jural minors, and their descendants were considered "like children," nobles were ideally supposed to behave "like parents" to them. This role entailed supporting them beyond biological childhood. Noble owners provided bridewealth payment for their slaves, and today, ideally, they still provide old-age security as well so as to back up immediate kin. As noted, Adoum's relations with individuals in his nuclear household did not go well, and he had long been separated from his matrilineal kin; thus he turned to his alternate "family."

Notions of social stratum extend into age groupings in several ways. In the Tamacheq language, class imagery surrounds much age-related terminology, and vice versa. *Amghar* denotes respectfully both elder and chief. *Tucherey* denotes old age. *Wa wachere* is more ambiguous; friends explained it to me as variously denoting an old person who is physically decrepit and in need of care or a head of family. *Teghafadley* refers to a firstborn child; *ililuwaten*, a lastborn child, is derived from the verb *alilui* (to rinse). The idea here is that a woman is "rinsed clean" after having her last child. *Telaqqawen* denotes subordinates, poor persons, and also members of one's family (verbal information, Alitinin Ag Arias, Centre de la Tradition Orale, Niamey, Niger).

The central idea here is the position of youths and, in the past, slaves, under authority. There is, in certain contexts, a cultural equivalence of youth and subordination. Specific folk beliefs about parenting and a child's group affiliation and descent are also class-based. If both parents are noble and the wife's first child is a daughter, the wife is considered "more noble" than her husband. If the child resembles the mother, there is also this belief that she is "more noble." If the child resembles the father, there is the belief that he is more noble.

While biology, including physical appearance and strength, is cited as age-related, there is much more to transitions over the life course than biology and chronological years. Authority in status as parent and household head, and in women's case as tent-owner, are key concepts here. My own lack of children was a constant source of consternation in Niger. My chronological age in years did not automatically confer *tamghart* (elderly female) status; as soon as individuals discovered my status as a non-parent, they hesitated to apply this term to me, even if I physically appeared to them "older" than most childless women. Yet women derive prestige from sources other than childbearing. Childlessness is not a stigma or a justification for divorce, and Tuareg recognize that male sterility can cause childlessness. Successful parenthood is nonetheless important for jural adult status because it presumably leads to affinal relationships that confer authority and security upon men and women in later life, regardless of social origins.

Adoum's domestic position, although precarious, also offered opportunities. During his estrangement from his daughter, he was able to activate fictive kinship ties with the relatives of his former owners, which was to his advantage, and to avoid becoming passively subordinate within his own household. Thus in interaction with former owners, as a former slave, he was in effect able to negotiate a more dominant, or at least more comfortable, role. Adoum is now deceased. Upon my return to the field in 1995, I learned that he had died of natural causes in 1994. Just before his death, he reconciled with his daughter, who invited him back to live near her and built him a small, conical grass structure just adjacent to her compound, where he died. At various times in his life, therefore, Adoum benefited from the care and affection of both fictive and nonfictive kin. Thus in Tuareg society, a variety of social ties provides alternative "safety nets" in later life phases, and cultural elaborations of aging mitigate household disruption, economic uncertainty, and physical decline.

Age is not necessarily viewed as equivalent to disease in local models. Yet some images of aging do refer to physical decline. A young man of noble origins compared the life course to the *abarkan* shelter-canopy in compound courtyards: "At age ten years, the human being, like a shelter, has vitality, with added posts and structural supports; after this the human peaks at age forty as parent and household head; then humans, like the structure, start weakening and losing foundations." Female herbalists recognize that after cessation of menstruation, the woman's body begins to "bend" and "become drier." Nonetheless, physical decline does not constitute the major, overarching definition of a person who is aging. For ideally, there is compensation for it in acquiring social and economic support from children's marriages and, in the case of some former slaves, from vestiges of client/patron relationships. These relationships until recently included economic obligations to nobles of domestic/herding tasks and harvest payments by ex-slaves and even their descendants. These practices have been breaking down. But their ideological counterpart—of noble obligations toward former slaves—remains modeled metaphorically on parent-child roles. This was shown in the noble chiefly family's obligations to Adoum as an elder of servile origins. It is this expectation that Kel Ewey implicitly recognize when they state, "The marriage of children depends on the conduct of parents." In effect, the making of affinal relationships—in particular, of mother-in-law and father-in-law—confers authority. Many elderly noble women told me that they wear *chileqaren*, small carnelian stones, because these stones "are not as pretty as silver." The red carnelian stone has symbolic significance. It is used in healing some wounds in the belief that it coagulates blood. In wearing these stones, elderly women in effect advertise their nonmenstruating status. Like elderly men who are less ostentatious in refraining from wearing festival face-veil styles, elderly women wear less and less silver jewelry, which is given to the bride by her mother and husband upon marriage. Silver is a metal believed to bring good luck and happiness.

In attitudes toward physical aspects of aging, there appears to be a slight double standard between the classes and sexes. Most residents agreed that men become "old" *(wa wachere)* much later than women; also, while older people may remarry, reactions to reports of older men marrying younger women were quite different from reactions to reports of older women marrying younger men. And, as observed, persons of servile origin are regarded by nobles as child-like throughout life despite their efforts to resist this through dignified personal dress and conduct conforming to more generalized Tuareg cultural typifications. During my visit with a smith friend upon my return fieldtrip after a long absence, we exchanged news of mutual friends, both in Niger and in the United States. One American woman who is now in the United States, who had formerly resided in the town of Agadez as an expatriate, had remarried after a number of years as a divorcee. Female divorced status is, in itself, not stigmatized by Tuareg; what is important is the conduct of the woman between marriages. In particular, she must not have an illegitimate child. The woman in question, now well into her fifties, had not given birth out of wedlock but had children by an earlier marriage. In the intervening years since she left Niger, the woman had remarried a man eleven years her junior. The smith friend became incredulous and disapproving when he heard this news. He laughed with disbelief and emphatically stated that such a marriage "was not good." I inquired why, and he indicated that, while some older men may marry young women, the reverse was "bad." He indicated that he himself had once married a woman "a little older" than himself but later divorced her "because she was old." The implications of this were puzzling, given that, as shown, women with married children enjoy enhanced ritual status and may also remarry, albeit in a "wedding of calm." When I questioned women about his comments, they indicated that perhaps this man pitied the husband because he assumed he would never have children. Here again, the point is to have children—who marry later and offer late-life assistance in a reciprocal, mutually beneficial parent-child relationship—not age or "old appearance" per se.

On another occasion, I asked another friend of mine, a woman of servile origins, about the reasons for one woman's spirit possession illness. She indicated that the patient undergoing this ritual had a secret love, but she was "now old"; and she added emphatically, "It is shameful for an old person to love." Indeed, this was one reason some residents held spirit possession rituals for older women: they could dress up, wear perfume, and attend an evening event featuring music and courtship, but only as patients in the spirit possession exorcism rite (Rasmussen 1995).

These reactions to male/female differences in aging also encoded efforts to maintain cultural purity and sociopolitical autonomy. Nobles around Mount Bagzan prided themselves, at least in principle, on contracting few marriages over their lifetime. Although polygyny is permitted by Islam and common among more sedentized gardeners and marabouts, nomadic households tend more toward monogamy, and women tended to idealize a single match throughout one's lifetime. In the beginning of my field research, very few local divorces, in particular of women, were reported to me; only later did I discover divorce rates were actually higher than initially admitted. Some men also claimed that their women were "purer," "more noble," and "more Islamic" than those of other regions, whom they criticized for traveling, going to bars, marrying strangers (e.g., outside the family), and divorcing too often "in order to keep the bridewealth." (Among Tuareg, it is considered ungallant for the man to request a return of bridewealth on divorce, though Kel Ewey differ from some other groups in that marabouts rule in favor of "whoever is not at fault" keeping it.) Local residents asserted that "our marabouts here refuse to remarry you too many times—especially if you remarry the same person [on reconciliation] more than three times." This has roots in precolonial notions of purity of descent. Rural noble girls traditionally married very young for purposes of descent. Men in the chiefly families continue to express a preference for very young brides and virgins, while smith and former slave women tend to marry later. One son of a local chief contracted a marriage to a cousin before the girl had even begun menarche, although the couple did not cohabit until after this event.

Thus attitudes toward male and female aging, expressed in an idiom of "purity/pollution" beliefs, marriages, and affinal relationships, constitute efforts on one level to amass personal support and economic security and, on another level, to consolidate descent interests. For example, menstrual restrictions are most strictly observed by noble women of childbearing age who are said to be in a state of "lack of prayer" (Rasmussen 1991a). These restrictions have two effects: first, they minimize these women's contact with gardeners, who are usually of servile descent, and smiths, both categories considered to be of lower social status. For example, menstruating women do not harvest crops or touch animal hides. Indeed, young childbearing-age women of noble origins are discouraged from harvesting crops at any time. In the past, slaves did this; nowadays, elderly post-childbearing women do this. Among Tuareg, in contrast to many other Africans, women do not plant, irrigate, or weed gardens at any age; this, like caravan trade, is men's work. These restrictions also underline the opposition between youthful, childbearing womanhood and males, nobles, and official Islam, for example, in taboos against praying and touching men's religious amulets and swords. In both instances, these express concern with guarding noble purity. Significantly, post-childbearing women may come closer to the mosque; they follow men there to pray and sing liturgical music seated beside it on Moslem holidays. These factors explain why elderly women may also work with animal hides and harvest crops, tasks usually associated with smith and servile statuses.

2

Aging, Gender, and Social Stratum

Emphasis upon purity of descent persists among many persons of noble origins, but this now tends to merge with emphasis upon generalized cultural autonomy. Both these emphases are subjected to considerable challenge. Threats to survival and autonomy are felt acutely, not solely by persons of noble descent but by all Tuareg. Erratic rains and diminishing pastures make it difficult to maintain socioeconomic security despite parents' efforts to arrange advantageous marriages for children. Colonial and postcolonial policies (taxation, censuses, enforced school registration, uneven development programs favoring gardening over herding) and armed conflict with the central government threaten local practices designed to safeguard security over the life course.

The issue, therefore, has been control and protection of the tent. Within Kel Ewey Tuareg society, this depends upon hiding one's true sentiments, or at least expressing them indirectly, and upon contracting official marriage and maintaining domestic household solidarity over the life course. Many ritual and jural changes over the life course address this dual problem of external and internal threats to property. Changing relations to tent and household, and efforts to protect them, are central in this scheme. Once children are of marriageable age, sexuality and childbearing are acceptable, albeit with some ambivalence, but open courtship and festival attendance are not. These principles extend into beliefs concerning health. Many elders indicated that if a person neglects to pray when older, he or she will become senile. A female herbalist felt that if a mother and daughter are pregnant at the same time, it is shameful because the older woman has a son-in-law. It is the son-in-law who makes this shameful, however, not the greater age of his mother-in-law per se. Other herbalists indicated that it is permissible for a mother and daughter both to be pregnant at the same time if this is the daughter's first child; if she has more than one child, however, this is shameful because her mother has a son-in-law with children already, the household is established, and these two persons would be "ashamed" to see each other at namedays.

Thus the emphasis upon steady progress toward religious devotion and reserve over the life course can be explained in part by jural relationships and bridewealth transactions and in part by wider efforts to cope with physical decline and economic uncertainty. On one level, the parent-in-law is an authority figure over the son-in-law. There is a relation between ideas about procreation and reproduction on the one hand, and power and property ownership on the other. Aging norms in private conduct, public performance, and religious ritual express this relationship over and above biological and physical aspects of age. This explains the practice of labeling women "elderly" (*tamghart*) before they are necessarily biologically postmenopausal. Many Kel Ewey classify a woman who has at least one child of marriageable age as *tamghart*. Whether or not such women are still biologically capable of bearing children is immaterial in certain social and ritual contexts. One such woman, named Abo, for example, had twelve children, the two oldest of whom were married, and she also had a year-old baby. But her social and ritual position in all other respects belonged to *tamghart* status: along with other elderly, post-childbearing women, this woman attended rites of passage in the morning, dressed with less jewelry and more closely drew her headscarf around her mouth, approached the mosque closely behind men and marabouts on Moslem holidays, and refrained from attending evening festivals or performing secular music.

The meanings of these transformations as socially constructed, rather than biologically based or chronologically determined, are reinforced by additional terms and the phases of life to which they correspond. *Tamtot,* the general term used for "woman," as opposed to "girl" or "adolescent" (*tabarart* and *tekabkab* or *tamawat,* respectively), is socially rather than biologically constructed. When I asked most women, "When did you become a woman?" they did not respond in terms of when they began to menstruate (as many American women would) but rather indicated this transition had occurred when they married. This concern is also shown in finer terms for age, thereby linking this domain to gender and social stratum affiliation: for example, *echku* (fem. *tachkut*), a special term, approximately denoting a "boy" or "girl" of servile descent but also connoting youthful (jural minor) status in general; *tamasroyt,* a special term meaning a single woman, whether never married or between husbands; *eleli,* denoting a noble (male) youth, unmarried but mature; and *tamtot-n-amas,* (literally "woman inside or within," meaning inside the tent), applied to a woman married longer than three years, when bridewealth and other obligations are completed, who separates her kitchen and herds from those of her mother, and with her husband may choose whether to remain in uxorilocal residence or move away. *Tamagergeri,* a married but childless woman, literally denotes a "woman in between." During the *amgharl tamghart* phase, the pattern for both men and women is similar. On reaching this phase in life, both sexes are expected to cease behavior associated with youth.

Both coming of age as an adolescent and growing old as an elder involve a control over personal expression that is applicable to both men and women. But to interpret these sanctions as "restrictions," "disengagement," or "deprivation," or to explain them in terms of dichotomies such as "expressive/instrumental" (Myerhoff 1978, 1992) or in terms of exactly linear and symmetrical gender dualisms such as "from aggressive warriors to peace chiefs" (Gutmann 1987) would be to impose, erroneously, Western values upon them and to obscure their mutually illuminating attributes as analytical "foils" for each other. For example, as adolescent Tuareg girls approach marriageable age, they are discouraged from revealing their choice of suitor. The bride is also forbidden to express preference as to whether to slaughter the bull offered by the groom and distribute it to guests, or to keep it in her herds. Later, as women age and their daughters approach marriage, the former are expected to shun amusements featuring music, dance, and mixed-sex gatherings. They are also discouraged from performing music regardless of the talent they had at this during youth. Many Kel Ewey state that elders, particularly women, must become more reserved in their personal conduct because many young people are potentially their future affines. Older men and women are also expected to practice Islamic duties of prayer more closely. Many aging Kel Ewey men take up professional study of the Koran. Although maraboutism is inherited within certain clans, Islamic scholars indicated that "anyone may become a practicing marabout by knowing the Koran, being generous, and practicing Islam better than others." One marabout and prosperous gardener told me, "When I was a youth, I attended songs, and I played music. I did these things until I had children. But then I abandoned these skills to my children. I go to the mosque and pray. I have forgotten all that I did during my youth. Now I only know Koranic study. I have abandoned all else since I have been old."

A woman friend named Chigdouane discussed these themes in the course of many conversations with me. She was from the *ighawalen* social stratum, which indicates a degree of servitude locally described as being "more like clients." These people were dependent upon nobles for protection but, unlike *iklan* or slaves, had not been recently bought or captured on raids. Chigdouane's parents, as descendants of captured people, performed gardening and gave a proportion of their harvest to nobles.[1] Chigdouane formerly played the *anzad* bowed lute. This is an instrument associated with women, love, and courtship, whose music is highly valued. But she told me that, due to her *tamghart* status, she had given up this instrument. Nor did she participate in evening festivals anymore except as an occasional patient in spirit possession rituals. When I expressed disappointment because I had wished to hear her perform on her instrument, and I asked her if she did not miss playing the *anzad,* she assured me this did not bother her. She insisted that her interest now that she was "old" was prayer *(emud):*

At the time I learned to play the *anzad*, I went to the home of women who could play it. I watched them play it until I learned. I was always in their home. I saw how they did it with their hands, and I watched. At that time I was a young girl. Now I am old. An old person does not play the *anzad*. It is better for them to pray. An old person is afraid *[eksode,* in some contexts used interchangeably with reserve or *takarakit]* and prays. Now prayer is better. A girl prefers the *anzad*, an old woman prefers prayer *[emud,* as opposed to menstruation, the term for the latter being *iban emud,* literally, "lack of prayer"].[2] Now the *anzad* is worthless! An old person needs to pray. I have abandoned the *anzad.* I prefer prayer. I'm here in my home, lying down [praying].

She continued:

Well then, youth and old age are not the same. Before, life was easy. There were herds, I was in a good situation, I found pasture [easily], had cows, goats, I had strength. I had milk. All I needed, I was capable of obtaining. Well, now people [in old age] have illnesses, they cannot do nomadism with livestock. And also, there are not even animals as there were before. There are a few animals that old people have, and those few they have, children lead them [to pasture]. Each day the children lose an animal. People have become weak. Before, all that you owned contained *albaraka* [benediction or blessing].[3] All that you wanted [to do], you did. Well, now life has become difficult [expensive]. Before, one worked, and now work is difficult for the body. So there is no more work. After that everything became expensive and difficult, and this made it difficult for all, and now money is necessary. The people in the past did not care at all about money; they exchanged items or bartered, they made their trade, they wove their palm fibers, they made their doum palms, they ate their leaves of the *agar* tree.[4] They were strong, in good health. They could do their work. Well, now people have abandoned all that. That's how life today is different from before.

At one time, we lived in Alga, three kilometers to the west of here. We did nomadism. It was good. We lived to the west. This [nomadism] was over a great distance. We did a very fine nomadism.

We could walk a lot. We were [at one time] also to the east [near Tabelot], and on the Bagzan. In the rainy season, instead of remaining in the big camp, it was better to be in the wild outside *(setakass).* In the cold season also, instead of remaining in the large camp, it was better in the wild. In the dry season, it was better to return to the large camp *[eghiwan;* among Kel Ewey, this denotes village, home, or camp], where water from the well was nearby.

That's what is different from the former times. The travel that I did was entirely nomadic with animals. I was young then. I used to travel. I was everywhere. I saw everyplace. I was a shepherdess. At that time, I knew happiness. When I walked toward the savanna, I watched cows, I saw animals. There was [plenty of] milk, it was happiness, there were cheeses as well, there were goats and donkeys. As I herded livestock, I led them with a long stick. I pulled at the trees with it, and the goats ate. The goats foaled a lot of kids only if they got enough straw to eat. When I returned home I put them in the enclosure so jackals couldn't eat them. In the morning I took them out to pasture. I milked them, and from their milk I made cheese that I hung from the tent roof [to dry]. I continued taking straw and twigs down from the trees, which the goats ate until full. They rested. Half the milk I usually made into cheese, half I drank. I let the kids inside the enclosure to drink their mothers' milk. Then I caught them.

I prepared my meals. I pounded *eghale* and put it into my gourd.[5] I put this on my back and left. If my animals grew, herds increased. I herded them all. That was how I accummulated my herds. During that time I was young, and so at night I could go out to festivities (songs and dances). Afterwards, we came home and slept. In the morning, we got up, pounded grain, and went to the well, and then we herded livestock. After dinner we often went searching for new sand for the tent floor and wood for fires. We brought straw for the *tettrem*. We built tents. We also brought palm fiber and grass for this purpose. At that time we could do this well. We had strength. We repaired our tents. That is youth, when you have the strength and you repair all you need.

But during the time of Kaousan, people died. They were killed, and their belongings were taken from them. We saw soldiers. We hid in the mountains. They were driven away, and some were made slaves. There was no millet. People were dying of hunger. We hid in the mountains. There were no clothes. People covered themselves with leaves and hides of goats. People ate doum palms, *aborak* fruit, and jujubier. There was no other food.[6] Europeans came. Kaousan fled. He was killed by Tubus. We went to Hausaland, which had lots of millet. Now life became better. We paid taxes, but the populations were calm. We returned to Aïr. Now people have stopped killing, [or] whoever kills anyone is thrown in jail.

At my marriage, there were cameliers with a bull and women on donkeys, well decorated. They [the family of the bride] invited people. We all put on indigo cloth. When they [the groom's family] came with cameliers, blacksmiths beat drums and sang praise-songs, and they ululated. These [traditions] are often neglected today. They don't always have bulls anymore. They do weddings more simply. They have drumming, praise-songs, and camel races and dances. But when I got married [for the first time], I was young. During my marriage celebration, I knew nothing. I was ashamed of it [the bride is said to feel reserve]. That's my "good route." When I was lying down [under a blanket in my mother's tent during the eight-day ritual], I closed my eyes. So I didn't know what was happening. Other people, not me, were celebrating. I did not understand anything. But I knew it was good. At that moment, I was young. I was not intellectual. When the wedding took place, people [of the family] pounded *eghale*. They [elderly female relatives] built the nuptial tent. The marrying couple arrived. They held festivities. The women put on henna, and people danced. The men dressed up, the camels wore beautiful harnesses. The women also dressed up. Everything was pretty. I wore indigo clothes, I received silver [jewelry]. I received millet. I filled up on milk.

My husband went to Hausa country. At first he brought me indigo cloth and black wooden bowls. As soon as these provisions were finished, he got me others. I would like to have a gardener. He would harvest tomatoes, wheat, onions, and all other crops. I would also like a caravanner. He brings millet. He goes to

Bilma. He brings back salt and dates. I would like to have goats, to drink milk. All three things are good. Yes, I like being married! Marriage is to have a man work like a slave! In one type of marriage, the man himself chooses *[tedua n elis]*, in another the people of the family choose. Marriages arranged by the family *[tedua n eghiwan]* are better than those "outside" [*essuf,* which also means "wild" or "solitude," is used here to refer to a marriage partner who is unrelated].[7] You won't be so likely to divorce because it is still the same household (where the bridewealth circulates and where you remain nearby).[8] Before, most marriages were within the family. Concerning polygyny, because one loves the man, one wants him to herself. If [some]one shares my husband, I want to strangle that other woman!

Despite her own preferences for monogamy and stable marriage, which are common ideals among most Tuareg women, Chigdouane nevertheless was twice divorced, and her second marriage was to a polygynist. This is a frequent pattern among widows and divorcees near Mount Bagzan. She commented that I should be careful, since during my own absences from my home on fieldtrips my husband "might marry a co-wife," and she asked me if I didn't worry about this. Indeed, polygyny was an overwhelmingly dominant concern in the region, a conversational topic women pursued in both seriousness and in jest. Once, when I brought along another American woman as a short-term guest to my research site, we approached Chigdouane and other women who were busy constructing a tent at a communal work party. The women teased me by asking me if the American woman was my co-wife. They commented, jokingly, that I had better be careful, since many men begin to search for new wives "once a woman has grown older." Another woman, married to the brother of a local chief for over twenty years and mother of five children, openly discussed with me her husband's plans to contract a second marriage, right in front of him. She asked me what I thought of this idea; she herself opposed it. Many women, when asked about their reactions to different phases of the life course, commented that, while they looked forward to the *tamghart* phase due to increased respect and prestige, they dreaded one aspect of it: they believe that many men tend to acquire second co-wives at this time. In contrast to some other African women, Tuareg co-wives regard each other with jealousy. They describe co-wives as "detracting from" or "diminishing" each other, "as water puts out a fire." Many women initiate divorce when their husband contracts a second marriage.[9]

Chigdouane is about seventy years old and recently divorced after living in a compound adjacent to that of her husband's first wife. In the Aïr, where polygyny exists but often meets with resistance from women, most co-wives reside in separate compounds or villages and do not share the same kitchen. Divorced again after several years as the second wife of Issa, Chigdouane was married to her first husband, Moussa, for eight years. She initiated the first divorce because, she indicated, Moussa did not provide for her economically. In such a case, the husband is ruled at fault, so Chigdouane kept the bridewealth. When she initiated divorce due to her husband's polygyny, however, marabouts ruled in favor of the husband keeping the bridewealth, for they do not consider women's opposition to polygyny a legitimate grievance.

Issa, Chigdouane's second ex-husband, is a marabout who recently retired as a caravanner and guide to the Tenere, a remote desert plain stretching between the Bagzan region and Bilma, a town where caravans go for salt and dates.[10] Chigdouane has two sons, still single, by her first husband. She had no children by her second husband, although he had several children by his first wife. The mothers of Chigdouane and Issa were cousins; she was unrelated to her first husband. Two nieces (daughters of her brother) sometimes board and help her with the housework, for she lacks daughters. She also is often ill, frequently doctoring herself with Islamic amulets and occasionally undergoing spirit possession exorcism rites, called *tende n goumaten,* to cure maladies believed caused by spirits. She does not visit often but is hospitable on my visits to her, exchanging small gifts of food with me, which is customary among women friends. Her frequent physical complaints are stomachaches and headaches. She says that she does not know whether spirits caused her physical problems, or vice versa. She indicates that spirits entered her stomach and moved in it as though living. Then they climbed up into her head, closed her eyes, and made her "crazy." But her first spirit possession occurred before her first marriage, during adolescence, while she was on her way home after attending an exorcism ritual held for another patient. The most recent attack occurred in the early 1980s. Chigdouane told me that the spirit attacks ceased after she had children but then returned in recent years.

Unlike Adoum, Chigdouane was not poor. She derived economic security from sources other than her marriages. She has about nine goats and four camels. In addition to owning and inheriting livestock, Tuareg women acquire property from preinheritance and gifts. Many women asked me if American women owned livestock. When I replied that most did not, they were incredulous and expressed pity for them. How, they wanted to know, could they live without goats or donkeys, especially in old age?

Even in the case of formerly servile persons, wealth may be accumulated from property passed down to descendants, now free, from original usufruct rights in client-patron arrangements. For example, some of Chigdouane's herds derive from stock that the noble owners of her servile ancestors left her family. After slavery was officially abolished, branches of her kin continued to cultivate gardens and date palms for nobles in sedentary oases near Chigdouane's seminomadic caravanning village until the early 1990s. Caravanning villages are predominantly inhabited by nobles and blacksmiths. Although nobles no longer had the undisputed right to collect tribute in the form of agricultural produce from the mainly servile residents of two nearby oases, until recently some vestiges of these transactions persisted in the form of gifts and services. When I boarded with a noble nomadic woman from 1983 to 1984, I accompanied her to the oasis and area of Chigdouane's kinspeople, where she collected baskets of vegetables from someone she described at the time as "a cousin." Later, upon taking censuses and genealogies, I discovered that her family and that of the oasis resident were actually unrelated. Instead, the resident was a distant relative of Chigdouane. My questioning on this matter initially yielded little information, for slavery is a delicate subject. Nobles in the seminomadic caravanning village of my long-term residence only alluded to some "sharing" between residents of the two settlements. Upon my return fieldtrip in 1991, close friends revealed further that residents of the caravanning villages formerly held tribute rights over the oasis and that a few residents of the oasis still gave some harvest to noble residents of the caravanning village. By 1995, however, they indicated that even these practices had ceased.

Chigdouane is of the Kel Eghaser descent group, and her ancestors first settled in Iferouan, an oasis to the northwest of the Bagzan Massif, near the mining town of Arlit. They tended nobles' date palms within their own cereal gardens there until they migrated to a small oasis five miles away, where she resided until her later move, due to a drought, to the caravanning village of her current residence. Chigdouane's ancestors fled to Hausaland after Kaousan, as did noble families. Thus Chigdouane spent a portion of her early youth in the South, between Kano, Nigeria and Zinder, Niger. She later returned to Aïr along with other families from this region. Many of her relatives continued to garden and herd for nobles even after the slaves were liberated. Her father, Hado, is now very old and resides with his matrilineal kin in the large oasis of Tabelot. Chigdouane and her family, however, like most former servile peoples, consider themselves Tuareg, speak Tamacheq, and dress and eat like other Tuareg of the region.

Chigdouane appears to enjoy, on the surface, social fulfillment and economic prosperity. But she has suffered from frequent health problems beginning in her youth. It is because of these problems, she explains to me, that she falls ill and needs medicine, gesturing toward an Islamic amulet wrapped around her forehead as a headache remedy. Because of these problems, she regrettably "cannot participate fully in the life of women." But the solution to this was not to be found solely in medicines; rather, prayer was important to her. She remarked that, indeed, many problems are caused as one ages if prayer is neglected.

Thus a combination of physical health problems, divorces, lack of support from daughters, and social norms of conduct surrounding age account for changes in Chigdouane's patterns of participation in public life. A number of persons who had formerly been famous musicians and singers, and who were still considered talented, refused to relate secular, non-Koranic folktales and nonliturgical music and songs anymore because of their *amghar/tamghart* status.

This retreat from performance was not solely due to physical fatigue or technical decline. One woman, a famed singer of spirit possession songs who had not performed for some time, was approached by her maternal nephew upon the spirit possession of his second wife, for whom an exorcism ritual was staged. After considerable persistence and appeal to their kinship relationship (a joking relationship—one of mutual affection and support), he finally convinced her to make an exception to her recent retreat from performance and sing at his wife's ritual. This incident shows that kinship relationships may sometimes modify age role expectations and the respect attached to them. Relationships with matrilineal kin are often relaxed, and individuals feel they can turn to such kin in situations when they could not do so with others. For example, the nephew could never have made such a request of an older female relative on his paternal side; between these persons a strict reserve relationship is observed. But except in rare circumstances, elderly women in general refrain from singing possession songs, which feature a chorus of young women accompanied by drumming on the *tende* mortar drum, often after midnight, before a mixed-sex and mixed-class audience whose conduct is marked by a license normally forbidden in everyday interaction and official domains of social life. Possession rituals are considered excellent occasions to meet persons of the opposite sex and arrange pre- and extramarital love affairs.

Older women must limit their participation in events of informal sociability—tea-drinking, eating, evening visits and conversation, and evening festivals—with young people, since all men at such gatherings are their potential affines. Many young men say they are "afraid" to enter compounds of women who have girls of marriageable age. Explaining this from another angle, one man told me that he felt a bit "ashamed" in the presence of the wife of his supervisor in an agricultural extension cooperative program because she was "a little like a mother-in-law" to him.

Chigdouane, while enjoying some economic security through livestock herds and her nieces' assistance with domestic work, lacked daughters altogether, and her two sons remained away from the region. This was a practical disadvantage as well as a source of personal sadness, for it deprived her of another source of security and prestige: that of the mother-in-law role. In accounts of her family, she only briefly spoke about her sons, one of whom had been lost for nearly twenty years and was now presumed dead, and the other of whom was away on extended travel and migrant labor in Nigeria.

> My parents lived around here. They stayed here in the village. We young girls were nomadic, we were in the wild looking for pasture [i.e., Chigdouane's mother and father were in the village; Chigdouane as a girl was more nomadic, leading herds to pastures]. All old people stay here at home. A young woman is strong.

An old woman has no strength for nomadism. I have become old. I do not do nomadism anymore. Today I cannot do goatherding. The reason why herding is good is that you have your animals, you have your cheeses, you sell them, you drink the milk, you have wealth. Wealth circulates and that is good. Now, I have become old. It is for that reason that I have abandoned all that goatherding. For the moment, I make my home here. A very elderly person does not make those decisions.

Now my father is in Tabelot. He is in his matrilineal family there, [to whom Tuareg can turn in times of trouble or old age]. These days, I tell my nieces (brother's daughters): "Go, take the herds to pasture, get water, pound millet for our guests." That's what I tell my family. It's our way of life. When it is Ganni [local version of Mouloud, a Muslim holiday commemorating the Prophet's birthday] and the festival begins, we take our donkeys, get dressed up, put on jewelry, dress our hair, and put pretty harnesses on the donkeys. We mount them, gallop, and run off to celebrate Ganni, ululating. In the morning, we return, take the harnesses off the donkeys, and rest.

I do not regret not having daughters, because it is God who did not give them to me. That's it—whatever God wills to give me, whether a son or a daughter. To have a son, ideally he travels and nourishes you, he dresses you, and he does anything you want. The value of a daughter is different: she tends the home, she leads the herds, she marries, she makes items for the home that are pretty. She makes her home and lives in it. My children, one son is very far away, around Lagos; the other, I do not know where he is. He has been lost [disappeared in travel many years ago]. My other son has been in Lagos for several years.

Initially I believed that the reasons for Chigdouane's reticence about her sons were several local cultural values: "speech by allusion," a practice of indirectly alluding to sensitive topics through metaphor; the respect/reserve relationship between mothers and their firstborn sons; and beliefs glossed in translation as "evil eye." For example, another woman friend of mine almost never referred to or talked about her oldest son, but not because she was disappointed in his character or activities or because she disliked him. Rather, most parents do not boast openly about their children who are successful or otherwise satisfying due to reserve toward the firstborn (particularly a son, whose name they cannot pronounce) as well as for another reason: fear of provoking jealousy with its associated malevolent forces, approximately equivalent to "evil eye." Friends explained to me that if people praise a child, for example, and "If someone says, 'she is fat and healthy,' they may activate forces called *tehot* or *tégaré*, and the child may become thin, sick, and perhaps die."[11] Chigdouane's reticence, however, stemmed not solely from these cultural values but from personal disappointment as well. For when I inquired further about her son in Lagos, mutual friends indicated that she had experienced some conflict with this son. According to men who returned from caravan trading expeditions, this son in Lagos had remained unemployed for a long period of time and had sold one of Chigdouane's riding camels to someone in the family of her (then) husband's other wife, who was paying for the camel gradually, in installments. The sale upset Chigdouane greatly, both because she needed the camel and also because she regarded the family of her co-wife as enemies.

A year later, she sent her brother to Lagos to see her son and tell him that this purchase was not all right with her. Use of an intermediary, often a brother by women and a sister by men, and indirect expression by allusion *(tangal),* is the usual preference in local cultural values. Sisters and brothers enjoy strong bonds throughout life and frequently serve as go-betweens in delicate situations, looking out for each other's welfare. Chigdouane's brother saw her son, but he was adamant at first, insisting, "This camel I have [kept] for us, and so I did with it what I wanted." Finally, Chigdouane resorted to less indirect means, dictating a letter to her son to tell him emphatically that she needed this camel to bring millet from Nigeria. She requested that he give back the installment advance and not collect any more of it. Finally, her brother intervened again, the son relented, and the camel sale was stopped. But the conflict was protracted and extremely trying emotionally for Chigdouane.

The experiences of Adoum, Chigdouane, and others underline the need, even in focusing upon specific categories such as "elderly" persons, to contextualize the subject of aging and the life course and to consider age-related roles not as "watertight" cabinets but as part of an interconnected network on several levels: first, one in which local typifications of gender, social stratum, and kinship crosscut, and second, one in which different "voices," emerging from local social participants and the presence and participation of an outside researcher and other intruding forces, register. These multiple registers continually reposition each other and reformulate experience. While old women are more reserved in public and before men and youths in general, they are less so in private with each other, before certain relatives—in particular, matrilineal ones (sister, sister's sons, matrilateral cousin, or, in Chigdouane's case, her brother and brother's daughters)—and in the nuclear household setting. Before young female cousins, also, older women may behave with less reserve; for example, they tease, engage in sham physical fights, and show more flesh (e.g., removing the headscarf or even, occasionally, allowing the bolero blouse to slip off the shoulder) in private within the tent. Old women dance at the women's nameday ritual held the evening before a baby's official nameday at the mosque, as elderly female relatives, holding the baby, go in counterclockwise procession three times around the mother's tent, led by an old smith woman who carries a tray of incense, dates, millet, and goat cheese. This tray is said to ensure the *al baraka* (benediction) of the child. At such occasions, old women dance with pestles and ululate loudly.

Thus like Adoum, Chigdouane provided insights into the Tuareg life course in two respects. She was typical of many older persons in her attitudes toward performance of music and attendance at festivals. But her social stratum enabled her, again like Adoum, to be less reserved with me than with local unrelated young women, and to speak explicitly rather than indirectly, early on in our relationship, about the intersection between the life course and other social processes. Like Adoum, her servile origins undoubtedly had something to do with this, but individual, personal emotions were also significant; for I also established friendships with women of noble descent, and Chigdouane was less open toward me on the subject of her sons. Chigdouane's reticence about her son resulted from emotions as well as cultural constraints upon conduct. Thus the context of interaction is important in bringing these to the surface. Very elderly men, even chiefs and marabouts, often similarly vary in role behavior. They joke intensely with small children as well as with both old and young cross-cousins and blacksmiths and ex-slaves of either sex. Smiths, in particular, are said to be "like cousins," and this confers on them the freedom to joke freely with both ex-slaves and nobles, regardless of age.

Having children who come to maturity themselves—especially in cases conforming to the ideal in which these married children remain nearby, provide economic security, and mediate between parents and outside world— entails a number of changes in status and role expectations that are salient for all Kel Ewey. While withdrawal from work such as livestock herding is a response to the decline in physical strength as well as external disruptions such as drought and war, withdrawal from festivals and secular verbal art and music has a different significance: it has to do with attitudes toward prayer, song, the sacred and secular in local cultural values, and changing jural and kinship relationships. Yet the assumption of apparently more religious, and less secular, activities is differently marked and produces slightly different results among women and men, among individuals of different social segments, and in varying contexts of social interaction. Many men become practicing marabouts, and a number of elderly women specialize in herbalism and also may approach the mosque more closely, following just behind men and boys, on Islamic holidays. This leads me to question the applicability of the Western-based dichotomies of "sacred/secular," "purity/pollution," and "taboo," much as these have recently been questioned (Buckley and Gottlieb 1988). Following these authors' position on the subject of "purity and pollution," I consider it more useful to explore these symbolic categories and associations multivocally, in differing contexts, and dynamically, as they pertain to men and women through the life transitions, rather than to treat them as rigid oppositions. This lends itself well to the poetics perspective in this study, of "doing" in order to avoid reification and essentializing glosses, and yet at the same time dealing with categories as salient social entities, having very real effects upon the people involved in their practice: namely, in kinship as well as gender and class roles, and during rites of passage as well as in daily social interaction.

3

Life Course Rituals

Rites of Passage, Rites of Containment

The ritual roles of Tuareg men and women and persons of diverse ages and social origins provide further insights into household cycles as well as patterns of participation and retreat over different phases of the life course. Rituals encode status manipulation and biological/jural permutations, rather than rigid dichotomies, between men and women in youth and old age, in sexual symbolism and Islamic observances. But they also demarcate boundaries: purity of descent, control of property, and preservation of autonomy are the concerns expressed in key roles elders play in these rituals. Thus these rites transform but also contain.[1]

As individuals age, ritual participation mediates tensions experienced over time and across different contexts. There are regional variations in Tuareg Islamic practices (Norris 1972, 1975; Casajus 1990). In some Tuareg divisions, in particular Kel Ewey around Mount Bagzan in Aïr, there is a strong influence of religious scholars and clans claiming descent from the Prophet, and residents are devout Moslems. Many rural Kel Ewey lament that formerly Niger was "more Muslim"—people had prayed regularly and abstained from alcohol—but that today, youths, ex-slaves, and (especially) townspeople "do what they want." Islam coincides with many local cultural values in that it requires practicing greater restraint in conduct: restriction of consumption and absorption of substances, namely food and drink; taboos against pork and alcohol; and enveloping oneself in voluminous clothing for protection and modesty. These injunctions apply, ideally, to everyone, regardless of gender or social origin. Although the men's face-veil does not derive from Islam but from local cultural values of reserve and gender role patterns, some men add an Islamic overlay of interpretation to this custom. A few men told me that one reason they wear the face-veil is "in order to resemble the Prophet, who wore a turban." But in addition to compatibility between Islamic devotion and local cultural values of reserve, Kel Ewey also experience contradictions between devotion to Islam and other values. These latter are class- and gender-based. First, there are tensions between religious devotion and two other other mutually exclusive sources of power: technical expertise, traditionally the province of lower-status smiths and servile peoples, and bravery in war, associated with nobles and tributaries. Casajus writes, for example, that nobles had greater reservations about conducting holy wars than raids because in holy wars, all Tuareg, as believers, were equal (1990:30).

Second, there are tensions between religion and local cultural values pertaining to gender typifications. The difficulty of establishing rigid dichotomies between women and men of various ages, classes, and kin categories in relation to Islam becomes apparent upon examination of the mulivocality of meanings of gender and sexual symbolism. For example, while menstruating women cannot pray or touch men's religious amulets or swords, on the other hand, young women of childbearing age only temporarily abstain from praying during their periods. At other times, women's devotion to Islam is seen as equally important as men's. Indeed, women become full-fledged, practicing Muslims only upon the onset of menarche, for girls do not begin to fast during the month of Ramadan or to pray at all until they begin to menstruate. Thus menstruation is, in this sense, a prerequisite, just as much as a limitation, to participating in Islamic observances. Furthermore, biological menstruation is used as a marker of life course social roles only in some contexts. As observed, many women in response to my question of "when did you become a woman?" referred to their marriage, not the onset of menarche; and a few married before menarche. Social/jural marriage, not biological processes, is significant.

Nonetheless, women's status undergoes clear-cut transitions upon the onset of menstruation and again later in life upon its cessation. Upon their first menstruation, women begin religious observances, but it is only upon marriage that they become full social persons. At this time, women begin to wear the headscarf. While this is not as obligatory or as formalized as the men's face-veil, it is nonetheless a marker of married women's status.

Menstrual blood's implied opposition to Islam, in its terminology, *iban emud*, denoting "lack of prayer," is problematic as well. Animal blood in sacrifice is also viewed as polluting; it must not touch the ground inside a family's compound. Yet in certain contexts Kel Ewey men do appear to regard women of childbearing age as dangerous or polluting. For example, once I handed a bowl of drinking water to a marabout, the father of four women friends, on a visit. He hesitated for several moments but finally accepted the bowl from me. Unlike those in some other confederations, Kel Ewey men and women do not eat together and tend to use separate containers for everyday meals. Yet as pointed out elsewhere (Buckley and Gottlieb 1988; Rasmussen 1991a), "polluting" does not necessarily imply dirt, but rather danger, from powerful forces that can be positive as well as negative. Local women themselves, moreover, consider menstruation a positive, empowering force. Herbalists told me that excessive periods (those lasting too long or recurring too often) were considered healthy, a sign of fertility. Only a few women gave an alternate idiomatic expression for a menstruating woman of "she is dirty" *(ta jerga)*. Women observe a taboo against washing during their periods. At the end, women remove their wrapper-skirt and wash it, taking care to go to the well and do the washing after sundown.

On the other hand, ritual references to red as a positive fertility symbol are recurrent throughout local cultural imagery. Women's bright red leather sacks (dyed from a vegetable base of red maize) are particularly elaborate, and leather amulet cases are also dyed red. These latter are worn to protect individuals at birth, during recently weaned childhood, on adolescence, on marriage, and on childbirth. Indeed, animal hides are more closely associated with women. Smith women manufacture leather amulet cases, whereas smith men manufacture silver amulet cases. Following childbirth, women are also given a bright red–colored liquid of leaves and roots, referred to as "mother's stomach medicine." Symbolism surrounding menstruation is multivocal and cannot be thought of as always consistently opposed to Islam or purity.

In men's circumcision and face-veiling rituals, there is a symbolic connection between male circumcision and ritual animal sacrifice, and between male face-veiling and marriage. Malam Boulala, about forty years old, of noble descent, currently a marabout and caravanner and husband of a daughter of the local chief, related his impressions of these events:

> All boys of age of three years, it is possible to cut [*agadam*, or circumcise] them. If they are cut, they will be able to take the knife and slaughter animals, either on Tabaski [the feast held to commemorate Abraham's sacrifice of a ram in Biblical and Koranic accounts] or on almsgiving. This process of circumcision, there is only one person who does it. He who knows that. When he begins to cut a child, he stretches his feet and places them apart and makes a hole in the ground between his two feet. There is a person behind him who closes the child's eyes so that he does not see the blood flowing, and in order to prevent him from running. The circumciser when he cuts and the child cries, this cry is said to hide his sentiments. If there are women in the village who hear, they respond by ululating. When the women respond by ululating, the circumciser pours on the child a product of the *agar* tree [fruits of this tree are also used to remove fur from leather hides]. He who closes his eyes then uncovers them and the child returns home. When he arrives home, his mother gives him a present. And now he is circumcised, he is Muslim. From now on, whether Tabaski or almsgiving, every holy ritual is his right, if he is eleven years, twelve years, thirteen, fourteen, fifteen, or after and he is at the age to marry.
>
> All those who aren't circumcised, if they slaughter an animal, it is like a cadaver [e.g., inedible]. If they receive a child, the child also is like living dead. His children won't slaughter a Tabaski or alms animal. [But] even if the child is three years old, if he is circumcised, he does not [even] need to veil himself yet. Everything he slaughters is correct. Even if he is very young, he can hold the knife. But normally, he says only, "God is great," and adults cut the animal. For

a large animal, one can slaughter it any way. No need to look to the east. But if you slaughter in the direction you look, it is correct. If it is a small animal [a goat or sheep], its head must be turned toward the north, and the feet toward the south. All men, if they have children, they are circumcised. He can circumcise them himself. There was once a certain man called Ahayo, my brother-in-law, and he cut them himself, his children. Not even one week passed, and they were cured [i.e., there were no complications].

Usually, it is the relatives [parents] of the children who go over there [outside the village or camp] for their circumcision. If it is someone who is not related who sees, that won't heal. One gives 500 CFA [about $2] to the circumciser, not the person circumcised. He must pocket this 500 CFA in advance for him to cut. The 500 CFA, the father of the child himself must give that and they must agree. If it is the child, the circumciser will not agree. If the child is circumcised he will spend seven days eating meat and everything that is good, like rice and macaroni. If the child skips or walks on the place where a menstruating woman has urinated, the cure will take longer. Medicine against delayed curing is thorns of the *taborak* tree and thorns of the *takonichite* [or Fr. *hérisson*] tree, rabbit and antelope dung, and also the *agar* tree to heal the boys' wounds. Boys recover back in the village. They cannot drink *eghale* during this time since it makes urination difficult.

Circumcision is called *asunuslummale* or *agadam,* literally "cutting" or "to cut." This is done to boys in groups once each year. Marabouts told me that they knew of only one group of Tuareg adult men, residing in a region northwest of Agadez, who had not been circumcised because their parents had neglected it; they viewed such a condition as "shameful." Only men are circumcised; there are no female genital operations among Tuareg. But some Kel Ewey men say jokingly that "the rabbit will circumcise women in the next life with a palm thorn." The rabbit appears in local folklore as clever, second only to the jackal as a trickster figure, and, as shown, its dung has medicinal use during men's circumcision. Heated rabbit dung and products from tree barks are believed to have healing properties when applied to the boys' wounds. Elderly female herbalists often gather medicinal barks. The boys' wounds cannot be seen by any woman of childbearing age or they will not heal.

Circumcision is performed at the end of the rainy season near a small mountain outside the village or camp. The cure takes place back at the settlement, but often away from the nuclear household in a resthouse usually used to lodge travelers, thereby underlining the boys' liminal status. Boys are usually between six and seven years old. This is done by a specialist/barber called *anagzem* (Tamacheq) or *wanzem* (Hausa); only rarely, as Malam Boulala indicated, is it done by an older relative. This job is a special skill but is not inherited or affiliated with any particular clan. One barber in the area, about seventy years old, also specialized in bone-setting. He inherited and learned this work from his father and began practicing it at about age forty, since, he said, "in order to heal, one must be an adult, since at this time one has a complete [fully developed] mind." He also indicated it is important for him to perform ablutions *(alwalla)* before touching his patients in circumcision and in bone-setting, as he would before praying. Healing from an older person is a kind of prayer and almsgiving. In this process, the older person transmits *al baraka* blessing. He added that circumcision wounds will not heal if a woman with an illegitimate child watches the ritual.

Thus fertility imagery permeates these rites, but it must be contained and controlled, or it becomes destructive. Yet despite the ideological valuing of women's biological fertility in cultural symbolism, there is no special ritual for a girl's menarche. Rather, traditionally there was a ritual of forced feeding of milk or *eghale*, the beverage made of millet, goat cheese, dates, and water pounded and mixed together that is important in rites of passage and served for *al baraka* blessing. Formerly, in order to hasten fertility Kel Ewey practiced this custom of force-feeding, called *adanay*. From descriptions in the ethno-graphic literature (Bernus 1981), adolescent girls, particularly nobles, were lit-erally forced to undergo this practice, regardless of personal inclination. Most Bagzan region residents told me that this is no longer done. But in the past, the idea underlying it was to hasten maturity and fertility, among nobles in particular, whose women married at a younger age than women of other classes. The value underlying *adanay* is, however, still very much alive. Fatness among women is still equated with good health and fertility from the view-point of both sexes. Women are constantly trying to put on weight, eating clay and drinking millet gruel and milk to effect this goal. But the formalized prac-tice of *adanay* is now rarer, due to the decrease in pastures and the scarcity of milk and cheese. One elderly noble woman, Amina, who lived next door to me, observed:

> A long time ago, people used to sometimes fatten up adolescent girls so they would get pretty. My family did not do this to me. Some did this. If, for exam-ple, you had a daughter who was thin, only to her did you do that. To her who was fat [already], this was not done. This is not done anymore today. Before, if you wanted to do this, you pounded *eghale* or gave her milk. You had her drink and drink and drink to get fat, very fat. But this was in the past; we don't do this anymore.

Other residents emphasized the idea of fertility and purity of descent asso-ciated with nobility. Noble girls were encouraged to undergo the ritual for the purpose of bearing children as soon as possible. Men mentioned other objec-tives, such as physical beauty and class-based physical ideals; for example, the belief that "[lots of] milk makes the flesh soft and white, whereas [a diet of solely] millet cereal makes the flesh hard, like that of slave women in the past."

Despite the emphasis placed upon women's fertility, most sexual symbolism over the life course addresses both men and women, and it centers around the social bond of marriage. Women receive a headscarf and length of indigo cloth (commonly called *pagne* throughout West Africa), worn as a wrapper-skirt, on marriage. Here again, as in other contexts such as women's attaining ritual as opposed to biological post-childbearing status, or former slaves' retaining jural minor status despite biological old age, age takes its primary significance from metaphorical and nonlinear attributes. The headscarf usually is a gift from the new groom, and the wrapper-skirt is from the bride's maternal grandmother. If a woman is not yet married by the age of thirty, an older female relative presents her with the headscarf, and a marabout pronounces verses from the Koran called *chimougraw*.

Like the woman's headscarf ritual, the men's first face-veiling ritual is associated with marriage. Malam Boulala, the young man of noble and marabout origins who had earlier explained male circumcision, described the first face-veil ritual as follows:

> Before marrying, he [a man] must be veiled. When he is going to veil, he decides and must tell his parents. This is not ordinary everyday cloth. When one first takes up the face-veil, they take him to a marabout, he reads Koranic verses and spits his saliva into the special indigo *[alechou]* cloth as a benediction, and in order to "calm the heart," and as a kind of protective amulet [against misfortune and spirits threatening the person during times of transition]. This is called the *tchimigraw*. After this, the marabout places the veil on his head. When he veils him, the man goes seven days without removing it from his head; this is medicine against spirits. If he removes it, there is the danger of being attacked by them. It is because of this that it is not good to remove the veil before that time. When the marabout comes to veil the face for the first time, one must give him alms. After having gone seven days without removing it, after that you can take it off. This period is called *issayat na nagade* or "the seven days of veiling." Now, after this [at between 15 and 20 years] you can seek to marry. Usually, one must wear the *alechou* [a fancy, indigo-dyed festival cloth] in order to veil in the Tuareg wedding style of veiling. One can start marriage negotiations without the veil, but as soon as one "attaches" the marriage [at the mosque], the man must have the veil on his head. When a person veils his face, he says to himself that he has become an adult. But if he does not know how to veil, at the Koranic reading and blessing of the marabout he gets this done [and learns how].

The ritual held for a man upon first taking up the face-veil is called *amangadezar*. A few younger men no longer undergo the formal ritual on first veiling. One young man, for example, told me laughingly, "I merely went to the market in Agadez, bought a measure of cloth, and wrapped the veil myself, unceremoniously, as I would getting a new pair of trousers." The traditional ritual is still important for most Kel Ewey men, however, and face-veiling, with or without the ritual, is a prerequisite for marrying. Malam Boulala discussed the two possible forms of marriage first alluded to by Chigdouane, thereby providing a man's perception to balance hers:

First, a noble man must—in order to marry, if he sees a woman in whom he is interested and he loves, and she is nice—he must ask her parents, using an intermediary [often a blacksmith who is a friend and confidante of the noble man] to tell them he likes their daughter: "If you agree, I want to marry her." And he also, if his parents agree, he marries her. This is "a man's marriage" [*tedua n elis,* the phrase Kel Ewey use to refer to a marriage of personal choice or love].

Now, another kind of marriage is that you can follow your parents, you can do what they want. If you want to find *al baraka* benediction [blessing or good fortune], you must do what they want. Even if you do not love the woman, you must make an effort to reconcile this in your heart and love her. This latter is a "marriage of the family" *(tedua n eghiwan).* Now you can find "blessing." In such a marriage, arranged by parents with close relatives, the husband's family is obliged to support the wife during his absence in travel, migrant labor, or caravan trade, whereas in an independent love match, they are not obliged to do so.

Smiths, who act as intermediaries for nobles not only in official marriage and bridewealth negotiations but also in illicit affairs, told me that, despite nobles' official preference for marriages arranged by the family and to partners within the family (usually close cousins), most Kel Ewey prefer to marry distantly related or nonrelated persons. Furthermore, one smith commented, "Only persons who lack suitors have a marriage of the family; others attempt to marry, insofar as possible, according to choice. You know how it is—some people have many suitors, others have only a few." But I noticed that many first marriages are arranged by the family, and subsequent marriages (either remarriages following widowhood or divorce, or men's polygynous matches such as that between Chigdouane and her second husband) are by independent choice. Women may indicate their own love preference, but only indirectly, through poetry and song, greetings at festivals, or intermediaries such as blacksmiths or friends. A woman may also veto an undesirable suitor, but parents may veto her first choice as well. Mothers-in-law prefer close cousin marriages, because in such matches the bridewealth remains within the family and presumably the relations between affines are smoother. Two sisters I knew who each had one child, a baby and a toddler, respectively, indicated enthusiastically to me that a future match between the children would be "very good."

One man I knew, Ado, a blacksmith, had wanted to marry a woman who was distantly related to him in a love match or *tedua n elis,* but his mother and her female cousin had already been trying to arrange a marriage between him and the female cousin's daughter in a *tedua n eghiwan.* The man cooperated "in order to please his mother." But later on, after several years of marriage to the closely related woman, he contracted a second, polygynous marriage independently with the more distantly related woman. His two wives resided in separate villages about twenty-five miles apart, which caused some tension in his marital life. Although there is an attempt to avoid problems of jealousy by giving a compensation gift to the first wife, staging the "wedding with calm" for the second marriage, and establishing separate residences for the women, Ado did not treat his co-wives equally: he spent nearly all months of each year in residence with the second co-wife in her village. Once, in 1983, he brought his second wife to camel races held in the village of the first wife during a Muslim holiday, despite heavy public criticism of him for doing this. The first wife frequently fell ill and became possessed by spirits called the "People of Solitude" (Rasmussen 1995).

By 1995, Ado had married again, to his third wife. Relatives in his village regarded her ambivalently. She was from a distant region, to the west of Agadez, and also from a different social stratum: she was of servile descent. This type of marriage, between smiths and former slaves, is still rare, for most smiths, as observed, marry endogamously and, furthermore, often contract marriages with even closer cousins than do nobles. At first, Ado kept this wife in her residential village, but during the 1991–1995 rebellion, he brought her to his home village to escape the fighting, which was particularly intense near her home. His first wife, still in the village next door to his own natal village, publically and vociferously complained about his polygyny to all who would listen, including myself, yet she did not request a divorce.

Ado seemed prosperous enough to support all three of his wives. He continued to practice successful smithing, making silver jewelry for nobles and, when the region became more peaceful for travel, also manufacturing soapstone knickknacks for the tourist trade. But his public economic success and private domestic tensions took their toll on Ado's health as he approached his fifties. His camel was stolen and sold by the thieves. He suffered from a heart attack (somewhat rare among the rural Aïr population) and had to spend three months in treatment at a hospital in Arlit, the large mining town northwest of Agadez. He also became plagued by eye problems, which were diagnosed as caused by sorcery activated by other smiths living around Agadez, who were rumored to be jealous of Ado. Ado saw a marabout, who cured his eyes by applying Koranic verses written in the form of vegetable ink as a make-up about his eyes, supplemented by herbalists' tree barks and gum arabic.

Close intermarriage, in particular between matrilineally related cousins— children of sisters—is favored by many Kel Ewey women, because in their view this fosters smooth relationships between affines, with whom there is ideally a reserve relationship, and also because it keeps the bridewealth within the family. Yet most Kel Ewey in practice prefer to marry distantly related or unrelated persons. This concern with keeping property as close to "home ground" as possible and with maintaining good relationships with affines is an important undercurrent in the changing social and ritual roles of persons as they age. Elders have an interest in negotiating close cousin marriages for economic and descent-related reasons. For affines are in effect in a relationship of uneasy truce, like that between partners in a business contract, at least until bridewealth payments and groomservice have been completed, and often until a child has been born. The mother-in-law can break up her daughter's marriage if she does not like the husband or considers early marriage obligations to be proceeding badly. Many women's kin are just next door and continue to interact closely with the new couple, particularly during the first two to three years of marriage. The newly married daughter also remains economically dependent upon her mother, as she shares her kitchen and her livestock herds remain held jointly with those of her mother. I noticed frequent visits each day by the neighboring mother and sister of the woman with whom I boarded during my first field stay in 1983. This woman had remained near her mother and sisters throughout her marriage, an option many more nomadic couples traditionally choose in caravanning villages near Mount Bagzan. In contrast, during my 1991 and 1995 visits, in the more sedentized household where I boarded, the female head had followed her husband to reside near his parents after the obligatory three years of residence near her own kin in a nomadic camp about seven miles away. In this household, although they were next door, the husband's mother and sisters visited and shared work less frequently.

Therefore, even in cases of good relations with parents-in-law, reserve limits their contact, thereby isolating the spouse who resides away from his or her own parents. The conduct, familiarity, and affection between a wife and her relatives, and the reserve and respect between affines, was also extended to relations with me and introduced a dimension to my field experience that at first puzzled me. The mother of my 1983 fictive "mother" adopted me as a fictive maternal granddaughter, frequently visiting me and giving me small presents and food. When my husband visited me near the final weeks of my fieldwork in 1983, we stopped by to visit my fictive "grandmother." I had forgotten that she and my husband would be considered fictive in-laws and thought nothing of his lack of face-veil until, on our entering her compound, she hurriedly covered her mouth with her headscarf as elderly women often do before affines, and on sighting him without a man's face-veil, fled with embarrassment into one of the tents. The mother of the husband in whose household I boarded in 1991 and 1995 was much more distant toward me, seldom coming by to visit. I initially misinterpreted this attitude as personal coldness but later realized it was merely an extension of her reserve toward her son's wife, whose age I approximated. Furthermore, as a younger person not in a close, familiar relationship, I was expected to approach and visit her, not the reverse. My field host explained the reserve relationship between affines by making an analogy between behaving with reserve *(takarakit)* before one's in-laws and relieving oneself outside the village or camp: he said *takarakit* is the reason why Tuareg do both. He said, for example, it is "embarrassing (translated as *honteux* in French) for the son and mother-in-law and daughter and father-in-law to see each other and think about their respective spouses and children at the same time." The new groom never eats, unveils his face, or pronounces the name of his affines or wife in front of his affines. The new bride cooks food in her mother's kitchen and brings it to her new husband inside the nuptial tent.

The beliefs that Tuareg men with daughters-in-law are not supposed to dance at evening festivals and that Tuareg women with sons-in-law are not supposed to sing at evening festivals, therefore, are extensions of these practices. They parallel and reinforce jural arrangements and property concerns in the domestic cycle. Although there is no abrupt point of disengagement, they are expected to gradually attend less and less as they grow older. Residents explained that their attendance grows "more and more shameful." Traditionally, the Tuareg husband could not smash sugarloafs or sugercubes (the frequent forms of sugar sold in the region) in his wife's village or camp because the loud noise would reach his parents-in-laws' ears. A brief tale associates reserve toward affines with the camel, in rural areas the principal form of bridewealth:

> The camel once had straight, extended legs rather than legs bent at the elbows or knees. While approaching his in-laws, he crept so as not to disturb them. Henceforth the camel has legs that are crooked at the elbows or knees; and thus began reserve.

The early years of marriage among Tuareg, therefore, are fragile and surrounded by tensions. Smiths told me that despite official ideals of close-cousin marriage preferred by older women who are cousins, and whose children would become economic assets, most young people marry distantly or unrelated persons, and those who marry too closely tend to divorce or (in the case of men) acquire second co-wives later. My own censuses and genealogies confirmed this. Young men told me that they find going to festivals in distant places "much more exciting" than attending festivals among close relatives in their home, or neighboring, villages or camps. Smiths, in discussing how "only those persons who have few suitors" end up marrying close relatives," described weddings for these latter types of matches as less elaborate than those held for persons from separate villages and camps, who also tend to be less closely related. For example, there was less drumming and dancing held at the wedding of a couple who were first cousins on the maternal side and who resided in the same village than there was at the wedding of another couple who were unrelated by kinship and resided in distant villages. There is much greater fanfare in cases where the groom is brought to the bride's village or camp than in cases when he already resides there, usually as a closer relative. This seems to contradict what one would expect to find, for close marriage is the preferred ideal of adults and parents, particularly sisters. Yet it reveals an underlying logic—the conflicts, tensions, and counterforces, the struggles between the wishes of parents and children, and conflicting considerations of love, property, and descent—at play in marriage.

Thus relations between the generations over time revolve most centrally around marriage, whose underlying goal is to guard the maternal tent space. Over the life course, temporal markers refer to spatial boundaries. The maternal tent space stands under threat, both from conditions internal and long-standing to Tuareg society and from external ones: male, patrifocal, and Islamic influences; the ambiguity and negotiability of social stratum affiliation, which complicates noble descent concerns; and encroaching central state policies of forced sedentarization, which jeopardize nomadic autonomy. On one level, there are struggles between husbands and wives and the latters' parents; on another level, nobles must struggle to maintain prestige as they lose material and productive bases of power; on still another level, development programs favor sedentarized gardening communities and penalize nomads. Elders' attempts to arrange youths' marriages reflect these concerns.

Another marriage practice involves an inherited marriage between a widower and a niece or younger sister of his former, deceased wife. This is common among Kel Ewey near Mount Bagzan, and I knew of several cases in the village of my long-term research and residence. A nomadic woman, married to a male caravanner about fifteen years her senior, had been the maternal niece of her husband's first wife. Smiths confided in me that such a marriage, while encouraged under the circumstances, was "somewhat shameful" in that the woman had no or few suitors. Noble men told me their view of this: if the man is very respected and there are women who "need" a husband, he is supposed to help them by marrying them after his wife's death, a motive similar to that given for some men's polygynous marriage to widows. But these types of weddings include only the Islamic ritual at the mosque, and there is no festival or musical entertainment held. They belong to that category called a "wedding with calm" or "wedding without noise," as opposed to a "wedding of noise" held for younger couples. The "wedding with calm" is also held when any older, previously married couple remarries after long-term divorce or widowhood.

Weddings and namedays are the most elaborate rites of passage. Other transitions, such as funerals and memorial services, are less elaborate. Rites surrounding property transfers upon the conclusion of the groom's obligations after two to three years of marriage—the disengagement of the bride's livestock from her mother's herds and the construction of a new, independent tent at a distance from her parents' compound—are also important. Certain symbolic elements recur throughout all these rituals, which underline jural changes over time. A number of processes symbolize separation and reconstitution of groupings in Tuareg society: the sexes, social strata, and different age groups and kinship groups. The roles of the sexes and different social strata often undergo reversal or inversion during these rites. Elders, marabouts, and black-smiths each play important roles in these rituals as mediators, facilitators, linchpins, and, in effect, diplomats or ambassadors between the major kin and class social divisions in Tuareg society. Different rites of passage alternately emphasize separation and mixing of various categories of persons in a con-trolled fashion: men and women, cognates and affines, members of different social strata, and old and young. The social segments come together at such times in genial exaggeration of affection, with smiths offering social commen-tary on each segment in praise-songs and dances. The roles of various age groups feature separation and the contrasting behavior of adolescents, newly married persons, and elders of either sex. For example, adolescents, particularly girls, and newly married young women do not attend rites of passage during the morning but instead go after sundown to the nightly festivities presided over by smiths. By contrast, older persons of both sexes attend the religious rites during the day with marabouts and ceremonies at the mosque but tend to avoid the evening musical festivals.

These contrasts impinged upon residents' positioning of me at different points in time and became apparent to me during their commentary on the rituals. For example, during my early stay in Aïr, I was guided by friends to the tent of adolescent and young newly married women wedding guests, and I was encouraged to participate along with them in the evening festivities. When invited to the bride's village or camp with the groom's side of the fam-ily, I was encouraged to rest along with these women in the tent set up for them and then participate in the late evening dances and songs organized by smiths. A few friends asked me, in a straightforward manner, if I wished "a temporary husband"; for, they explained, a recently married, childless woman separated from her husband over a long term in effect is considered single, albeit temporarily. On my later visit to the field, local perceptions of my changed situation were vividly illustrated to me. While I was attending smith women's wedding songs featuring much buffoonery and ribald humor, a prominent marabout passed by the compound. He greeted me cooly, all the while remaining at a distance outside the fence, gave me a stern look, and asked, "Prayer is better than this [smith performance], isn't it?" Elders and marabouts tended to avoid the smith festivities, emphasizing instead other phases of the wedding, in particular, praying at the mosque. Subtly, the marabout was telling me I should think about changing my focus in attend-ing these events as I grew older. At about the same time, women began to question me more often about why I did not have children, who would assist me when I grew old, and who would inherit from me.

Central to the wedding is the theme of the groom's role as initially servile to his mother-in-law. Symbolism in the wedding ritual conveys the idea that the groom's access to the bride depends on his relationship with his parents-in-law, in particular, the mother-in-law. Tuareg marriage is enacted in slow, progressive, and tentative stages rather than accomplished in a single event, and the position of the groom is similar to that of a new apprentice. The wedding is itself a smaller rite of passage within a whole series of rites of passage surrounding the strengthening of ties between affines, through exchanges of property and services, over several years.

When the family of the woman and that of the man prepare for marriage, Kel Ewey say that they form the same "head" *(eghef)*. This means they are happy about the marriage. They send a smith who tells everyone in the neighboring villages and camps. Then the smith goes to the mosque and he cries three times *"Azalaf!"* ("Marriage!"). That night, people come to pound millet and the smiths prepare the meal. They slaughter a large animal from the herd of the bride's mother, either a lamb or a goat. The smiths organize a musical event *(tende,* also denoting the mortar drum featured at these events, which smiths usually play); young women sing and men guests dance. This lasts about two and a half days. When it is concluded, the *chidegalen* (female affines) "guests," who are often, though not always, from another village or camp on the husband's side of the family, prepare an *edew* nuptial tent that is made larger each successive day. The women on the side of the bride reconstruct it bigger and bigger each day for three days.

After about half a year or later, the husband pays the bridewealth completely *(taggalt).* Three years later, he may make a home apart from his in-laws. Before this, however, the *chidagalen* prepare one tent for sleeping (later called *ehan*), one for storing food provided by the husband, and perhaps one for rest during the day. The husband brings millet and buckets, other food, jewelry, and so forth to the house of the wife's mother, called *tamegi,* from the day of the marriage onward for about one year. The bridewealth usually consists of one camel and clothes. The camel is kept in trust by the father of the bride.

Just before marriage, the girl gives her fiance one ram. He, in turn, gives it to his mother's herd. The mother of the bride gives a refined goatskin water bag called *anwar* to her son-in-law upon marriage. This is made by a local blacksmith woman attached to the family. The mother of the groom gives large, black wooden bowls to her future daughter-in-law upon her marriage to her son. These bowls are variously called *alkada* or *enkes* and are made by smith men in the region near Zinder, Niger and Kano, Nigeria. Most are undecorated, but marks on the rims of some bowls indicate the identity of their manufacturer, like livestock brands or artisan signatures. These bowls are considered fine dishware, served to guests and used on holidays. Friends explained the traditional purpose of these bowls to me: they are used in combination with wooden spoons and ladles so that the husband's parents-in-law cannot hear the sound of the new groom's eating, which is considered highly shameful in their extreme reserve relationship.

Thus for the first few years, the couple live at the bride's parents' home, in the nuptial tent a few yards from the parents' compound. There is emphasis both on extreme reserve between the groom and the bride's parents and also on the exchange of goods and services between the two families. The bride's parents build her nuptial tent during the seven-day wedding ritual. This tent is repeatedly torn down and reconstructed, larger each time, during the seven-to-eight–day wedding. About two to three years later, if the marriage is considered stable by the bride's mother, the couple's friends construct another tent that is bigger and located independently of either the man's or the woman's side of the family. It may be located in the village or camp of her parents, but at a distance from their compound, or in the village or camp of the groom's parents, according to choice. This shelter or *abarkan*—the same metaphor used for the individual's changed constitution over the life course—is used for cooking and reception.

In the Bagzan region of Aïr, many couples choose to stay near the bride's parents because many men depart on caravans. During my earlier field residence, I noticed that many women refused to follow husbands who moved, and eventually these couples were divorced. This practice varies, however, and recently seems to be changing in favor of more numerous moves away, particularly among gardeners and other more sedentized couples. Indeed, postmarital residence after the first two to three years can become an arena of struggle; for although women own the tent and men the mud house, the land beneath these structures is owned by whoever resides near his or her own kin. In addition to economics, interpersonal factors may influence where a couple resides after the initial uxorilocal residence.

Thus the stakes are high, and the spouse who succeeds in imposing his or her residential preference is usually able to do this through sheer force of personality (having a stronger will) or being from a "stronger" family, or in local terminology, a stronger "tent" (i.e., more prominent or prosperous, or both; or viewed as "saving" the other spouse from some unhappy situation in her home). Two examples illustrate these possible outcomes. One prosperous merchant, of noble descent and from a maraboutique family, had a store in Agadez, where he usually resided in recent years. His two wives resided in the rural Bagzan region, one in each of two neighboring villages. He had married his second wife, from a nomadic camp several miles from his own village of origin, after about eleven years of marriage to the first wife. The second wife's mother had numerous health problems and was defined by local residents as "crazy": she was even rumored to be physically violent, frequently striking people, including close relatives. Her family, including the son-in-law, tried a variety of methods to cure her. The new wife remained with her mother in the nomadic camp for the prerequisite first two years, and her husband visited her there, fulfilling his obligations as a new son-in-law. Mutual friends indicated, however, that this man's relationship to the mother-in-law required "less reserve than usual" because she was the mother of his second, not first, wife. They said the husband practices "the most reserve" with the mother of his first wife. But the mental state of this mother-in-law undoubtedly also affected this. After two years of remaining with her family, where the husband visited her at intervals, he established his second wife in his own village, next to his mother. He thereafter alternated between his two wives' villages, but spent most of his time in Agadez, conducting his business. Another man, a smith who owned a small store in his maternal village and combined tailoring and gardening with tourist crafts, married a woman from a neighboring village. As usual, this couple spent the first year or two in residence with her family. Although this woman's mother was not rumored to be "crazy," the smith told me during one evening visit that, although all went well initially, he later "had great difficulty" getting along with his mother-in-law and soon moved his wife to his own village. Both these men were in a position of economic strength.

A few women, after being married to prosperous gardeners for many years and residing near their husbands' relatives, eventually even give up their nomadic tent, but this practice is still rare and is considered "unfortunate" by most residents because of all that the tent still implies: psychologically, culturally, and economically, it remains the centerpiece of women's autonomy. Yet even though most women retain this tent and own livestock herds, continual effort on the part of men to pull women away from their nuptial residence, and frequent resistance to this by many women, suggests that residence is crucial, if only as psychological leverage in disputes.

These tensions are shown in the *techawait* ritual, held when a couple moves away from the wife's parents. This rite is enacted expressly, smiths explained, "to bring the wife to the home of the husband's family." During the rainy season of 1995, I accompanied relatives of the husband and their attached smith man leading three camels, one on which the wife would ride back to the wife's village, about five miles away, where the couple had heretofore resided. The camels were decked out in colorful, elaborately embroidered saddles, harnesses and trappings; the smith led by the bridle a white riding-camel intended for the wife. The husband's relatives, men and women alike, were dressed in their best festival clothing, similar to that worn at the wedding, including women's headscarves made of iridescent blue indigo cloth and men's face-veils. The women wore red and yellow ocher facial make-up. En route, no songs were sung, and conversation was casual. Several individuals asked me where American married couples reside, and they expressed mild shock when I indicated that usually, couples in the United States prefer to reside independently, sometimes far from relatives on either side, and that sometimes, American men even joke, disrespectfully by Tuareg standards, about their mothers-in-law.

Approximately midway to the wife's village, we encountered a large group of men from the wife's village carrying on their shoulders her nuptial tent, detached from its wooden posts, toward the husband's village. Upon our arrival at the village, there were formal greetings with the wife's relatives, as at weddings and namedays. The smith disassembled the couple's bed and loaded this, along with other prepacked belongings, onto the two pack-camels, reserving the riding-camel for the wife. The wife, closely veiled with indigo cloth (contrary to everyday practice when only men veil the face), emerged with a woman friend, and her male in-laws placed her upon the riding-camel behind her friend. Both women were careful to keep their heads covered, due to reserve. As we left her village and relatives behind, with the smith leading the white camel that had the two women on it and carrying her husband's sword, and with another man carrying the husband's lance, the wife's female relatives began lamentations, crying softly. When I later inquired about the women's crying, men's and women's responses were very different, thereby revealing marked differences in perception of this situation. Men told me matter-of-factly that the women's cries were "not real (grief), only ritual cries," whereas by contrast, women told me that the women were crying from very real grief "at seeing their daughter leave."

Upon arrival in the husband's village, the wife's affines took her off the camel and carried her into the husband's home (in this case, he had constructed a mud house). She remained inside with her friend, still closely covered with the cloth, as brides are at weddings. Later, men and women also contradicted each other in accounts of who "decided" where the couple would reside: men insisted that this is the husband's decision, while women told me firmly that the mother-in-law, "at least a strong one," decides.

Thus postmarital residence and ownership of land and buildings, as well as some men's polygyny, are sensitive points in the life course for many couples and are the primary causes of divorce. This was shown by substantial numbers of women who refused to follow husbands, and also earlier, in the case of Chigdouane, who married a polygynist but eventually divorced him following conflict with his first wife's family over sale of her camel. Many marriages, however, endure, whether monogamous or polygynous, regardless of where couples reside. In these successful marriages, more residential structures are eventually added, wherever the couple decides to live, enclosed by a fence or wall.

The preferred season for weddings is the rainy season (in the Nigerien Sahara, from June to August or September). Reasons given are that, at this time, all kinspersons are together; the women are home from the pastures and the men are back from their five-to-seven–month absence on caravan trade expeditions to Bilma and Kano; camels are "strong and beautiful" (it is their rutting season) at this time; and it is planting time in the oasis gardens. The emphasis is upon fast camels for racing at the camel *tende* during the wedding and upon plentiful food. Thus both symbolic and practical explanations address fertility in the timing of weddings. Early in the wedding ceremony, announcements begin, accompanied by a rhythm of the smiths' *acanza* hand drums and *tende* mortar drum, identical to that played at nameday rituals for a new baby. Women and children gather around the smith players in the afternoon. Beginning in early morning, old smith women prepare *wayna* (wheat pancakes) and a dish combining rice and macaroni that is associated with rites of passage. At smith weddings, there is role inversion between the social strata, and old noble women prepare and serve the food. This holds true for babies' namedays as well. There is also gender inversion at weddings and namedays, where men pound the millet for the ritual drink called *eghajira* or *eghale*, the infusion of crushed millet, dates, goat cheese, and water. There is never, however, inversion of age roles. Smith men grill the meat of a sheep slaughtered at dawn by the marabout.

Toward sundown, many guests—mostly young men and women from distant and neighboring camps and villages including the groom's side of the family—arrive, stiffly dressed up. These persons are referred to collectively as *imartayen* (the masculine form of the feminine *chimartayen*). In the case of a more elaborate *aduban n ezgar* (bull wedding), at which the groom's family gives a bull, women guests arrive on decorated donkeys, all filing around the nuptial tent in counterclockwise direction. The wedding ceremony and festivals are about seven days in duration. Kel Ewey say that more distantly related brides and grooms have more elaborate weddings "because more guests are involved in this (i.e., not solely persons within the family, as would be the case in a marriage of closely related persons)."

The first day of the ritual, the parents of the couple go to the mosque, where, with the marabout but without the couple, they "attach" the marriage. Kel Ewey indicated that smiths cannot touch the drums announcing the wedding until this is completed. Older persons and marabouts are prominent during this phase, which highlights official marriage, Koranic verses, food preparation, and the roles of parents of the couple. The father of the bride, in particular, must be present. In the meantime, the groom and bride each remain at home in their respective parents' compounds. Henna is applied to their hands and feet by a smith in the case of a noble wedding, and by a noble in the case of a smith wedding. The smith woman who applies henna is called a fictive "sister" to the groom and bride. At one wedding I attended between closely related cousins from the same village, I observed henna application during late afternoon in the groom's compound. The groom was inside a mud house protected from the spirits, like the bride, by a knife stuck in the ground and Islamic amulets placed nearby; but unlike the bride, who lay concealed beneath a blanket throughout the ritual, he was said not to feel "ashamed" and not to be "in hiding." The smith woman who applied henna to him arrived with other smith women, and after the application, before they left the house, they sang smith praise-songs called *tedaban* and performed smith dances called *tabategh.*

Their performance began with drumming in the courtyard of the groom's compound, joking and singing as the young noble guests present gave the smith women money and millet on trays, and some also sprayed perfume on the soloist. I also gave money, and my name appeared in some verses. The soloist, whom I'll call Adaoula, made a dance gesture with the right hand upward, extended in a begging motion said to be "self-denigrating." This is a reference to smiths' role as important go-betweens in marriage and also to their marginal social status and position as clients supported by their noble patrons. The performance is also intended to be buffoonlike, for smiths lack reserve and comment freely about Tuareg society, mocking each social segment in turn, including themselves. There were mock fights, chasing, attempts to rip off men's face-veils, and satirical references to individuals in the audience in the women's songs. Adaoula ate some raw millet with comic abandon as this was offered and placed the rest of the millet in a heap on a cloth on the ground. Later, the smiths present divided the money and millet among themselves. Following this was a performance by smith men and women of praise-songs out in the open, called *chiluba,* as men raced their camels around the circle of smiths.

Each night at dusk old women on the bride's side of the family take down, and then reassemble, the nuptial tent; at first, it is intentionally incorrectly constructed, and too small, to be enlarged and improved at each successive reconstruction. Elderly noble women are believed to be expert at tent construction, whereas the grass *tettrem,* later added to the couple's compound, is viewed as less demanding to construct and is the province of younger women, who, until recently, had assistance from former slaves. On each night, beginning with the second day of the wedding ritual, the groom arrives first at the nuptial tent, led by male friends in a slow procession, chanting Koranic verses. The bride follows, after about twenty minutes, in a procession of female relatives. They go around the wedding tent three times, in counterclockwise direction, led by a young smith woman carrying incense, dates, and millet on a tray to repel spirits believed jealous of the bride and to promote *al baraka* blessing. This is called *asoghele* or "circling around." The crowd ululates and smiths beat their small hand drums, and later, after looking in from the front of the tent (the bride enters from beneath the side panel of the mat wall), they close the door. Smiths then beat against the tent door with sticks, saying "Bissimillallah," an Islamic benediction. This is also believed to ward off spirits and bring good fortune. The crowd of youthful guests then attend a music and dance festival led by smiths near the tent set up for female guests, at some distance away from the nuptial tent, which lasts until very late (often around

4 A.M.). During the first year of marriage, the married couple meets in this nuptial tent at night only, and each returns to his or her own parents' compound during the day.

For six nights, the bride enters the nuptial tent on its side, crawling under the tent mat wall. She enters by the front door only on the seventh night. Throughout, close female relatives and men pound millet for *eghale*. The bride remains, for all seven days of the wedding, secluded underneath a blanket in her mother's tent. She often wears a white cloth tassal called *takarkart* around her head. Near the bride's head is an Islamic amulet with Koranic verses inside, small presents, and sometimes a knife stuck in the sand to fend off spirits, as during a baby's first week of life. A close woman friend stays with her. The bride does not speak to anyone except to the friend, secretly, with whom she also eats in privacy. The bride does all this because, according to Kel Ewey of either sex and all ages, "she is ashamed." The bride remains physically apart from the celebration, particularly morning wedding rituals that are seen as primarily the affairs of elderly women and men.

On the third day, the mother of the bride provides a goat or ram for slaughter. Male guests of the groom gather by day in the tent near the mother's compound; here, young women are less visible. A smith man grills the meat, and (at noble weddings) smith women cook food and serve it.

On the fourth day of a wedding, there is an event called "passing the day," when young men and women visit in the groom's home to play games, chat, and eat festival food brought by older women. In late afternoon, inside the nuptial tent, the young people play a game called *taba* featuring two teams (men on the right and women on the left side of the tent). The objective is that all sticks, after being thrown, should land with the same side up. The loser of this game is jokingly called a "donkey's husband." The outcome is sometimes ambiguous, so there is a lot of dispute. Afterward, there is more singing and dancing outside with the *tende* provided by smiths or women. Young persons go out more often in late afternoon and evening during weddings; older persons attend in mornings, pray and prepare food, and do not as a rule attend evening festivities.

The bride's mother pays for mats for the nuptial tent's walls, and the groom purchases wood from smiths for its frame. The mother of the bride organizes this tent construction and provides the women with a communal feast. At a wedding I attended as a guest on the bride's side in the village of my research, at sunset I accompanied the women out into the oeud (a dried riverbed) to greet the women who came along with other guests on the groom's side as they brought the groom to the bride's home. On their arrival, we ran stealthily through the oeud in the dark to greet them. Two friends, Mariama and Tima, urged me to extinguish my flashlight but also to run fast (a somewhat difficult feat, I found), "because," they explained, "there must be a sudden surprise," and if we were not there exactly when the guests arrived, the guests bringing the groom could, in principle, become angry and go home. This went smoothly; guests were served dinner and tea, and later, the groom was brought to the nuptial tent.

Throughout weddings, smiths play prominent roles, indicative of their important go-between function in negotiating marriage and bridewealth for nobles. *Salikhu* are smith women's songs performed in early afternoon on the second day of the wedding to continue to announce the wedding and to invite guests. This is done near the bride's home as henna is applied to her hands and feet. The *tedaban* songs are performed by a group of men and women smiths of varying ages in the evening on the second day of the wedding, near the tent housing the female guests from the groom's side where young wedding guests attend the festivals with music, dancing, and singing. *Chiluba* songs are performed by smiths at the camel race called *ilugan* in the late afternoon, led by an elderly smith man playing the drum with sticks made of braided palm fibers. During this event, men of diverse social origins (formerly mostly nobles, but today anyone who has a riding camel) parade their camels counterclockwise around the group of smiths. Dances representing each social segment are also performed at this event, and money, tea, and sugar are given to the smiths. On the third day of the wedding there is another camel race and smiths' praise-singing in the morning, and repeated dances and songs near sunset after young persons' games and conversation inside the nuptial tent.

Several features stand out at the wedding details. First, there is a marked contrast between the behavior of the new couple, and that of the young guests, after sundown. The new couple are not supposed to consummate their marriage until the seventh night, or at least no earlier than the fourth night, "so as to become accustomed to each other." Smiths gave another reason: "because, on the first night, the bride is your sister, on the second, she is your mother, on the third, she is your mother-in-law, and on the fourth, she becomes your wife." At the *tende n tagbast* (dance festival) held after midnight at some distance away from the nuptial tent with the couple inside it, there is an atmosphere of extreme license, which stands in stark contrast to the everyday conduct between the sexes. Men make blatant passes at women, flirting openly and aggressively, for example, pinching them. There is rowdy joking. Flashlights are beamed on women's faces, and there are mock swordfights. Young boys dress up in men's face-veils at this occasion, before the age they normally wear them. No one is reprimanded for what would be considered highly insulting behavior at other times. The audience present at the festival is predominantly under the age of thirty, unmarried or newly married persons of either sex. A few older children also are present. Elderly persons (with children of marriageable age) and marabouts are conspicuously absent. There are many travelers from distant regions. Elders warn youths to be careful at weddings, where "people have no reserve (or shame)." Sometimes there are thefts. Many Kel Ewey believe that a person's character changes during travel, while far from the maternal tent and from the constraints of official kinship and social stratum roles.

On the third night, guests at the revelry play a game in keeping with this carnival atmosphere called *ekesen taqubut* ("taking off the headdress"). This calls for any unmarried woman to try to tear off the veil of a married man once he is inside her tent. Whoever wins the ensuing struggle receives a prize of perfume from the loser. Significantly, a man's own wife cannot play this game with him.

By contrast, the bride and groom, at least in principle, are expected to observe rather stringent rules of conduct. Friends told me that a child believed to have been conceived before the seventh night, or at the very soonest the fourth night of the wedding, is shameful, called by a special term, *elgenagougou*. This derives from *eljenan* (or *djinn,* spirit). Only after this initial phase does the bride change her hairstyle to that of a married woman, wear the headscarf regularly, and wear her husband's presents of silver jewelry and indigo cloth. Emphasis after this is upon covering her hair. There is a parallel between this reserve emphasized during the initial phases of the wedding for the couple and the idealized attitudes attributed to the older population, and a contradiction between all this and attitudes and behavior encouraged for youthful wedding guests and youths in general. These attitudes address cultural typifications of gender and age that transcend the context of rites of passage. Nicolaisen (1963:475) and Lhote (1955) report similar attitudes, but do not explore their meanings. Casajus (1987), in his analysis of Tuareg kinship, does not analyze marriage in relation to age or the life course. Several questions emerge here. First, why the parallel between the restraint demanded of the new bridal couple at the wedding and elderly persons in general, as well as at the wedding ritual; and why the contrast between the demands on the bridal couple and the elderly, and the behavioral license encouraged for the rest of the evening wedding party? How does this fit in with the wedding ritual and marriage as a whole, the underlying code and principal actors? Second, how does it fit in with local notions of gender, kin and age statuses and roles throughout the life course?

During the day at weddings and namedays, there is age and sex segregation: this is strictest during eating and least strict during camel races. Older men and women tend to remain in groups by sex, especially at the home of the groom, and younger married couples arrive at weddings separately, as "singles." Young unmarried and newly married men and women, again initially segregated by sex until sundown, go to the home of the new bride. Women guests sleep in a large tent with a smith man "guarding" them until later on, after midnight, when a carnival ambience takes over: men come to awaken the women, flirt with them, and then men perform dances, and the women sing songs accompanied by the *tende* mortar drum (usually played by a smith). The emphasis at these evening festivals is upon youth and interclass; illicit courtship and liaisons, with blacksmiths playing an important organizing role; extreme freedom in conduct; and the right to associate with whomever one prefers. There is also freedom to insult and joke with those toward whom one is normally circumspect, in reserve. By day, particularly at the mosque, at animal slaughter, and at meal preparation in the morning, older age groups and marabouts predominantly practice stringent codes of restraint by emphasis upon prayer and formal greetings between affines.

In this light, the smiths' utterance concerning the ideal postponement of consummation expresses underlying principles of interaction between men and women, old and young, and cognates and affines at given times over the life course. The focus in early years of marriage is upon the relationship between husband and affines. Encounters are marked by caution and even apprehension. Since movement away from familiar settings (cognates) and known interlocutors engenders increased caution and changing functions in utterances (i.e., here, the groom moves into the home of his affines), identification is crucially important. There is conflict between affinity and the awareness that interaction is not always harmonious. The utterance concerning the reasons for the postponement of consummation therefore, on one level, expresses cautious circumlocution in seeking identity: in the man's life course, first he is the close associate of his sister, in the prominence of matrilineal elements (female founder/ancestresses) and brother-sister ties in mythology; then, his mother becomes more prominent in his circle of affective ties and rights and obligations; then, his mother-in-law prevails over him for goods and services and bridewealth, and finally, his wife becomes a "real" wife to him in the finalized, recognized marriage. Thus in the marriage utterance resides a panorama of relationships over time, condensed into its imagery. The order of mention of each kinsperson, or female relative, used respectively as tropes for the new bride, corresponds to the order of prominence of each of these persons in the life course, in terms of a developmental cycle of domestic group and personal identity. Sisters continue a close relationship with brothers as moral counselors and intermediaries. Mothers continue to predominate in affective ties, and the matrilineage is associated with sentiment and moral support (as opposed to the patriline, which is associated with discipline and economic support). The mother-in-law, upon marriage, becomes dominant, and access to the bride depends upon the quality of the groom's relationship with the mother-in-law in the first few years of marriage.

This theme is reinforced in other ritual contexts by other persons. During the days preceding the final day of the wedding, the groom does not have the right to enter the area during daylight. In one small rite within the wedding, an old woman may come to sit at the side of the groom in place of the bride. Her role is to "fool" the spirits: by this subterfuge, the old woman attracts to herself all the influences that menace individuals at transitions, particularly during the establishing of a new household. The old woman is believed to take the spirits with her by leaving the tent some moments before the arrival of the "real" bride. Older women also perform, in another ritual of a baby's nameday, a dance with pestles resembling the men's dancing with lances at evening festivals. In effect, during these inversions, old women are acting as mediators and linchpins of social groupings, distracting the spirits of misfortune and dissension that are believed to hover around the new relatives. Another small rite occurs when the bride's first cousin on the matrilineal side attempts to block her passage to the nuptial tent during the wedding and requests that the groom give him a pair of sandals, allowing him to enter the tent when he complies. Another mock blocking occurs after the wedding, during joking between nobles and smiths and cousins of the bride and groom at their evening visits and tea-drinking sessions. Once, I saw smith women attached to the noble bride's family doing this; in another instance, a female cousin of the bride did this. Ritual postponement of marriage thus has symbolic analogies and permutations in diverse contexts.

Weddings therefore develop very slowly, with many interruptions, barriers, substitutions, inversions, and reversals. The bride and groom are brought together, to be separated again before finally being united in a correctly erected tent. The bride must first enter the tent in reverse fashion, through a side panel, a very narrow space. It is tempting here to introduce Freudian interpretations (perhaps this symbolizes the consummation?). This, however, would not explain other elements of rites of passage and the life course. For example, the same time lapse exists between birth and naming as it does between marriage at the mosque and consummation of the marriage (seven days); the visual imagery of counterclockwise circling at both weddings and babies' namedays; and the recurrence of the number three (in circlings). Here, it is instructive to recall other social factors that relate to these features in a pattern. The break of the married woman with her family is not abrupt and, in the region near Mount Bagzan, often never occurs. The couple, in effect, live outside the community during their wedding, as do the mother and her baby during a forty-day seclusion in the tent following birth. Interpersonal relationships modified or stabilized in these processes only partially explain their reference to aging and the life course, however. Additional considerations address the classification of persons over time.

At marriage, there is concern with classifying the bride. This has a double sense: it involves who she is not as much as who she is in relation to the groom before finalization of marriage. It also involves who she is metaphorically. The bride is not classified as wife at one stage of marriage but rather as metaphorical sister, mother, and mother-in-law progressively, for she enjoys a unique relation to the matrilineage. Murphy (1967) has discussed the problem, in Aïr

Tuareg kinship, of persistence of a matrilineal kin nomenclature in an altered social structure. Cousin marriage, in a system of underlying matrilineal ties, presents individuals with double-binds and contradictions. Endogamy may have been introduced by Islam with its preference for the father's brother's daughter marriage, which, under the impact of matrilineal institutions, Kel Ewey could subsequently have extended to the mother's sister's daughter (the ideal frequently expressed by women to me, though, as shown, not necessarily followed by children in practice as often as their mother would wish). Affinity, common descent, and kin group membership thus become difficult to separate and sort out. The data indicate a vagueness of genealogies beyond the second ascending generation. *Tawsit* (section or descent group) bonds are those of client-patron relationships, such as smith to noble, and (until recently) former slave to noble, ranked in loose political confederation.

Therefore the major ties of consanguinity and affinity are within the kin group. Role differentiation has always been ambiguous. The utterance at the wedding thus appears to express the masculine viewpoint upon marriage of role differentiation of female kinship ties. On this level, it states what the wife is not, at this point in time: she is not the sister, the mother, or the mother-in-law. But this constitutes only part of the message. The remainder is the metaphorical implication of who she is. On this latter level, the utterance alludes to the shift in focus on various female relatives as significant others to men in the life course. During engagement and bridewealth negotiations, when the fiancee is still technically a cousin (whether close or distant), the focus is upon the sister dimension of her relation to her fiance: as a source of friendship, in joking, and also as a source of moral support. In the case of close cousin marriage, there is, many local residents admit, some latent discomfort with having grown up together and having engaged in a joking relationship, and this must be transformed into the respect relationship between husband and wife. During the residence in the home of the bride's family, the in-law dimension, particularly that of the groom's mother-in-law (called *tadagalt*), becomes prominent in the man's universe; emphasis here is upon "pleasing" the mother-in-law through gifts and labor and general reserved conduct in etiquette until bridewealth obligations are met. The mother image in the wedding utterance therefore represents the more inclusive category of matrifocal and matrilineal kinship: the matriline, submerged and challenged in daily economic and jural life, has moral and affective values that need reaffirmation upon marriage.

Thus the husband-wife relationship revolves around several foci over time. These involve competing obligations to other closely related females that dominate different phases of life but that themselves face interference from patrilineal economic ties. Throughout life there are tensions pulling husband and wife in opposite directions—that of his kin and hers and the crosscutting ties of morality, inheritance, subsistence, and residence, each alternately under-lined through ritual framing. For example, the brother-sister relationship, highlighted in matrilineal ancestress/founder myths, tends to become sub-merged and highlighted alternately in different contexts. A man is obligated to give his sister's son animals and personal possessions in times of need. There is outward extension to other villages and camps of the nephew's right to replen-ish or maintain his own productive resources through activation of his matri-line, which tends to be dispersed through other villages and camps in bilateral descent and inheritance and postmarital residence. Many men go for extended visits to agnatic kin during the rainy season when obligations are fulfilled. Uncles frequently joke with their small nephews in a manner that highlights differences between Tuareg conceptualizations of the father and the maternal uncle: the uncle pretends to beat the nephew with a stick and jokingly says, "I am his father."

Special relationships between diverse kinspersons at different times, with concomitant rights and obligations, become important in a high-risk environ-ment and subsistence system: loaning, sharing, and the giving of animals, credit, and insurance over the life course when needs arise. But these relation-ships are not always clearly defined every day due to their dispersion in time and space. The marriage tropes and ritual inversions concerning age- and kin-based roles bring into relief the underlying structure. In a system of partially revealed genealogies, bilateral descent and inheritance, marriage and other transitions necessitate the awakening of sometimes dormant relationships, through contrast, transformation, and juxtaposition. Thus not solely ambigu-ity but also flexibility and multivocality of ties are conveyed here as important in property considerations. Rites of passage, therefore, while transformative (Van Gennep 1905) and also reaffirmative (Crapanzano 1992), are evocative of negotiability and multivocality.

Several other rites of passage mark the gradual and contingent nature of marriage. A smaller rite of passage related to marriage, taking place after the wedding, is called *taneqait*. This is held on the occasion when a wife visits her affines. They slaughter a bull and stage a camel race. Another ritual marks two or more newly married women's disengagement of livestock from their moth-ers' herds and their setting up of an independent kitchen, with the mothers' permission and recognition that the marriage is stable. An animal, given by the parents of the husbands, is slaughtered. This ceremony may, but need not always, coincide with the establishment of a separate compound for the mar-ried couple. In many cases the establishment of a new compound occurs well before the disengagement of herds and true adult independence. Such steps all ultimately depend, however, upon the groom "pleasing" his mother-in-law and may entail some tensions.

Consider the case of Takoro, a woman of about forty-five years of age, who had twelve children. She was married to Enfa, a former caravanner who had taken up gardening and also practiced maraboutism. Takoro came from a family of chiefs and prominent marabouts who claimed some Arab ancestry on the maternal side (a prestigious claim, in the Aïr region) and took much pride in this feature of their genealogy. Yet the family belonged to what may be termed the "poor nobility," that is, they were respected but without much material wealth. Takoro had only a few goats, all owned jointly with her older daughters, who, though married, were still new brides who continued to share their mother's kitchen. Takoro's household, indeed, consisted of a large number of daughters, many of whom were single due to the difficulty poor nobles among Kel Ewey have in marrying off daughters in such circumstances. Two married daughters were brides of men of somewhat unequal economic means. Takoro was said by residents to be troubled by having so many daughters to marry off, by her precarious subsistence, and by her sons-in-law, who were of differing economic means and brought varying amounts of millet to their mother-in-law's storage house. One son-in-law worked in her husband's new garden a mile away, and the other was often unemployed, doing sporadic masonry work on mud houses. Their unequal contributions caused jealousy, resentment, and tensions in the household, especially among her daughters, and also made Takoro's role as an ideally dignified mother-in-law difficult, for in order to accumulate wealth, wealth is needed to begin with. Tuareg say, "The marriage of children depends upon the conduct of parents." To make good marriages for their children, parents need both prestigious descent and economic prosperity; this ensures, in turn, proper matches with husbands of similar status who will make generous sons-in-law. But nowadays, although the cultural ideal is still class endogamy, many nobles are poverty-stricken due to diminishing herds and pastures, and consequently some are compelled to marry daughters to lower-status men whom parents would not ordinarily have accepted in the past. Indeed, this theme recurs as lamentations in verses of both ancient and recent spirit possession songs that I recorded from rural areas (Rasmussen 1995) and in the new songs by Tuareg nationalist/separatist guerrillas that Bourgeot (1990) recorded from Agadez.

Thus, as new brides, Takoro's daughters were caught between their husbands and mother. Mother and sisters were frequently ill, with disorders ranging from very real physical ailments to types of depression locally attributed to possession by spirits. Tensions affected relations with extended kinspersons as well. Takoro suspected that her recent health problems had been caused by the sorcery emanating from her female cousins next door, who had been angered by the intrusion of her goats onto their property and the ensuing damage. A diviner told Takoro to move a few feet away from them, after analyzing her problems with the aid of cowrie shells.

Another woman of noble origins, about fifty years old, whom I will call

Chimo, was the mother of five daughters and two sons and the wife of a prominent, successful marabout. Their sons worked in the garden of a daughter's husband and received 50 percent of the harvest to take home. Chimo herself, of outgoing and generous disposition, was also well-to-do: she had four camels, fifteen goats, a donkey, and five ewes in addition to other livestock owned jointly with her newly married daughters, who continued to cook in her kitchen. The eldest daughter was married to a school supervisor, whose salary (and later, whose retirement pension) was high by local standards and whose household lived throughout the school year in towns, returning to the countryside during the rainy season (June-September) school vacation. This husband was of mixed social origins, from the town of Agadez. He enjoyed social acceptance locally, due to the force of his individual personality and his prestigious occupation. Eventually, after he retired, he and his wife settled next door to Chimo, her mother. This move home to the wife's parents, rather than to Agadez near the husband's, reflected the strong economic position and personalities of this household, particularly Chimo as mother-in-law, in contrast to the cases of weak mothers-in-law presented earlier. Another daughter was married to a man who gardened and did some tailoring, who came from the local community, and was of noble descent. The third daughter was married to a primary school teacher in a distant oasis, and this couple, also, resided near the husband's work most of the year. Her two other daughters were married to a caravanner/itinerant merchant and a gardener, respectively, both of noble descent and from the local community.

Thus most of Chimo's married daughters resided near her all year, but several husbands, while in a better geographic position to contribute to their in-laws' support, were less prosperous than the husbands who initially resided at a distance. Only one of the three daughters living near Chimo had disengaged their herds or kitchens from those of their mother by 1983, and one of the remaining two had done so by 1995. The last daughter's husband continued to have obligations to his in-laws longer than usual due to his prolonged absence on trading expeditions.

Therefore a multiplicity of factors impinge upon the process of the married couple's disengagement and independence from the bride's parents. Although interpersonal relations play a role, residence and socioeconomic means also are important. As shown, often sons-in-law of greater economic means, regardless of descent, tend to pull wives to distant regions away from parents. Those sons-in-law who remain are sometimes more closely related and of more similar descent and prestige but are not always prosperous. These conditions frequently cause tensions within the household between husband and wife and between affines.

There is the need, then, to constantly reaffirm ties and contain or minimize conflict. The highly elaborated, numerous marriage-related rituals after the wedding itself focus upon this effort. For example, the ritual called *tineseslem* or "greeting the tent" vividly illustrates these points. It features sisters-in-law of the bride arriving one year after their brother's marriage in order to see his wife and, in the words of residents, "to show her that they like her." This follows the construction of a new tent for the married woman, located adjacent to her parents' compound. Participants are said to "greet the tent" at this time. This idea reinforces, again, the groom's position vis-à-vis his in-laws. One woman I knew, whom I will call Tana, who had married the previous year and was residing in a village neighboring the one where I lived, held this ceremony in the rainy season of 1991. The arrival of her sisters-in-law was followed by a *tende* drum musical festival after sundown, where special songs identified with this event were performed. This festival was attended by cognates and affines, persons on both the bride's and groom's sides of the family, but almost all persons were under the age of thirty, except for a lone traveler I saw, a man who was about forty years old from a distant settlement, who told me that he regularly attended such events "in order to meet strange women [from afar]." The few older, married men who do attend such evening festivals often do so in order to begin illicit, extramarital affairs. Many residents say that such goings-on are tolerated after dark, and, in particular, affines can only mix with ease after the sun sets; at other times, "they would be ashamed to encounter each other [in such circumstances of song and dance]." At this event, men still are careful to keep their face-veil in place, however. The importance of this was clear to me once when a young man who accompanied me part of the way as guide, because my flashlight batteries had failed, left me at the edge of the village and declined to continue or attend because he was not wearing his veil.

During the festival, the young female choral singers sang, accompanied by the *tende* drum, as men danced, facing the chorus in pairs with lances held above their heads. Upon the conclusion of the dancing, the men sprayed the women in the chorus with perfume. This gesture has several meanings. It is sometimes a sign of hospitality; as a visitor in homes, I was sometimes offered perfume. At rites of passage, particularly weddings and namedays, people saturate themselves and others in incense and perfume in order to ward off spirits, which are believed to be jealous of participants. On the other hand, references to repelling the "evil words [jealousy] of strangers" (recall that the Tamacheq term for this, *imagaren,* is synonymous with guests and foreigners) appeared in some song verses. Thus, on this occasion the gesture may have been a pun, with a double meaning: it was part of the general flirtation between the male dancers and female singers but also served to protect against possible conflict and ill feelings.

Prior to this point, the marriage was not complete jurally, and the couple, in particular, the new bride, was viewed as essentially of jural minor status, with the groom as a kind of raider, or at least an outsider, to the tent. Young girls told me that what they most looked forward to in life was "to build a new home, apart from my mother's home but also nearby it." The mother herself must decide when this is appropriate. Older persons' security, largely dependent on new sons-in-laws' obligations to bring in food, tends to encourage the unspoken ideal of always having a new son-in-law. This ideal may in part be realized by numerous marriages of successive daughters, or alternatively, by the remarriage of a single daughter. Some strong-minded mothers are rumored to encourage daughters to divorce often for purposes of accumulating bridewealth property and groomservice benefits. Thus the daughter's transition from active bride to successful wife, the son's transition from active groom to successful husband, and the bride mother's transition from active motherhood to successful affinity are controlled by the mother-in-law in a system in which preinheritance is as important as inheritance, and where someone other than the couple (the mother-in-law, except if she is weak or incapacitated, as shown) decides when a marriage is stable. This contingency of attainment of adult status is expressed euphemistically, in the exclusion of young girls from participation in daytime rites of passage and in the predominance of elderly women alongside men and marabouts in them, at namedays and mortuary ceremonies as well as at weddings. This expresses a notion of youth as standing at the threshold of a series of tests, upon the passing of which full adult status is contingent. The status of an elder, in particular, an older woman *(tamghart),* is ritually prominent and celebrates the double-edged victory of passing these tests but also abandoning the freedom of expression of youth.

Marriage draws individuals into a network of obligations resembling client-patron relationships between superior and subordinate, and relationships in the household take on dimensions of the class system. The reverse is also true, as seen in Adoum's case: relationships between the social strata and client-patron roles are not only described in an idiom of metaphorical kinship but also take on kin and household aspects in their actual dynamics. Thus age and social stratum interweave in processes of boundary definition and negotiation in Kel Ewey Tuareg society.

Smith woman applying henna to bridegroom's hands and feet at wedding.

Women and children celebrating Muslim holiday.

Men carrying wife's nuptial tent to husband's home, in *techawait* ritual.

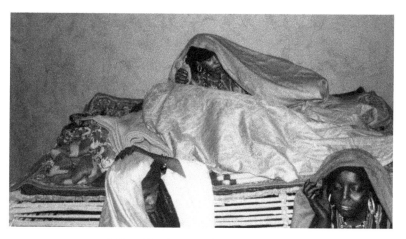

Wife and friends on arrival in husband's home.

Part Two

Repositioning Self and Others

The Poetics and Politics of Aging

4

Intergenerational Relationships
and Intercultural Encounters

Thus marriage and other rites of passage allow some manipulation and negotiation but are in many respects strategies of containment. The roles of older
persons in them have to do with preserving purity, power, and autonomy, as
well as idealized solidarity between cognates and affines and between members
of different generations. Furthermore, metaphors of kinship, age, and social
stratum are interwoven in the idiom of rituals of the life course. Social stratum
imagery pervades age, and intergenerational relationships are imbued with
hierarchical and client-patron tones. Hence the need arises for facilitators in a
system where some forces tend to undermine linkages. As Turner (1967:265)
and Crapanzano (1992:267) stress, in such rituals there occur not only changes
in the status of the person and a realignment of roles but also reaffirmation and
reintegration of important social relationships. In the past, subjugated peoples
who today comprise formerly servile and tributary peoples, as well as smiths,
became integrated into the local social structure on a kinship and age model as
"children" and "cousins" to paternal nobles. Their roles and relationships with
nobles have traditionally featured institutionalized joking. A number of scholars have documented Tuareg society as originating in an agglomeration of specialists in client-patron relations resulting from successive waves of conquest in
the past.[1] Nobles are ideally expected to support and protect smith clients and
formerly servile peoples, as parents do children. Cultural values in general, furthermore, emphasize generosity and almsgiving *(takote),* particularly on the
part of high-status persons such as Islamic scholars and persons of noble
descent. In this setting, problems arise when what is wanted (status symbols,
property) must be hidden or else there will be pressure on those who monopolize resources to redistribute them. Yet the suppression or concealment of
property entails failure to actualize self-respect, namely, conspicuous consumption and also generosity, in a society where there are contradictions: on
the one hand, hoarding and accumulation are expected normal behavior in an
environment of scarcity and unpredictability; on the other, giving is also valued. Blacksmiths, themselves from outside and of uncertain origins, who are
metaphorical cousins to nobles, traditionally brought tribute to nobles from
clients and acted as "ambassadors" between chiefs in delicate political matters.
Currently, they aid chiefs in contact with central state control schemes: for

example, in food relief distribution, during which outside functionaries accompanied by soldiers often give political speeches, and in tax collection. In this system, there is local emphasis upon buffers, go-betweens, and intermediaries, and balance between hierarchy and complementary interdependence, particularly in situations local residents perceive as intimidating. Joking relationships encode this condition. Thus the historical origins of attitudes regarding age, kinship, and intergenerational relationships are located in processes of empire-building and resistance to it.

Non-nobles, such as smiths and ex-slaves, and all youths of diverse social strata lack reserve the important noble cultural value. Precisely because they lack reserve, such persons are often buffers between nobles and outsiders (including researchers, tourists, and other expatriates) and in transitional and liminal situations, in order to diffuse potential conflict. Hence the problematics of conducting research on the life course and aging. Many rural residents did not immediately perceive the difference between France, the former colonial power, and the United States, my own country of origin, until I explained to them how far the latter was from Niger. On one level, I was absorbed into some local client-patron structures; yet on another, there were always limits to this, due to my being childless, my non-Muslim outsider status, and residents' identification of me with external colonial hegemony.

Anthropologists, as ambiguous, outside intruders who interact closely with local residents, appear to local residents as rather like smiths, lacking in reserve. Smiths' lack of reserve enables them to cross sex, age, and class barriers and to create alliances (for example, they serve as go-betweens in love affairs and also, along with marabouts, in official marriage negotiations for future in-laws). Yet while the anthropologist also displays, in the local noble and adult viewpoint, a lack of reserve, as do children, slaves, and smiths, the anthropologist's work—ethnography—tends to benefit primarily the anthropological enterprise. Thus local residents tend to feel threatened, or at least ambivalent, about these contradictions. On the one hand, I evoked images of outside paternalistic colonial and central state control over resources (not solely material wealth but also, and perhaps more important, intangibles such as knowledge, a forum for opinion, and representation). Within local social institutions, "joking" is the usual response to economically asymmetrical yet negotiable relationships between social strata and different age groups. On the other hand, as an anthropologist I was perceived in some respects as anything but powerful. I was viewed as childlike, that is, not yet mature in ways that correspond to local typifications of a jural adult at the same point in life. Residents respond to this perception in several ways. They use strategies of constraint of the researcher, whom Tuareg sometimes view, for historical reasons, as an invader or would-be conqueror.[2] But since very real friendships form during field research, local residents also seek to protect the researcher.

For these reasons, the longer I remained in the region and the more frequently I visited there, the more knowledge I acquired, yet at the same time the more problematic my participation in specific domains of Tuareg culture became. Local commentaries on life transitions in many respects became symbolic-interpretive elements in their own right, an articulation of local views of an anthropologist's own life as well as their own. Mutual discussion of passages through life provided an arena in which social relations and sentiments, not solely among Tuareg but also between Tuareg and myself the outside researcher, coalesced.

Local residents expressed their ambivalence toward my ambiguous role by alluding to themes of marriage, sex, children, religion, and property during interaction with me. Much of this took the form of jokes. Their joking often addressed the important local cultural opposition: a social universe separated by singlehood versus marriage, cognates versus affines, parenthood versus childlessness. They also alluded to prayer, albeit more seriously, which is seen as more important as one ages. I, the researcher, was drawn into these dialogues. Early in my residence as a single Peace Corps volunteer in the town of Agadez, individuals continually asked me why I went about without my husband. At a functionary party at the Prefecture, guests were divided into two sides, seated separately: single and married. My search for a particular brand of perfume in boutiques (where women at that time customarily did not venture alone) was interpreted as looking for a husband, requiring smith go-betweens who eagerly tried to take part in the intrigue. Upon my return to the area for doctoral research, by which time I had married, a smith friend teasingly reproached me for having married outside Niger, beyond the reach of smith go-betweens. When my husband visited me briefly during my residence in rural Aïr, there were different reactions. We were not supposed to walk together alone away from villages and camps; this is considered "shameful," for it suggests possible illicit places of sexual activity (outside the maternal tent, under moonlight) and its possible consequence (according to local belief) of birth defects. My husband was not, furthermore, supposed to enter the compound of my fictive maternal grandmother (mother of my fictive mother, the woman with whom I boarded), especially without a face-veil; fictive affinal relationships were superimposed onto visitors as well.

Although Tuareg men and women may freely make visits to each other outside marriage for purposes other than romantic interest, nonetheless courtship is an important, highly stylized institution. Local residents tended to assume that the mere condition of any woman being alone (without husband or children) was an invitation to courtship. One evening, during the early part of my research, I awoke to find an unknown figure with a flashlight entering my tent from beneath the side wall. Fearing a burglary, I cried out in alarm, and the figure retreated hastily. When I mentioned this incident the next morning to my hostess and her sisters as we crushed grain for the noon meal, they exchanged knowing looks and laughed, telling me that the "intruder" was probably a male suitor. In rural areas, it is customary for a man to enter the tent of a woman who interests him and "awaken" her. But he must leave before morning and avoid being seen by her parents, and the woman may reject his advances and throw him out of her tent if she wishes. If the relationship proceeds toward marriage, smiths play an active role in negotiating the bridewealth. Smiths matter-of-factly told me that since my husband was far away, and I was as yet a newly married, childless woman, I should take a second, temporary husband locally. This would be logical, in their view; for as shown, marriage obliges individuals to observe client-patron and other relationships of reciprocity (for example, with affines and smiths), thereby absorbing them into the local protective structures. Local residents, in effect, felt more comfortable the more they were able to draw me into such structures and attempted to resolve my ambiguous, somewhat anomalous status (as non-parent and non-Muslim) by these means.

Joking and humor versus respect and reserve are cultural values that are polar opposites in Tuareg society. Each attitude is identified with members of different social strata, age groups, and kin roles, and each is emphasized or deemphasized in conduct between them. For example, persons of noble descent, Islamic scholars, and affines are ideally supposed to practice reserve in conduct with each other. Cousins, regardless of social stratum affiliation, are supposed to practice joking with each other. Smiths are said, by nobles and smiths alike, to always lack reserve, and Tuareg say that "the smith is like a woman . . . you don't get angry at smiths, but joke with them." Joking is particularly prominent in relations between smiths and nobles and between cousins of all social strata. This attitude prepares cousins within the same social stratum for their roles as potential marriage partners. Youths should not joke with elderly persons on their paternal side or with most persons in adjacent generations, yet may joke with certain other older relatives, for example, the maternal uncle and the grandmother on the maternal side. Youths may also joke with elderly smiths and former slaves. In interaction with me over the long term, these metaphorical age and class roles were given expression.

Even before the recent nationalist/separatist movement, important social roles within Tuareg society have addressed outside intruders.[3] The symbolism of weddings, as shown, suggests that even marriage is not always connected to congenial confrontation with outside forces, and even the young groom is a kind of invader. Transitions over the life course and relationships between persons of different ages incorporate the imagery of war and raiding by nobles and other forces. As outsider and anthropologist, I was frequently incorporated into this process. As Casajus observes in his study of Tuareg marriage (1987), marriage brings into contact different camps of a *tawsit* (descent group or section, literally denoting the wrist with the fingers spread out, or a stem). War brings different Tuareg descent groups into contact with one another. It also brings all Tuareg into contact with the rest of the world. Descent group sections of the same political confederation did not engage in war and in principle refrained from raiding each other's livestock, but there is a connection with war in the annual tributes and other payments formerly given noble overlords and the protection nobles provided tributary and servile groups in return. Both marriage and war are therefore an expression of a relation with the outside world. Whereas marriage normally takes place within one and the same *tawsit* (Murphy 1964; Bernus 1981; Casajus 1987; Claudot-Hawad 1993), war is carried out exclusively between different *tawsit*. A *tawsit* border is the dividing line between realms where intermarriage is made and where war is waged (Lévi-Strauss 1963).

Contact between the ethnographer and insiders is analogous to that associated with war but also the rite of passage of marriage in Tuareg culture. This idea responds to Said's idea of the anthropologist as colonialist (Said 1979a) but adds the dimension of alliance and the active, rather than passive, role of local residents. Local residents as research subjects are not passive but rather active in the process of ethnographic representation, particularly in mutual repositioning over long-term field research. The potential for war is continually transformed, through mutual reassessments and negotiation, into alliances that defy an outcome that would enable the actual exercise of unequal power. It is in this sense that the contact between ethnographer and insider is analogous to war and alliance. This is ambiguous and thus can and must be continually renegotiated, like bridewealth in marriage. This negotiation places the so-called other (Said 1979a) on an equal or even more powerful footing with the ethnographer, who, in a turning of the tables, ironically becomes the "other" from the viewpoint of the subjects researched.

Well before I consciously focused upon the topic of the life course, local values, institutions, and rituals pertaining to the life course subtly impinged upon my relationships in the field in my trips to Aïr between 1976 and 1995. After serving in the region as a Peace Corps volunteer in the late 1970s and conducting informal language and culture study, I returned to conduct "official" anthropological field research for my doctoral degree and then to do postdoctoral work. As an anthropologist, I initially introduced myself through a letter from a mutual friend (a marabout or Islamic scholar and agricultural extension agent from a neighboring oasis, who had attended secondary school in Agadez). I first described myself as a teacher who had authorization to write a book about Tuareg culture, curing, the spirit possession rite, and women, and to study the Tamacheq language. The plan, as I viewed it, was to drop into a local community with a systematic field method and theory to test, to totally immerse myself in the local culture, and to follow, quite literally, in whichever direction the wind carried me. Superficially, my experiences at first seemed to confirm some conventional earlier anthropological theories about the field-worker as standing completely outside local boundaries (Bohannan 1964; Briggs 1970). I seemed often able to cross social stratum and gender lines, and local residents seemed comfortable in their positioning of me—for example, I ate alternately with men and women. Age boundaries were more problematic, however, and residents found my position with respect to age disconcerting because of the disjunction between their notions of transitions and my own position as traveler, guest, and scholar with, in effect, a kind of double life inside and outside Niger. But my data in retrospect seem to follow more close-ly recent emphases on the more mutual and dialogical aspects of knowledge construction in the field experience (Stoller and Olkes 1987; Gottlieb and Graham 1993).

This mixture of mutuality and disjunction sometimes caused problems both of social integration and epistemological interpretation. Almost all devout Muslim residents, in particular as they grew older, noticed that I did not pray at Islamic holidays. In addition, elderly women were initially distant from me, although later they became friendly. I found that revealing to local people that I was married, while not a social stigma in itself, caused some older Tuareg to disapprove of my travel and reproach me for leaving my family behind for so long. So initially I was seen as a person who was "not serious," who had reneged on my adult domestic responsibilities (centering, in the local residents' view, on household labor and social obligations of client-patron, as well as filial and affinal relationships) in my own culture, despite my continual efforts to participate by helping women with their daily domestic tasks such as gathering firewood, fetching water from the well, and pounding grain in a mortar. In retrospect, I now realize my presence was in some respects associ-ated not solely with outside threats but also with entertainment, due to the specific topic of my early research: spirit possession rituals, featuring music and song. My methods included the intensive recording of music, dances, songs, and other oral art. At the same time, however, many Tuareg viewed me ambivalently due to their very unhumorous history of contact with outsiders (French, Tubu, central government, tourists), marked mostly by invasions and conquests—actual physical destruction massacres and what some local resi-dents view as exploitation in forced school registration quotas, taxation, and uneven economic development of different regions in Niger. Yet within Saharan societies generally, even before wider contacts, the major social process was conquest and subjugation, of sedentary peoples by some nomadic nobles, for tribute and services. More recently, residents have seen the anthropologist and other outsiders as new kinds of raiders wandering into the setting. Yet this only partly echoes Said's (1979a, 1979b) idea of the anthropologist as colo-nialist and his or her contact with the insider as analogous to war, for, as shown, it is also analogous to an alliance. Indeed, some anthropologists have married into communities they have studied, and others, such as myself, have continued long-term associations with these communities in letters, medical aid, and other assistance that far transcend the formal researcher/subject relationship. Researcher/subject relationships, ambiguous and negotiated, can substantially change the vantage points of observer and observed.

Children invented myths about my field relationships with adults. They called me the "sister" of my transcriber assistant and asked if it was true that I gave him his shoes, if he gave me bic pens, and if my fictive mother's children "stole" from me (Tuareg cross-cousins and maternal nieces and nephews may take each other's belongings in a joking relationship). These rumors, debated heatedly among children at play, revealed their own view of me integrated into the local system. At first, low-status persons and schoolboys filled my tent as visitors. As it gradually became apparent that I planned to stay longer and was somehow different from the occasional tourist, higher-status persons—older women and adults in the noble chiefly families—came to visit me, and finally the chief's wife and primary school director visited. Prominent male marabouts, by contrast, although courteous upon meeting me and hospitable upon my own visits to them, never sought out my company or came to visit me. Other local male residents tended to relate to me as an opposite-sex person from alternately different social strata (whether noble, smith, or descendant of slaves), depending upon the context, because of my ambiguous status.

Sometimes, I was assigned go-between roles. Women friends, for example, were shy about approaching certain outside male medical specialists directly themselves and so often sent me to bring them back medicines such as traditional perfumes (believed to have aphrodisiac properties) from Agadez healers and medicines from first aid clinic workers. I was a woman alone, not unusual or disapproved of in itself in rural Tuareg communities, although I had left my family behind and this was subject to some mild disapproval; I was non-Muslim, a fact frequently commented upon, but I did not fit into the categories that traditional local African religions Tuareg think of when they label someone *ekafir* (infidel). I was married, but childless; I did not appear young, but neither was I considered old. I was a "child" of my Tuareg "fictive mother," but too independent to be truly considered a ward; and I seemed to be a "sister" to some men and women who assisted me regularly with projects. I was no tourist, but then neither was I a permanent resident, committed to coping with the long-term effects of a life that, while deeply fulfilling in many ways, was also a physically difficult one by middle-class American standards. For although I gladly dispensed medicines and treated small wounds and other minor ailments at any time, everyone knew that I would leave and seek better medical care elsewhere. Letters from friends and field assistants over the years sadly reminded me of this, for example, in news of local residents about my own age who had gone blind, become ill, or died when, in many cases, this could have been avoided had they resided nearer medical assistance.

My field research on aging brought into focus various status conflicts that overlap and become opposed to each other. The ethnographer discourages or even prevents some persons from participating fully in their normal social roles. For example, a primary school director experienced some mild ridicule from older male Islamic scholars for running to assist me with transcribing song texts. But gossip controlled me only temporarily; local residents would have to contend with it long after my departure. As an ethnographer, I had only approximate precedents in local historical experience, but residents in effect "rewrote" me into these processes. I followed the intrusion of colonial and postcolonial powers and also introduced new roles into local society that, inchoate, needed to be defined and acted upon. Thus residents continually tried to dissolve my status, not solely for purposes of role reversal, as is often assumed in the literature (Huizinga 1950; Gluckman 1965), but to remind me of my obligations to them (and perhaps also of theirs toward me) and to fix and identify me. As an ethnographer I, in one sense, represented potential betrayal and compromise.

Others have compared the anthropologist to a trickster (Geertz 1973; Rabinow 1977). My own experience continually exposed a different quality, of go-between, an object of suspicion until absorbed into the alliance structure on multiple levels. Attitudes toward me were really a response to this quality. I appeared sympathetic but was as fleeting and uncontrollable as a nomadic warrior. Though I was clearly not there for tax collecting or school registration, I, like smiths, gathered information that could be used to those ends and did not appear to be constrained by reserve. Yet, like a child or former slave, I was completely helpless and totally dependent on them in the field site. I was vulnerable and powerful at the same time. In Kel Ewey Tuareg society, the reason that go-betweens and mediators are usually of low social status (smiths, slaves, children) is that they are viewed as impartial due to their being outside the system of alliances. Thus residents attempted to draw me into more general client-patron relationships with their associated age imagery. On one level, I was analogous to low-status clients and mediators and children; on another, I was a potential marriage partner and, by extension, affine. Admittedly, the ethnographic purpose, although not featuring conquest from the individual ethnographer's viewpoint, seeks knowledge and is therefore also acquisitive.

But to view power in terms of repression alone, from either end of the dialogue, is a point some refute (Foucault 1980; Abu-Lughod 1990), arguing that it obscures the productive aspects of power. Power is exercised over subjects who are faced with the possibilities of several ways of behaving or reacting. As Tuareg played with images of sexuality, marriage, and war, they were aware of these processes. Thus there is a complex interplay when power is at issue, because there is a relationship between power and freedom, and the "power-less" can sometimes refuse to submit, not necessarily through silence or ostracism but rather through integrating the outsider into local power struc-tures. Indeed, this is the way even precolonial hegemonic processes worked: by absorbing subjugated peoples into the local kinship system that emphasized reciprocal rights and obligations. As shown, even servile peoples could inherit, as fictive "children," from their noble masters, as their fictive "parents." And nobles as fictive "fathers" were obliged to arrange, through smiths, marriages of their slaves as fictive "children" and provide bridewealth for them as well.

Thus in constructing boundaries of difference and commonality, self and outsider, Kel Ewey extend age metaphorically. In self-definitions and moral concepts of personal destiny, elders refer to children and parent-child roles and relationships: "The marriage of children depends on the conduct of parents"; "in the past, slaves were like children (to noble parents)." Yet as all persons age, regardless of social status, elders are supposed to fulfill more closely noble ideals of reserve and dignity and to avoid senility by adhering more closely to Islam and prayer. Children, for their part, are without reserve or dignity but also without sin.

Interpreting the implications of these themes of age requires alternating reg-isters of focus in data analysis, which include an alertness to ethnographic counter-transference (Devereux 1956) as well as intersubjective factors in field-work (Rosaldo 1989; Blacking 1990:121–30) and the mutuality of the field encounter (Stoller and Olkes 1987; Gottlieb and Graham 1993). Age referents extend over a range of alternating registers of field experience and the types of knowledge it produces (and is, in turn, produced by). Aging and life course issues require, in the epistemology of interpretation, a discussion of how knowl-edge about age is constructed. Life course knowledge intrudes, perhaps more than many other topics of study, upon the anthropologist's own life course, regardless of what "official" research topic brings him or her into the field. Age impinges upon the limits of ethnography, as local residents seek to contain but also absorb the ethnographer into the contours of their own life course.

I was continually struck by this in the field by my experience of one rela-tionship in particular, the triangular parent-child-ethnographer relationship, and in the multivocal extensions of paternalistic intergenerational metaphors into class and ethnic domains. Given the Tuareg emphasis upon intergener-ational and interclass metaphors in aging imagery, the conventional separa-tion in anthropology between studies of "child development" and those of "gerontology" emerges as an artificial separation, based upon Western linear and chronological notions of the life course. At this juncture, it is instructive to examine adult-child relationships for several reasons. As shown, Kel Ewey Tuareg mark the entry into adult status by marriage, not strictly biological processes, for either sex; and they mark the achievement of "older" (i.e., "postmenopausal" status for women and "leader" status for men) by having children of marriageable age. Thus children are crucial in local formulations of adult transitions in later life. Perhaps the most vividly memorable interaction in the field occurs between adult anthropologist, local children, and local adults as parents. With few exceptions (Read 1959; Richards 1956; Rabinow 1977; Stoller and Olkes 1987), this interaction remains hidden in the data—relegated to field diaries, notes in margins, and letters home.[4] This gap in knowledge is puzzling, given that many current reflexive concerns in ethnographic analyses are relevant to studies of the life course. Conversely, studies of the life course also open up new perspectives on these concerns, which include problems of detached observer versus emotions in ethnographic representation, and questions of how adequate intersubjective personal experience is as an analytical category in ethnography, as opposed to emphasis upon self-contained entities in time and space.

As Rosaldo points out, ethnographic knowledge tends to have the strengths and limitations given by the relative "youth" (or, this could be refined to say, the social youth, according to local values, that is seen by residents as disjunctive with increasing biological age) of fieldworkers who, for the most part, have not had the same experiences as local residents and could not have personal knowledge of the consequences of these experiences (Rosaldo 1989:7–9).

The foregoing analysis of the poetics of aging—personal narratives, aging symbolism, wedding rituals, and residents' commentaries and jokes pertaining to the most culturally central rite of passage, marriage and the metaphorical extension of age imagery into other social relationships—reveals local cultural messages but also a turning of these messages outward. I now examine more closely the experience of cultural encounters, in terms of both mutuality and power relations, through the medium of life course processes and images. I also show how intergenerational attitudes and practices through the life course have a potentially disruptive as well as integrative role. Relevant here is the role of Kel Ewey children as adult representatives, part of the local adult response to colonial and postcolonial structures.

In the following pages, therefore, I continue to explore the interplay between social stratum and religion in aging, but I concentrate more intently upon two interrelated strands of this experience: local adult residents' responses to outside authorities' frequent treatment of them as "children," on the one hand, and anthropologists' position as "childlike" in the value systems of their communities of research, on the other. The mediators in this dialogue are local children as social actors. Thus in addition to the literal categories of "aged," "elderly," "old age," "children," and "childhood" as culturally defined and experienced, I also explore those metaphorical parent-child relationships that are central to Kel Ewey culture as they diffuse out into local stratified structures and beyond. The latter emphasis is complementary to the poetics emphasis in the foregoing chapters and is in keeping with the focus of this book: the life course not solely as an entity in itself but also in relation to inter-subjectivity as an analytical category impinging on the process of constructing knowledge about this entity.

Pioneering studies of relationships between the generations in field research, with reference to local perceptions of outside adults, exist in the literature on childhood and children as social actors more extensively than in the literature on the aged per se. Many works addressing children explore how adult attitudes and behavior toward children are a consequence of external social, political, and economic conditions imposed on adults (Aries 1962; Levine 1980a, 1980b; Scheper-Hughes 1987; Mull and Mull 1987) and how aspects of the life cycle are shaped by internal cultural concepts of person (Levine and Schweder 1984; Riesman 1986; Fortes 1987). Furthermore, as Croll (1990:147–55) notes, local experiences of parenting, with few exceptions, are understudied. Many of these studies tend to concentrate either upon positivist analyses of child development and survival or symbolic analyses of children's games and rites of passage. The first set of studies have shown that in the tropics, where uncontrolled infectious disease, food shortages, and vestiges of colonial and postcolonial exploitation have interacted to make human life particularly precarious, cultural practices of infant-tending are organized primarily around health and survival goals (Scheper-Hughes 1987:8). In societies where economic subsistence poses a greater risk than infectious disease or other natural dangers, parental child-rearing strategies and goals may be organized around the eventual economic viability of children (Scheper-Hughes 1987:8). Scheper-Hughes summarizes the macrohistorical, ecological, and demographic trends exerting a profound influence on parental goals and on child-rearing practices: in Europe from the early to the modern era, deaths became more controllable. This trend was accompanied by new perceptions of human life and its meaning, parenthood, and the relative value of the individual measured against that of the family, lineage, and community. New images and representations of adult-child relationships appeared (Aries 1962, cited in Scheper-Hughes 1987:8–9).

Imagery of youth and age in contexts of class and gender relationships, and parents' manipulation of these images in confrontations with outside intruders, receive scant attention. Yet researchers recognize that in many communities where they work, children play important economic roles and are highly visible participants in adult life. Aries and Scheper-Hughes argue convincingly that, given a world of great uncertainty about individual human life, parents share a common understanding that subordinates the survival of the individual to the survival of the larger domestic unit (ibid.:10), thereby making possible a greater understanding of those conditions that cultural representation and the treatment of children reflect and of what local beliefs enable parents to do. But these authors stop short of sorting out these variables from the local perspective, because they tend to ignore or underplay multiple levels of interaction: between local residents and cultural beliefs, macrohistorical trends, and visiting researchers.

A number of studies (Riesman 1986:71–138; Le Moal 1973; Ottenberg 1982; Rabain 1979; Cartry 1978) have made valuable contributions toward understanding the expressive role of play and rituals in relationships between the generations, specifically, in parent-child relationships: for example, in conveying messages about who participants are, the content of adult ideas about what children and the person are, the meaning of parenthood, and key ideas and notions of society, property, and relationships. Special emphasis has been placed upon the ways childhood-related attitudes and practices communicate, in the socialization process, officially sanctioned values of society. Riesman (1986:73) has pointed out the need for studies of concepts of the person and the life cycle, particularly in Africa, that analyze the relation between symbols or symbol systems and the "realities" to which they refer. In my view, these studies, while valuable and richly descriptive, also suffer from limitations. They tend to place too much emphasis upon the passive socializing functions of childhood activities as these reproduce the social structure through the child as malleable object or conduit. In his recent critical survey of studies of concepts of the person and the life cycle in Africa, Riesman (1986:71–138) discusses how rituals and play as well as work communicate what it means to be a man, woman, or child. For example, Ottenberg (1982:170–84, cited in Riesman 1986) has shown how, in Nigeria, Afikpo children's masquerading reflects their social and psychological maturation. These children's groups play an essential part in educating people for adult life and responsibilities well before puberty initiation rites occur. It is shown that these practices express key ideas and notions of society and person. Yet they may also have a political basis, overlooked thus far by some researchers.

In the following section, I reflect upon my relationships with local residents, who overwhelmingly are adult, married parents with children rather than mere "subjects" in a study of the life course, in order to open up new perspectives on the role of different generations in the world of nonrelated, as well as related, adults. I hope this approach provides more vivid portrayals of cultural encounters along several dimensions: between Tuareg adults and local children, between Tuareg adults and adult outsiders, and between Tuareg children and adult outsiders. This is in keeping with my goal of portraying the life course in ways that conform to local formulations of it.

Parents and Children, Anthropologist and Residents

In casual interaction with me, as well as in local exegesis of life course beliefs and practices, older adult residents introduced three topics most frequently: religion, marriage, and children. Thus it is instructive here to examine definitions of childhood in Tuareg society. Adults appeared to allow small children to take some risks, for example, to walk on burning sand without sandals, to wear scanty clothes in cold season sandstorms, to play with dangerous objects, to go for lengthier time periods than adults without bathing, and to eat leftover food. Although material poverty certainly enters into these practices, it does not explain them entirely. Once I gave a long shirt to a year-old girl who normally went naked during the cold season. Her parents dressed her in it on several occasions, and then the shirt vanished. When I inquired about its whereabouts, I discovered that they had given it to a cousin, an older child who already had several items of clothing. Gender did not explain this either, for girls are as much valued as boys. When I questioned adults about children who were playing outside in the hot sun one afternoon, they suggested that children enjoyed a kind of compensation or protection: "Small children are in less danger of pain than adults because they have no sin *(abakat)*." Tuareg children may rummage through garbage and play freely with sharp throwaway industrial objects such as wire to make toys and traps (e.g., cars from sardine cans or wagons from thong sandals). Yet in contrast to their seemingly casual attitudes in supervising everyday children's play, adults practice numerous ritual measures to protect children.

Another practice I noticed was that adults of all social strata allow children, as they do adult smiths and former slaves, to closely approach outside visitors, researchers, and other strangers. This occurs despite cultural values admonishing children to be reserved and respectful toward local adults and also despite some ambivalence felt by local adults toward outsiders. In these encounters, I argue, children act not solely as go-betweens for adults but also as buffers and, on occasion, even agents of active resistance. In towns, some teachers complained that Tuareg school children were intractable and posed "discipline problems." Many Tuareg adults traditionally opposed secular schools for reasons I outline in subsequent pages.

In order to make sense of beliefs and practices pertaining to children as social actors, childhood, parenthood, and relationships between adults and children, I proceed on two levels of analysis. First, I explore local associations of children with power, risk, danger, and vulnerability. I also explore some wider cultural and political issues these associations raise, such as cultural autonomy, hegemony, resistance, and subjectivity in ethnographic representation. In the course of my long-term fieldwork it became apparent that certain aspects of my own life were not taking the same paths as those of my "subjects" of study, and friends and assistants became more aware of this upon each visit. This issue was addressed in much behavior of children and adults toward me—in the ways mothers, fathers, and children related to me as an adult, married, but childless woman and a friendly student of Tuareg culture but also as a representative of potential domination from outside. The entire topic of childhood, as well as its complements, marriage and parenthood, became of focal interest in conversations with friends and acquaintances, more of whom had become parents on each successive visit of mine to Niger. "Why don't you yet have children?" friends wanted to know. Didn't I like them? My display of photos of my own nephews back in the United States reassured them somewhat but not entirely. They were amazed to discover my age in years, and some residents at first thought it was an error in Tamacheq; upon verifying the number, women surmised that I "must be well-nourished" and added hopefully that, because of this, I undoubtedly would remain capable of having children for some time yet. But with worry they asked me what my own old age would be like without children and in-laws to take care of me, and they recommended amulets to cure childlessness. Thus my position as married but childless researcher on the life course, and theirs as subject-parents, caused concern and also stimulated testing of my attitudes (and by extension, those of my cultural traditions) about parenthood, childhood, and the wider sociopolitical relations these evoke.

This gap in mutual experience became an arena for residents' testing of my own character according to their value system, conducted through observing my responses to their children, for example, when I was continually surrounded by staring children. On still another level, children and childhood activities were frequently used to express adults' unofficial, hidden, or muted viewpoints—not solely their official, voiced norms—when in the presence of, and addressing, outsiders. In this respect, it differed markedly from two other activities culturally marked as crucial in life course symbolism, religion and marriage, which provided a forum for expressing the official "voice" of Tuareg culture. Relevant here are adult ideas about what children are within society and also what they can do for society in confronting the outside world. Children in the field site simultaneously participate in local ritual and political strategies of bridging and containment and thereby express impressions of contact with others that adults do not express directly.

Beliefs about childhood and the treatment of children are related to two processes: efforts to underline status and descent distinctions (of age and social stratum) locally, in a community that is changing but still characterized by marked stratification of inherited, endogamous occupational groups; and political responses to central state government authority, including how to oppose it, benefit from it, and channel it to local advantage, while preserving cultural autonomy. Tuareg attitudes toward children and concepts of the parent-child relationship have traditionally revolved around concern with (Islamic) religious purity and the guarding of prestigious descent and social status before biological needs. Furthermore, children are a potential force of resistance that adults deploy at specific times and places against what adults perceive as foreign intervention. The roles of lower-status persons, including children, have expressed resistance, first against French colonialism and recently against some government control schemes. It is instructive here to examine these processes on two levels: cultural factors in Tuareg children's life conditions (health, play, work, education) and their interaction with political processes through their relationships with adults (local residents, myself, and other outside figures).

Thus theories of resistance are complementary, rather than antithetical, to a poetics framework of the life course. Bourdieu (1977) conducted research on French farmers' domination by the French educational system. His early work included a study of ways in which the French educational system replicated society and inculcated dominant values. This author's interest was in how people react to and resist the school system. Bourdieu's notion of symbolic violence, the incorporation of ideology that informs behavior, is useful but does not fully explain processes of resistance (Bourdieu 1977). Relevant here is De Certeau (1984) and his concept of tactics: how people play with the structure behind the scenes. They appear to follow, but backstage they resist—for example, children in the classroom. This connects with wider state processes. In such resistance, there is not passivity but refusal to cooperate. Scott (1990), similarly, defines everyday resistance as constituting unofficial private discourses and behaviors that subvert and undermine official public ideologies and actions. These are "hidden transcripts" not readily apparent in official transcripts and onstage behaviors controlled by elites. Here the emphasis is placed on manipulative behaviors among subordinates, suggesting that they are not always victims of false consciousness, mystification, or internalization.

Furthermore, the focus on youth is complementary to—and produces a more nuanced and balanced view of—power, domination, subordination, and the resistance process in growing old. In Tuareg society, there is a connection between notions of the child and cultural/ethnic identity and autonomy in two senses. Older residents give a commentary, through children, on power relationships. They also gauge, through outsiders' responses to children, outsiders' attitudes toward Tuareg culture specifically and authority/hegemony relationships generally. This is shown in birth rituals and other rites protecting children and in social interaction between elders, youths, and researcher.

Most Tuareg children are born in a rural, seminomadic household. Among many Kel Ewey, this is matrifocal economically for about five to seven months of the year. Groups of mothers and sisters living next door to each other cooperate in subsistence, cooking together, sharing food, and herding and merging livestock. During this time period, many men are away on caravan trading expeditions. The household is more patrifocal (that is, defined and managed as a subsistence unit more in terms of a nuclear, male-headed household) for the remainder of the year while men are home.[1] In the early 1990s, the nationalist/separatist movement caused some men to travel away from home as they took up arms and joined the rebellion, while some left for migrant labor and others emigrated to refugee camps. But most residents near Mount Bagzan in Aïr have not been uprooted, and even those who left have recently been returning to the region.

The mother's female kin are prominent in birth rituals. Ideally, first babies are born in the mother's maternal home. If the couple has moved away from the wife's parents, the woman usually returns to her mother's tent to give birth to the first child. Often, however, the first child is born before the marriage has been ritually recognized as stable by the bride's parents and therefore before many changes in household structure and locale. The mother of the baby's mother, or some other elderly female relative, buries the child's umbilical cord underneath three stones to the east of the compound. Old women gather the fruit of the *agar* tree and bathe the child in this fruit and water. Protective amulets, made by a marabout, and a knife are placed on the ground near the baby's head to ward off spirits, as they are near the bride during the wedding, and mother and child enter their state of seclusion, interrupted only by naming rituals. The new mother and baby are considered particularly vulnerable to spirits at this time and are secluded for forty days following the birth in the mother's tent. During this time, the new mother neither washes nor prays. There is often a windscreen erected inside the tent that physically separates the pair from the outside world. The underlying purpose of this screen is not only to shield the mother and child from wind and sand, but also to protect them from malevolent forces, articulated metaphorically as spirits but seen as emanating from antisocial human agents as well. This time period is called *amzor,* during which mother and child live in a symbiotic relationship. A knife is stuck into the sand directly above the baby's head to ward off spirits. Sand, referred to as "mother's medicine," is also placed on the mother's bed. Tuareg believe that the baby should, for good fortune, be born literally on the ground or sand.

The new mother is given a mixture of leaves and plant roots called *tisset;* it is bright red in color and is called "mother's stomach medicine," believed to have properties that heal the stomach following childbirth. An association is made between the red color of this medicine, ritual references to menstruation, and the prominent maternal ties and the matrilineage. Within twenty-four hours following the birth, a smith woman disassembles the bed and takes it far outside the compound. Then she cleans the tent and compound, and the family begins preparation for the baby's nameday *(isem),* to be held a week later.

Cultural beliefs and practices pertaining to early life reveal that perceived needs depend on social status rather than strictly on biology, and protective measures taken are primarily religious. During the first week of life, the baby is fed goat's milk only. Closely related women soon join the mother in her tent and sew Koranic verses written by marabouts into cloth squares. Later, a smith woman inserts them into leather envelopes for the child to wear around the neck, from about the age of one to two years. The significance of the protective roles of the child's mother's mother, female affines, and smiths is apparent here, as at other liminal points in the life course. Even young children are aware of this, as apparent in this account of the event from a schoolboy:

> When a woman has a child, her mother cleans the house. She prepares food and tells the [female] in-laws that her daughter has had a baby. The female in-laws, cousins, everyone, also smiths, come if it is a first-born child. Namedays are held for all children, but the most elaborate are for the first-born child. The smiths organize a big festival like a camel race and some games and songs, and people give them money. When they gather at the home of the mother, people bring food. When the marabout arrives, he cuts the throat of a goat or ram, and smiths grill the meat. People eat the meat. Both the marabout and the women on the father's side of the family each give the child a name. When the marabout cuts the animal's throat, he also pronounces [simultaneously] the child's name, the one given by the marabout and the father at the mosque but not the name given by the women. He then goes to the mosque with the men, where they pray for a good nameday. At the child's nameday, guests are supposed to give money only to the mother of the father of the new child. Guests are supposed to celebrate [eat and drink tea] with the side of the family who invited you.

Prominent in these rituals are the child's mother, older female relatives on the child's father's side (called "in-laws" from the viewpoint of those on the mother's side), smiths, and Islamic scholars. Maternal and paternal grandmothers play much more prominent roles than the mother and father of the child. The maternal grandmother, for example, receives the money for a nameday from those guests invited by her side of the family; the paternal grandmother receives this from those invited by her side of the family. Emphasis at the nameday rites is upon giving money to smiths as well, during their play-ing of the hand drums and *tende* mortar drum and their singing of praise-songs, as at weddings. Smiths are, again, key go-betweens: when they cry out the news of the birth (similar to their crying out the news of the wedding) and when they circulate among their patron families conveying this news individ-ually, constituting an invitation to attend the nameday.

The night before the official nameday ritual, at sunset, another, unofficial naming ceremony is held called *asegherle* (denoting, literally, "going around"), when the child (though not the mother) is temporarily removed from seclu-sion and taken around the mother's mother's compound three times, in coun-terclockwise direction, "in order to see the world." A procession of older women relatives file around the home, at a brisk walking pace, led by an old smith woman carrying a tray of dates, millet, and goat cheese, which sur-rounds burning incense in a clay potsherd. Kel Ewey state that the purpose of this "going around" rite is also for the good luck (blessing, *al baraka*) of the child. These items are called, collectively, *takote n barar*. In translation, *takote* has the general sense of alms or offering, donation, or gift, and it conducts good luck or blessing. Thus *takote n barar* denotes the "the child's gift of good fortune and blessing." This is a recurrent element throughout Kel Ewey rites of passage: in weddings, at mortuary rites, and on numerous other occasions marking transition or transformation in status. It is strongly associated with female relatives of post-childbearing age and reinforces matrilineal kinship ties.

When a small child dies, for example, his maternal grandmother serves the important festival potion, *eghale,* consisting of dates, millet, and goat cheese, to visitors offering sympathy at her home. Three days after the child's death, there is held a *takote n barar;* in this context, this entails a feast held featuring food identical to that at weddings and namedays, but guests do not dress up or wear elaborate jewelry, and no music, dancing, or camel racing is held. Elderly female relatives on the mother's side gather at the home of the mater-nal grandmother in the morning and roll *eghale* dough into small balls, undi-luted with water, to be distributed later among the deceased child's relatives who attend the ceremony, which, again, is called *takote.* The number of balls made is said to equal the number of joints *(eserghis)* in the body, by extension metaphorically referring to kinship links. Each guest at the mortuary feast takes these home to persons in the immediate household.

During the *asegherle* ceremony, the women ululate loudly as they go around the house three times. More women arrive, until those present represent both sides of the baby's family; the *chidegalen* or "guests" (affines) arrive to join the others just as the sun sets, from their village, camp, or (in cases of close mar-riage between families residing nearby) from their compounds. Soon the el-derly women dance, waving pestles as others beat on washbasins and continue to ululate. Here women's encircling also replicates a recurrent theme throughout Tuareg rites of passage as well as other collective activities: for example, at weddings, young men encircle the bride's camp on camels, and young women encircle it on donkeys; formerly, during raids, male warriors encircled the enemy camp on camels before pillaging it. The drum beat on the washbasins is identical to that played by smiths on hand drums to announce weddings and official namedays.

During this unofficial naming, the elderly smith woman leading the procession chants a few verses, opening with the phrase "Chiketaw, chiketaw," meaning, "The stomach is full, the stomach is full" (derived from Hausa). On one level, this signifies that at rites of passage, food is plentiful and everyone, particularly smiths, eats well. On another level, it alludes to the role of the stomach (*tedis* in Tamacheq, *ciki* in Hausa) and older maternal female kin in forging children's identity and destiny, both conceptually and jurally.

Several features of the women's *asegherle* merit closer attention. The dates, millet, and cheese symbolize health and prosperity; incense, burned on festive occasions generally, represents celebration and is also, along with perfume, a protection against spirits. The burning of incense outside the ritual proceeds in a specified manner: a circle of friends, usually young men and women, gathering in a tent to celebrate an occasion such as a marriage, pass the incense around in a small container, and each individual wraps his or her robes in a tentlike fashion over the incense; the idea is to saturate one's clothing with its scent. But incense in these contexts does not merely serve to provide pleasant scents as an end in and of themselves, although these are highly valued aesthetically. It also evokes unity and protection from outside dangers, specifically spirits believed to hover around persons in times of transition because they are jealous of them.

The old women's dancing inverts the usual age, class, and gender roles. It contrasts to the older women's everyday role ideal of dignity and restraint in public. Men are absent from the *asogherle* rite. Normally, older persons of either sex, and women of all ages, do not dance with such abandon in public. Young men dance at evening festivals with lances held high above their heads, and young women sometimes also dance, but elders, especially older noble women, do not dance with pestles. The pestle is associated with the mortar, and both have associations of precolonial servile domestic labor. Elderly women also imitate men's style of holding lances, in their jubilant wielding of pestles above their heads. In effect, they are enacting roles of successful parenthood and, simultaneously, ritually ambiguous gender status. Several women indicated that women "become like men" in certain contexts, for example, as mothers-in-law and upon reaching post-childbearing status in the occasional covering of their mouths with the headscarf that resembles men's face-veiling. Meanwhile, during this rite and at a distance from it, male relatives gather, pounding millet for the *eghale* to be served at the official nameday the following day. Thus the women at the unofficial pre-nameday rite become more "man-like," and the men, who in everyday tasks normally do not pound millet, become more "woman-like."

Here it is tempting to interpret these acts in terms of late-life gender roles and instrumental/expressive inversions (Myerhoff 1978, 1992; Gutmann 1987). But I caution against overgeneralizing these processes. Rather, their use in the specific ritual context, and their kinship and jural meanings, not strictly their gender meanings, are important. Here the older adults reaffirm the maternal element in kinship and the symbolism of the mother's tent. The pervasive theme puts emphasis on the child's grandmothers as even more significant than the child's mother and father, in terms of affiliation with the newborn child and rights in the marriage itself. In this way, the power of mothers to make and unmake marriages, and the privilege of grandmothers to joke with and "feed" their grandchildren in early life, and later to monopolize their in-laws' labor and gifts, is given ritual expression.

By contrast, the slaughtering of the animal at dawn on the following day is "to celebrate the marabout's official naming of the child." The marabout bestows the name at exactly the same moment that he cuts the goat's throat, while the baby's hair is shaved by the smith woman attached to the family in a separate women's gathering at home. The baby's hair is shaved for the purpose of severing the child's ties with the spirit world. The child receives more than the single name pronounced by the marabout, which is given by the marabout and father and considered to be his or her "sacred name," usually a Koranic (Arabic-derived rather than Tamacheq) name. Old men say this name "replaces" the women's name given the previous evening, but old women dispute this, indicating that the secret name is important. The marabout pronounces only the public, official Koranic name as he cuts the throat of a ram.

There are a number of customary guidelines for the Koranic name: names for the day of the week on which the child is born as well as Muslim holidays. For example, a child born on Tabaski is called Al Hadji (fem. Hadjia or Hadjua); on Ganni (Mouloud), Mohammed (fem. Fatimata or Amina). Yet each child also receives a name bestowed in private, usually Tamacheq, by maternal female kin in the separate *asegherle* ritual held the evening before the official nameday. Older women told me that this name is the name the child, especially if the first-born, is addressed by later, particularly by the mother. Until these two ritual namings, one by the women and the other by the father and marabout, the baby is often called "stranger" (*amagar*, also denoting "guest"). Alternatively, a girl is called by the mother's, and a boy by the father's, name. This conveys the tentative, contingent nature of his or her existence: the baby may not live. Until the child has survived a nameday, he or she is not yet identified by an individual name. Unless a child cries at birth, no funeral is held. If, however, the child cries, a funeral is held, even for a child without a personal name. The multiple names with different origins, alongside other ritual beliefs and practices, suggest that social personhood is gradual and results from an accumulation of several identities, kin- and class-based. These identities in effect "layer" the person protectively against outside threats to the maternal tent: Islam and men's patrilineal interests threaten ancient matrilineality, and sedentization threatens the tent.

These names have very different meanings in terms of identity of the person. The name pronounced by the marabout in public at the official rite represents paternal kinship and Islamic religious affiliation, given public expression in the open pronouncement. This Koranic name constitutes public aspects of the child's personality, though they are shameful for the mother to pronounce. Maternal ties and the domestic, secular, and profane are seen as part of the child's hidden, submerged dimension. In the bilateral system of the Kel Ewey, although Koranic inheritance and patrilineal descent predominate in everyday jural practice, herds called *akhu huderan* are a type of inheritance meant for women that counterbalances Koranic inheritance. Matrilineally based affective ties underlie the former throughout the life course, emerging in particular contexts: for example, beliefs regarding affliction with some types of spirits of the wild, which are believed to be passed from mother's milk.

Thus the paternal and Islamic naming establish the child's identity in official kinship and jural domains, but henceforth it is shameful to allude to this directly, especially for the mother of the child. By contrast, the maternal name is the name subsequently used for the child by many persons, but especially the mother, in everyday conversation, both in reference and in address.

Numerous everyday incidents clearly reinforced these notions, initiated during nameday rituals, of what it means to be a child. At a women's tent-construction party early in my residence, I was given a bowl of food before others ate. (This was customary initially, while I was still considered a guest; later, as residents became more open toward me, I ate with most adults, usually women, but occasionally men as well. In Kel Ewey communities, men, women, and children usually eat separately in public, and a new guest is usually separately served first.) On that occasion, I accepted the bowl, but feeling slightly uncomfortable about eating first and with all eyes upon me, I asked if the other people present wanted to share it with me, indicating with an inclusive gesture women and children seated nearby. The women laughed and referred to the small children as "not people, but children." This implies a view of children not as inhuman but rather as incomplete social persons, who are yet important mediators between the human and spirit worlds. Adults say small children have no reserve *(takarakit)* and also "lack a head." This latter expression denotes intelligence and is tied to principles of descent and social stratum.[2] Although ideally intelligence is supposed to be inherited and class-based, according to social stratum affiliation that is, in turn, based on descent, individual character traits may modify this. Furthermore, although the social strata are supposed to be endogamous and traditionally were associated with different, inherited occupations, nowadays there is frequent intermarriage and combining of subsistence patterns. Thus a child's personality configuration and local theories explaining it become complex and are subject to a great deal of negotiation. In principle, if a child's parents are of mixed class origins, the child is supposed to take on the affiliation of the father's descent group; on this point, Kel Ewey differ from some other, more matrilineally conscious Tuareg divisions who state that "the stomach colors the child." Yet Kel Ewey display some contradictions, and cases suggest that children's physical and character traits can be manipulated to suit different goals. For example, individuals of diverse social origins told me that a child inherits intelligence from the maternal uncle. A noble man from an *echerifan* clan who claimed descent from the Prophet had two wives, one of noble descent, the other the descendant of a slave. He pointed out to me how the child of his wife of servile descent was more obedient than the child of his noble wife. He attributed this quality to his *echerif* descent, however, rather than to the servile side of descent, and he also indicated that the obedient child acted "more *echerif* and more noble" than his other child. Some Kel Ewey allude to physical traits in cases of mixed parentage: if a child's hair is fine, they consider him or her "more noble"; if less fine, they consider him or her "more servile" in descent. Religion and descent are therefore strongly present in concepts of what shapes character, personality, and appearance. Even today, judgments of behavior sometimes allude to social stratum identity. Nonetheless, descent-based ideology is not always reflected in individual achievement and destiny, and there is considerable flexibility in actual practice.

Thus there is a "feedback loop" between, on the one hand, notions of personal destiny, that is, the fate of the person over time as a component of the moral person (Fortes 1959, 1987), and, on the other hand, symbolism in the nameday rituals, in particular, the prominent roles of elderly persons as gatekeepers. Following the naming of the baby at the mosque by the marabout, the smith woman attached to the family comes to the mother's tent to dress her hair. Throughout all this, the mother of the father of the baby dances intermittently, usually only in the presence of closely related women and smiths, after the men on the father's side have left for the baby's home, or, from the alternative kinship vantage point of the mother's side, while the men are away pounding millet. Lots of very rich, sweet, well-blended *eghale* (*eghajira*) is made by both sides of the baby's family. Individuals at namedays wear elaborate dress—silk blouses, indigo veils—and place brightly decorated trappings on camels. If the baby's father resides in a different camp or village from his own parents (usually the case on the birth of a first-born child), the in-laws prepare for a journey to the baby's mother's home, timing their departure so as to arrive at sunset, as at weddings. The mother of the father of the baby gives a kid from her herd to the family of the baby's mother at the nameday. Guests' gifts of money constitute economic compensation for the celebration expenses, as well as ritual recognition of ties.

When I accompanied a group of women on the father's side to a first-born–child's nameday in the mother's village, a small oasis about seven miles from the father's village of origin, the women stopped frequently along the way to make up their faces, rearrange their clothing, and nurse their babies. The women went on foot, the men on camel. The women approached the oasis slowly, as the sun was setting. In the encounter between these women and their affines, elderly female relatives on the baby's maternal side who came out to welcome them before they actually entered the village, there were lengthy and formal greetings and much covering of their mouths with the headscarves, almost in the fashion of men's face-veils. Later, the women guests from the father's side were lodged in tents, again as at weddings, separate from the baby's mother's relatives and also separate from men on both sides of the family. The guest affines rested, chatted, and were served, after the men and the maternal relatives, festival dishes identical to those served at weddings: rice mixed with macaroni, wheat dishes, meat, and the *eghale* drink. Afterward, they drank tea, prepared and served by smith women (the reverse occurs at smith namedays, as at weddings: nobles then serve food and tea).

Later on in the evening following the nameday, the younger people (adolescents and the newly married) of both sexes, including local residents of diverse social strata and also relatives on both sides of the baby's family, attend singing, drumming, and dancing that is organized and led by smiths. Again, the central instrument at these evening festivals is the *tende* mortar drum. This is often played at festivals featuring mixed-sex, mixed-class flirting and courtship and said to house Iblis, the Devil, whom Kel Ewey hold responsible for illicit love as well as reproductive force. Again, as at weddings, elderly persons (especially male Islamic scholars and older women) are conspicuously absent from these evening festivals. Men dancers approach the women's chorus in pairs, performing the dance waving a sword or lance. Others circle the performers and seek out romantic partners on the sidelines. In contrast to the daytime *isem* (official nameday) ritual, both sides of the family and both sexes freely mix together at the evening *tende* festival (named for its accompanying mortar drum). There is an atmosphere of license, and it is openly acknowledged that the activity called *tambur* (denoting "picking up women") goes on during and after the festival. Secret signals are used for flirtations. The point here is that namedays' nightly festivities provide ample opportunity for mixing across class lines with the partner of one's personal choice, on the basis of achieved rather than acquired characteristics, whereas such free associations are forbidden in other contexts. The only restrictions and segregations that continue to operate at this event are those based on age.

Smiths also sing praise-songs at namedays, as guests give them gifts of cash, sugar, tea, and millet. The next day, guests rise before sunrise, according to residents, "because they are at the home of strangers." In this feature of the nameday, there is a parallel with the behavior of the male suitor before marriage. During courtship practices of conversation and flirting inside the woman's tent, the man may spend the night with the woman, but he must be gone before sunrise and must avoid being seen by members of her family, in particular her mother. If he is not, this is a cause for great shame. I heard of a case where the suitor had been found the morning after by his sweetheart's mother, and he was accused of rape. The seriousness of this accusation is apparent when it is noted that rape is extremely shameful and rare in rural Aïr. While there was some question as to whether this was in fact actual, coerced rape, or solely the accusation from the suspecting girl's mother, and the man was not prosecuted or otherwise punished, his relations with the woman's parents were nonetheless damaged. The mere accusation illustrates the gravity of his offense, of being seen by his potential affines.

In the morning, the female affines/guests drink tea and *eghale,* then apply make-up and rearrange their clothing, and greet the mother of the baby and other female relatives on the maternal side who drop by, remaining at their tent door to chat. There is again emphasis upon lengthy and formal greetings to elderly women, in particular. Toward mid-morning, the male affines and other male guests go home on camelback, the women on foot.

During the nameday ritual, therefore, the family of the father and that of the mother of the baby are kept strictly segregated during the day and while eating, drinking tea, and sleeping. Men and women as well as old and young, are also segregated, particularly during eating, chatting, and tea-drinking. But at evening festivals both groups are mixed together, except for the elderly, religious scholars and very small toddlers. This pattern conforms to that at other rites of passage: weddings and greeting the tent. Single and newly married persons predominate at evening festivals, while older and long-married persons predominate at the daytime rituals.

Several additional features of namedays are noteworthy. The giving of offerings of money to the grandmothers is considered of utmost importance. Lack of funds is a serious matter and prevents individuals from attending. Beautiful clothing is also considered essential; there are many comments on how attractive each guest appears, men as well as women. Even the newborn baby is given cloth and jewelry, mostly beaded bracelets, strung by the baby's father's mother and other older women. Finally, dances are also considered essential. People judge a nameday's worth by how "lively" the dancing was. The point here is that the birth of a child, particularly a first-born child, is a victory for the mother of the father of the baby. For Kel Ewey, marriage, enacted in slow, progressive stages, is tentative and fragile in its early years. As shown, the position of the groom is similar to that of a new apprentice, and his access to the bride depends on his initially servile role toward her mother. Thus the meaning of ritual separations and mixing and inversion, at both namedays and weddings, becomes clear: these encode the new relationships of various men and women.

Babies are carried about, at first mostly by mother and grandmothers, in a leather cradle, sling, or diaper, made for the first-born by the grandmother in order to express gratitude for the child and made for subsequent children by a smith woman. This method of carrying the baby in a sling is called *egechik*. It differs markedly from the method so widespread in other parts of Africa (including towns in Niger) of carrying babies on the back in a cloth. In rural Aïr, the sling is frequently detached from the mother's shoulder and suspended from a tent post, in hammock fashion, thereby allowing slightly greater freedom for mother and child. Mothers usually carry babies along with them when they do housework but may leave them behind with older siblings and female relatives for the duration of a day while herding and gathering outside the village or camp. But in other respects, there is close physical contact. Babies sleep with their mother while the father is gone on caravans. There is a joking, playful relationship with the maternal grandmother, such as teasing and mock-feeding, for example, pretending to nurse or to offer tobacco to the child. A smith told me the purpose of this was "to reinforce the child's relationship with the matrilineage." But fathers, also, display a great deal of affection for babies and small children, though they never take a child from the mother during tantrums; the mother comforts a crying child with games, sung rhymes, and nonsense words.

Ideally, there is no younger sibling until after two years; if there is, this is considered shameful for the parents. Babies are weaned at between 17 and 20 months, with no transitional baby food. Following weaning there is a decrease in protein intake and an abrupt retreat of the mother from physical closeness. The child is left much on his or her own or in the care of older siblings, even while the mother is at home, for the mother is busy with often arduous domestic tasks revolving around food processing. From very early on, emphasis is upon courageous trial and error (toddlers are allowed to play with potentially harmful objects, like bits of wire); invention (they make their own toys); and fatalism (God cares for a child). Parents say, "Where there is a mouth, Allah will feed it": for example, one woman already had four children and limited resources but insisted that God would provide for however many children she eventually brought into the world. It is also important for adults to give to the child: relatives are to be generous and offer alms *(takote)*, such as food. Until about four years of age, when the children are dressed in long cotton gowns, small toddlers' clothing is scant, but they wear many protective religious amulets. Mothers at this time begin to encourage children to leave the compound with siblings to relieve themselves away from the village or camp, and children begin to form play groups.

From an early age, children are trained through example and anecdote (for example, in evening folktales related by mostly women and smiths) to survive in an unpredictable physical and political environment. There are many tales portraying the testing of youths in outwitting treacherous villains. For example, on the deep structural level, a series of tales about a character called Aligouran, an uncle who attempts to trap his maternal nephew in continual difficult tests or tasks, addresses kinship relationships between brother, sister, and maternal uncle and nephew that are based in ancient matriliny. But residents in their own local exegesis emphasized to me its overtly didactic purpose of teaching youths survival skills and testing their intelligence, while also emphasizing that the nephew inherits intelligence from his mother's brother.

Attempts at behavior modification of toddlers involve fright and shaming. The four-year-old son in the first household where I boarded, whom I'll call Mohammed, once climbed into a mortar full of millet that his mother was about to pound. His mother and her sisters lifted him out and then laughingly reprimanded him verbally and also by playfully aiming a knife at his penis. To teach her year-old son the danger of fire, his mother lit a straw and brought it near the baby (but still at a safe distance, too far to burn), exclaiming "hot!" In each of these incidents, the women told me that the children in question "had no head." I saw only three cases of physical punishment of small children: when a child of about six years urinated in a water container; when a small boy grabbed goat cheese without asking; and when a girl of about six years persistently stared at an older, adult woman on the paternal side of her family. Children are not supposed to initiate greetings with adults (though they should respond to the latters' greetings) or stare at adults directly in the eye. They usually eat following adults. These practices convey the respect or reserve *(takarakit)* children are encouraged to begin expressing toward elders generally, adults in adjacent generations (except the mother's brother), and adults on the father's side. In these cases where I saw children severely punished by local standards, adults said the children in question "had no shame [reserve]."

On the other hand, adults often appear to accept children for what they are, particularly in situations involving an outsider. Tahirou, who sometimes informally assisted me with transcribing verbal art, was explaining to me the meanings of a song text when his children appeared and began playing boisterously nearby. He stated matter-of-factly that children do certain things "because they are children" and did not attempt to stop them, yet continued calmly with transcriptions. I noticed, however, that several of Tahirou's male friends had recently teased him about "working for the woman guest" at a time when the purpose of my presence in the area, still novel, was not fully understood by most local residents. Tahirou may have felt ashamed to be ridiculed by other men whom he referred to as being in his "clique" (his age and class cohorts, and also many members of a small circle of chiefly and maraboutique families) and later somewhat sheepishly suggested to me that, as "an older adult and parent," he needed to spend more time "educating" his children. He then arranged for a younger relative, also highly competent, to assist me on a more regular basis.

Concepts of age-based responsibility were also expressed through blaming children as scapegoats in incidents that adults wished to distance themselves from, and social types they wished to separate themselves from, in order to illustrate social differences in matters embarrassing in the presence of outsiders. Soon after I arrived at the field site on my first extended research project, introduced through mutual friends in neighboring villages and camps but still unknown to most local residents, I found some small toilet articles, soap and perfume, missing from my tent. My hosts, who were warmly hospitable and genuinely concerned with my welfare, often attempted to "protect" me from persons considered antisocial. They insisted that theft by adults was rare in the region, except by "slaves," and theorized that children had taken these items. They named one child in particular, whom I'll call Idrissa, a child of about ten reputed to be difficult. Adults lamented that he "had no shame." But Idrissa rarely came by my host family's residence, and to my knowledge, he would be unlikely to have taken the items without being noticed. It appeared Idrissa was a convenient scapegoat who took on all the "sins" of others. Although his mother was matrilineally related to the mother in my host family, she occupied an ambiguous, marginal status, having never remarried after being widowed and raising her children without a father. When older children disobey, this is sometimes explained in terms of having no father or a father who is absent for prolonged periods.

Idrissa was somewhat of a pariah in the community—he was constantly blamed for mishaps, got into fights, and was considered a troublemaker generally. The boy did not seem intentionally antisocial to me but rather somewhat slow and solitary. But his presence gave residents the opportunity to divert responsibility from others and to save them from embarrassment in an unpleasant (if minor) incident with an outsider guest. Residents indicated that Idrissa had inherited evil spirits from his father, which affected his head. Residents also said all children in that household were "strange." One daughter, in fact, had committed suicide. The tragedy had occurred before my residence for reasons unknown or hidden.

During my return visit years later, I saw Idrissa, now a teenager, lying still and alone in the open oeud, a dried riverbed where people often walk with herds or when traveling but where they seldom recline alone. His body appeared oddly stiff, lying face down with toes pointing into the sand. I expressed alarm to friends, wondering if he was ill, but they said his spirits caused these episodes. When Idrissa's fits occurred, they said, he always lay motionless, "as though he were dead. . . . He does not speak, and eats sand." Only the insane or mentally deficient would attempt to eat sand. When I inquired whether he had seen a marabout for treatment (customary among Tuareg men who are believed possessed by spirits), they indicated he had not, for treatment was expensive. Despite membership in the chiefly family, and despite women's ownership of herds, he and his mother and sisters were poorer than most of their relatives because they were cut off from male kin who normally help raise money for such expenses. Adults pitied Idrissa and did not often punish him, but all age groups shunned him socially and tended to scapegoat him.

One day, Idrissa wandered off in the desert. Although people searched for him for two days, no trace of him was found until shepherdesses came across his body, by then dead from dehydration and exposure.

The important point in these vignettes of socialization and other interaction is that judgments of children's actions are used to underline the social identity of other, older persons both inside and outside the community in terms of both distinctions and commonality. Children who are considered unrestrained, greedy, and disrespectful in the presence of persons standing in specific relationships to them, yet who are otherwise considered normal and healthy, are said to "have no shame." This is viewed as controllable, to be developed in socialization, even if occasionally through punishment. But they are held less individually accountable when they are said to "have no head," a trait viewed as uncontrollable, associated with very young children, the insane, or those possessed by spirits—all defined as incomplete social persons. But although these latter persons are not usually severely punished, they may be socially shunned and scapegoated. "Having a head" is bound up with social identity, traditionally class- as well as age-based. In the past, nobles considered themselves the most highly developed in this trait.

Gender distinctions also enter into responses to children. Mild disobedience by boys is tolerated slightly more than by girls, in particular toward mothers. I saw boys occasionally slap mothers, who merely laughed at these acts, but such behavior by girls, or by children of either sex toward fathers, would never be tolerated.

This may be the reason why several divorced fathers I knew took their children away with them by force upon leaving the region, despite the principle that on divorce children are supposed to stay with the mother. Unless they themselves are considered antisocial or, like Idrissa's father, possessed by spirits, present fathers are more likely to command respect from their children and to receive credit when their children display proper respect. Absent fathers are more likely to be blamed when children do not display such respect.

Furthermore, later on in life, fathers and patrilineal kin are important in assisting the groom in raising bridewealth. Thus, despite competing ties with women, the father-son tie is not easily dismissed.

Aside from really blatant violations of respect and reserve, small children are exempt in early years from the bulk of adult role expectations and responsibilities. Most young children of either sex spend time playing and watching their mother's goats. Yet learning goes on during these activities. Girls around six years old play with female dolls that they make from palm fibers and stalks and bits of cloth and that they dress in exact replicas of Tuareg adult dress. Small boys build miniature wells in the sand and build trucks and cars from discarded cans and sandals. Boys and girls build a miniature *tende* drum and enact play versions of performances. They also play at giving each other medicine, riding camels with branches, and imitating animals such as goats.

Gradually, children begin to help more with adult chores according to gender and class divisions of labor; these include herding (recently, with the introduction of poultry to the region, children begin to prepare for herding by raising small chickens), gardening, caravanning, cooking, hunting small birds with simple traps they make themselves from a bowl and string pully device, fetching water and firewood, and gathering clean sand for tent floors. At about this time, emphasis is placed upon repressing one's true feelings, especially anger.

A combination of several factors—emotional attachment, a contradictory perception of children as simultaneously a drain on resources and a contributor to economic welfare, and requirements to share scarce resources and assist with a heavy workload—encourage a great deal of informal adoption of children by older relatives. Children from Mount Bagzan come down to attend local primary and Koranic schools, board with relatives, and perhaps help out with chores while in residence. There are similar arrangements for those few who continue on to the CEG (middle school) and lycée (high school) in Agadez. Sometimes, a grandchild or grandniece is adopted by an elderly female relative to stay with them and help with housework. She may be childless or may lack children of both sexes. This is particularly true when there are no daughters (as in the case of Chigdouane, the woman portrayed in the preceding section) or after all daughters of an elderly woman are married.

As previously related, descendants of slaves, even as adults, are thought of as adopted or fictive children, but this is not necessarily denigrating. Like Adoum, a number of them are adopted and cared for by descendants of former masters. Individuals of noble descent frequently stated directly that "slaves are like children." Formerly, slaves, like children today, performed herding, gardening, and domestic labor. Although slaves like Adoum spoke the Tamacheq language and were culturally Tuareg, their lifestyle was far less opulent than nobles', which was characterized by conspicuous consumption. Slaves were not free but were owned by noble individuals and descent groups.

Yet there was opportunity for negotiation: the offspring of a noble and slave could inherit from the noble parent. Furthermore, since slaves, along with smiths, have stood outside the official descent and alliance system, they have traditionally acted as go-betweens and mediators. Recall how Adoum's freedom of verbal expression and his joking relationships with nobles illustrated this vividly. The question arising here is, exactly how are children's roles in certain respects similar to the servile roles of the past?

This analogy is complex. Children, and formerly, slaves, as jural minors, are both said to be deficient in reserve or shame and to lack "a head." Mothers openly admitted to me that they want children for the purpose of helping in domestic work and as old-age support. Although there are, without a doubt, strong affective ties to children, in contexts of work and subsistence children are nonetheless seen as nearly equivalent to slaves. Here, I wish to emphatically qualify this statement. This is not to deny the presence of an emotional attachment between parents and children. Of course, parents love children. But regardless of social stratum affiliation, all children are in a metaphorical sense slaves, and all parents are in a metaphorical sense nobles. In other words, youth and age have social stratum metaphorical entailments that result from precolonial relationships. Nowadays, since domestic slavery has been abolished, women's workload is heavy, particularly that of married women in semisedentary gardening settlements, whose most time-consuming tasks consist of cereal-processing (namely, pounding millet in a mortar and, except for those who live near recently built mills in some villages, crushing wheat and corn between two stones). Rural women spend much of their day performing these tasks, fetching water from the well, gathering firewood and palm fibers, weaving mats, constructing and repairing tents, and cooking. Some adults lament having to perform tasks formerly performed by slaves and value children as contributors to daily subsistence. Parents spent much time demonstrating to me how to motivate small children to do work by promising some reward, for example, by making them an amulet. This is quite an incentive, since spirits are said to threaten all young, despite (or perhaps precisely because of) their sinless nature.

Yet older adopted children, even relatives, seemed to me to be treated with less affection than parents' own children. I frequently heard adults speak sternly to them and give them orders, rarely smiling at them or playing with them. For example, Tina, a small girl who was the younger sister of Habiba, the woman friend with whom I boarded on a recent return to the field, stayed at her sister's household during the first part of the rainy season. Tina performed more work than the neighboring children, related on the husbands' side. I could not help but wonder whether these patterns had to do with my own presence as guest, with increased requirements for water and firewood, or whether they would have occurred in my absence and had to do with the proximity of paternal rather than maternal relatives. Habiba and her husband, Khamid, had initially resided at a nomadic camp about seven miles away with Habiba's parents, until Khamid had completed his bridewealth payments. This couple had subsequently moved near Khamid's parents in a semisedentary caravanning village, where they now resided after five years of marriage. Habiba was still childless and needed assistance with the housework. Eventually, Tina accompanied Habiba on a visit home, and Habiba returned a week later without the child. When I inquired about her, Habiba told me the girl felt angry at her because she had once spanked her and had asked to stay with her parents. So the analogy, or metaphorical connection, between slaves and some children, especially adopted ones, is not too far-fetched, but of course the equivalence is not exact.

On the one hand, the presence of a guest in the household may have created the need for more domestic work, for despite my efforts to help, this was considerable in a compound without children. Furthermore, Habiba's affines, due to reserve, were not expected to display as much affection for the child as were other relatives, in particular on the mother's side. Habiba and her mother-in-law, Tamata, observed strict reserve/respect relations, and Tamata visited more seldom than did the mother of the woman with whom I had boarded during a previous stay, who had had assistance from nearby female kin as well as from five children of her own. Mothers assist more than mothers-in-law, because between mothers and daughters there is no reserve. While Habiba's sisters-in-law assisted her, sisters assist and pool resources more closely. Children, like smiths and servile peoples, tend to perform tasks that are either unfinished due to others' absence or are avoided by others.

On the other hand, despite Tina's subordinate, ambiguous position in Habiba's household, the child was not coerced by her own parents into returning there. For this conflicted with the competing principle of mother-daughter solidarity and, of course, with emotions of very real love and affection. Moreover, like former slaves who, in the past, could change owners (Nicolaisen 1963), children have opinions that are not entirely disregarded in such matters. Children are never abandoned completely to the whims of the nuclear household in disciplinary matters. And in the past slaves also had some "escape hatches," as Adoum's resistance to being exchanged for a camel illustrated. Thus in the past, slaves were seen as "like children," but, although children today contribute to subsistence in performing many domestic tasks, the exact reverse is not true. Rather, precolonial nobility and servitude are social stratum attributes evoking metaphorical and economic paternalism and maternity in parent-child relationships, extending into political/jural domains. They enable individuals to benefit from the system in the long run and negotiate their own fate. Yet children do, like smiths and former slaves, often take blame, and they express sentiments and actions from which others distance themselves.

Children thus stand at the nexus of internal relationships of social structure—in particular, class—and external relationships with the outside, non-Tuareg human, and spirit nonhuman, worlds. Adults tend to use metaphors of paternalism, dominance, and subordination to explain young children's actions by reference to their wider place in the system—in terms of descent and social stratum, and the presence or absence of attributes of that place, such as having no head, no shame, no sin—rather than by individual motivation. I was struck by this on one occasion in particular, when, consciously wishing to discern the extent to which Tuareg and American values were similar, I inquired whether a small boy of three might possibly be jealous upon the birth of a new sibling, as is sometimes believed in the West. The father expressed astonishment at the very notion. In this respect, Tuareg concepts of the child as a relational person rather than an autonomous individual do not differ markedly from those reported elsewhere in Africa (Riesman 1986). But previously, reports have largely concentrated upon kinship relationships and have omitted dynamic descriptions of how these relational concepts—how the child is perceived in relation to outsiders and the groups they represent—are channelled over time, throughout the life course, and outward, toward the external world.

Among Kel Ewey, cultural autonomy, status distinctions, and related rights and obligations, particularly generosity, are explicitly inculcated in children. They are encouraged to display and use elaborately carved wooden spoons made by smiths and associated with dignity and reserve in eating. Children participate along with adults in life course festivals, rituals, and religious holidays, dressing up like adults and wearing adults' jewelry in fashions associated with their respective social origins. On holidays, boys carry fathers' swords, prized possessions inherited from fathers and uncles. At all other times, however, children wear age-appropriate dress and accessories and are, above all, encouraged to begin to practice reserve toward local adults.

These patterns extend into the distinctive beliefs and practices surrounding special children. In contrast to some other African societies, Tuareg have no elaborate rituals or myths about twins, called *ikanewen*. But friends told me they were not so keen about twins because they entail a lot of work and are a drain on resources. This is due to the belief that twins must be treated exactly equally and that people must not make a twin angry, or there will ensue misfortune. I observed a smith woman pick up both her twin sons and nurse them at the same time, and then arrange them in the same sleeping position. Tuareg also give twins special, alliterative or rhyming names toward this end. Another special child, called *eljenagougou* or "of the spirit," is conceived either before the seventh night of marriage, or alternatively, under moonlight, in a forbidden place associated with the wild outside the camp or village, and in an illicit love outside marriage and legitimate descent, symbolized by the nuptial tent. Illegitimate children are not stigmatized, but their mothers are, for they violate values of purity of descent. Illegitimate boys are viewed as more disadvantaged than girls because they lack male relatives to help raise bridewealth. Tuareg often name an illegitimate child Yessuf, or "child of the wild." This has two senses, which further illuminate the poetics of aging. Mothers often attempt to hide such children outside their camps or villages of residence, and such children are seen as "of the spirit," as opposed to Allah, the tent, and official marriage. Spirits are believed present at courtship and mixed-sex festivals, events that are permitted but also are viewed ambivalently by the Islamic scholars. Although there is free social visiting between the sexes and women are not secluded, women must not give birth out of wedlock or they are socially ostracized.

Thus the child is both powerful and vulnerable as a mediator between the human and spirit worlds. Furthermore, I argue that, far from being devalued or deprived, children are similar to former slaves and contemporary smiths in that they are valued in performing important subsistence tasks. All these persons are free of reserve, thereby pronouncing what others cannot. All these persons also act as social and spiritual go-betweens and can enter places others cannot or that they prefer to avoid.

The living are endowed with spiritual components that link them in a number of ways with other people, predominantly living relatives, and also with the natural world. The world of spirits is an ever-present undercurrent of the Islamic world and realms of official marriage and descent. This is clearly seen at transitions, in efforts to control potentially anomalous tendencies. When a child begins to suck his or her thumb, parents place a shell bracelet on the wrist, in the belief that this will stop the thumb-sucking because the hands are not the same in appearance. If a child displays a tendency toward left-handedness, this is seen as antireligious, so adults lightly tap the left hand whenever the child uses it to discourage this. When a child loses a tooth, parents bury it in a camel footprint so that a new one will grow in soon. When a child crawls for the first time, there is held a small *takote* or celebration with offerings. Women make seven balls of *eghale* to distribute among friends, a recognition of this first step but also a symbolic protective measure: for this beverage and its ingredients are also prominent at weddings, namedays, and funerals, which are the occasions when spirits threaten most. They conduct *albaraka,* the mystic blessing force.

When a first baby died on the day of his nameday, he received a name, a funeral, and a memorial with offerings *(takote n barar),* but this nameday, in recognition of the tragedy, was a simpler event than one held for a living child. Residents indicated that even if a child has no name, if he or she makes a cry at birth, the funeral memorial ceremony takes place after seven days, at the same time the child would normally have the nameday. If a child is stillborn, only the burial is held. Unless asked to specify, women counted only living children rather than the total of deceased as well in response to my question of "how many children have you had?" Thus, despite memorials, there are ritual efforts to cut the child's ties to the spirit world that indicate how precious and precarious life is. Everyday child-rearing practices, for their part, emphasize primarily children's independence and their taking up appropriate kin- and class-derived roles.

Alongside these practices, there are efforts to strengthen children for confrontation with outside powers. During gestation, after weaning, and during adolescence, they are believed vulnerable to spirits who may be jealous or to the alleged mystic powers of smiths (Rasmussen 1992). Birth defects are usually attributed to Kel Essuf or *el jenan* spirits, or to smiths' alleged *tezma,* a force automatically taking effect upon a refusal to give them a present. In such cases, children may become ill or die. The brother of a traditional chief had two children, a son and a daughter, who were born mute. The son, the older of the two, about fifteen years old, was called by a name referring to the glands of the throat. People used sign language to communicate with him, although he also read lips. This boy went on errands and brought garden produce back for different related families. Local residents explained his and his sister's congenital muteness as the result of "a bad fate" and spirits, and someone's grudge against their father. Specifically, the power of "evil words" *(togerchet)* caused this condition. Birth defects in a child can also be caused by spirits' exchanging of the real baby for their own, replacing the mother's normal child with their child who is defective. When I inquired if close in-marriage could cause this, residents said they do not believe this, though some individuals had read about this theory in school textbooks.

As observed, children wear many amulets. These have several functions, primary of which is guarding children from spirits seen to threaten them at weaning and other dangerous points in life. The power these practices hold endures, indeed even persists, in recent upheavals, for example, armed conflict and massacres. A small Tuareg boy encountered by a reporter for *Africa Report* wore a bullet as an amulet around his neck. When the reporter inquired why, she was told that his father had been shot by Malian soldiers and the bullet was believed to confer protection from a similar fate (Rowland 1992:44).

Thus attitudes and strategies toward children express key ideas and notions about the person, destiny, and society. They reveal local adults' struggles for autonomy from control by outside forces beyond local-level kinship but also competing Islamic efforts, long-standing and internal to Tuareg society, to extricate children from local pre-Islamic religious, kinship, and class influences. They are also a response to material conditions of scarcity in an unpredictable environment that predate colonial and postcolonial eras. They express experiences of contact between Tuareg and other societies. Adults are aware that the way others respond to children may be an indicator of the way they view Tuareg society as a whole, and residents thereby formulate their own theory of ethnography within a framework of resistance against paternalism. Here, following Scheper-Hughes (1987), my data indicate that local older persons' attitudes about the phase of childhood and behavior toward children are in part a consequence of external social, political, and economic conditions. But I argue further that these are imposed on adults whose authority is respected in their own world but challenged in facing the external world, and that notions of the locus of parental responsibility, expressed in class, gender, and religious metaphors, are embedded in power relationships, both within Kel Ewey society and between Kel Ewey society and other societies.

These concerns are expressed in beliefs about vulnerability, the waxing and waning of powers, and the protection of powers over the life course. In Tamacheq, there exist several idiomatic phrases for pregnancy: one denotes "to have a spirit," another "to have a stomach," and another "she is not alone." Although there are not many food taboos during pregnancy, women indicated that they avoided certain "bitter medicines" of non-Koranic curers called *bokas,* who treat illnesses with plants and perfumes, and preferred mountain plants and acacia bark and leaves of local female Tuareg herbalists *(tinesmegelen).* There is also the belief that, if a man pronounces Koranic verses before sexual intercourse, he can protect the unborn child. Alternatively, some other verses act as a contraceptive. Local theories of conception are not elaborate. One belief, related to me by a woman friend spontaneously during observation of a toddler at play, states that if a small child bends down and looks backward between his or her legs, this means that the mother will soon become pregnant again. Some women indicate that menses become children and are gradually "used up" through successive births. Menstruation represents strength and health; spirits can take away menstrual periods and prevent conception. Each woman has a predetermined number of children that can potentially be born, and upon completion of this number, her period stops definitively. Thus periods and births are seen as limited according to personal destiny. Childbearing is also equated with youth. When the body stops bearing children, there is the perception of its becoming drier, diminished, and rinsed. After the last child is born, the woman is "rinsed clean." Yet there is the continuing wish to have children around not solely to provide assistance but also to be fed. Feeding is emotionally associated with love and nurturing, with motherhood and grandmotherhood. Tata, an old smith woman I frequently visited, had children who were already married but not yet parents. One day she lamented to me that she had no grandchildren yet and "no children anymore at home to feed." She said "an old woman needs to feed a small child."

There is the belief that a pregnant woman should not be made angry or she will suffer the possibility of miscarriage. Pregnancy "wrinkles" are considered a sign of beauty. There is also the belief that if the woman is carrying a defective child, this causes problems during pregnancy. There is a danger of this if there are unrestricted sexual relations in any place (outside the tent, under moonlight, in the oeud) or if the pregnant woman is angry (the illness called *tourgoum*). Tuareg say that to refuse what a pregnant woman wishes will cause her problems during labor. Other images used to describe threats to a healthy pregnancy and normal newborn are "pricking" of the stomach by a bad fate or sorcery, and misfortune "flying" at the victim from the heart of an offended smith.

6

Aging, Power, and Resistance

In sum, children and child-related beliefs and practices delineate older persons' social and moral universe, according to trustworthy insider/untrustworthy outsider social forces. These forces are conveyed in an imagery of social stratum, gender, and cosmology (e.g., the spirit world). Those who are close should show solidarity and protection from the outside world; if they do not, this is an anomalous state with disastrous consequences that are embodied by children. Children are deployed as spiritual and social mediators in moral testing in struggles for autonomy and control. During a new mother's seclusion, she must speak the truth, or else whatever she pronounces will become true. The general term for children or younger family members *(talawaqqan)* also denotes clients or subordinates. Mothers practice a reserve relationship with their first-born child. The mother never pronounces the official Koranic name given to this child but rather uses an alternate Tamacheq name invented by other relatives, sometimes describing some situation surrounding the birth. Her first-born son, in particular, is shameful, equated with the husband (whose name she cannot pronounce either) because he is an heir. Some women friends, approximately my age, with whom I shared a joking relationship, sometimes teased me with questions calculated to induce me to pronounce my own husband's name.

Children are the external manifestation of adult moral conduct. This explains why children are deployed in moral testing. In times of natural disaster or political threats from outside, they are marshalled to protect identity and resources. In such contexts, they are associated with spirituality and the ancestors through the additional mediating link of elders. This view is expressed in a brief legend I collected from an elderly woman in a marabout family. She related this story of how a child of the *icherifan* clans brought rain during a drought:

> One year there was a great drought, there was no more food, not anything, neither water nor food, there was nothing. And the people, the servants of God, they implored God to give them a drop of water, a single drop of water so that they could refresh themselves. During the drought all their animals had disappeared. There was a person, Akhmed, who had two small girls. These people were *icherifan*. He told people: "These little girls are going to visit their relatives, but the relatives are in their tombs [i.e., deceased]. They are going to visit them." Upon arrival at the cemetery, he addressed the tomb, "My little girls visit you in

aranizoum [alms after the Ramadan fast that people request at homes of paternal relatives, such as dates, goats, or other items]. They search, but the alms of water are what they want [i.e., of all things, they would prefer water as their alms, because of the drought]." The girls' father gave an offering to his ancestors on the tomb [customary if the descendant wishes something], and he left. They were on their way back home. They were walking until they arrived at a certain place. A girl said to them, "There is a cloud over there. Hang up the water container to catch rain." The father told her, "Our wish to the ancestors is almost accomplished." Before they arrived home, the small cloud became water. It began to rain hard, pouring on every side. All the oeuds flowed with water.

To this tale, her husband added the following brief epilogue, indicating it was confirmed by Islam: "And God made them a drop of *albaraka* [blessing], everyone drank and ate and was satisfied, and the oeuds flowed with water for one month." *Icherifan*, viewed as "celestial sponges," possess special protective power against outside dangers, deriving from their own and their children's special relationship with the ancestors. As will be shown, this power can be extended to political resistance.

These relationships between older and younger Tuareg, and local beliefs and practices surrounding elders and youths, parents and children, became central to my own experiences with local residents in social interaction. I, as a childless adult working among parents and children who were "subjects" for my "studies," had crucial significance in the construction of knowledge about age. Local perceptions of me were shaped by the two principal roles I occupied in Niger at different times—teacher and researcher—as well as by Tuareg encounters with outsiders prior to my presence. Rosaldo has suggested that ethnographers should not assume themselves to be "blank slates"; inevitably they are "positioned subjects," contributing a perspective on different cultures that itself is highly cultural (1989:206). I would argue for the added dimension of "political" here. Rosaldo also reminds us that the subjects of social analysis are also active, analyzing subjects whose perception must be taken as seriously as we take our own (ibid.). Thus there arises the problem of the resonance between the experiences of researchers and other long-term visitors and that of local residents. The ethnographer, as a positioned subject, grasps certain human phenomena better than some others. He or she occupies a position or structural location and observes with a particular angle of vision (ibid.:19). In a very different context and expressing a contrasting viewpoint, another ethnographer, Margaret Mead, observed in the film *Taking Note* that once she had become a mother, she became "a very poor observer of (others') children." This latter position is now widely disputed, in calls by scholars like Rosaldo to abandon the stance of the objective, omnipotent, and distant observer.

While I am sympathetic to these recent calls, nonetheless I find a problem with them. The question is how much of oneself to interject into others' experiences without distorting, or worse, dominating others' experience; could this become self-defeating and perpetuate a form of the old authoritativeness that anthropologists now wish to avoid, thereby becoming a monologue rather than a dialogue? Does the research subject merely become background scenery in this approach? Yet there is no question that age, gender, marital status, parental or nonparental status, and identity with a particular outside regime or local social status influence what the ethnographer learns. In my own experience, however, it was precisely gaps in experience (e.g., adulthood and parenthood) that provided me with much data on these subjects, since these "gulfs" gave rise to reflection and conversations about this experience and may also have even detached me somewhat from paternalistic adult figures associated with external colonial and postcolonial control schemes. Thus contrasts between identities and experiences, rather than their exact congruence, produced insights; but at the same time, I could not act as omnipotent, detached observer even if I had wished to do so. I did not easily fit into local life course categories. Although a researcher's own experience as a nonparent in certain respects poses limitations upon entry into a local community of research, it also equips one to imagine local experience of adult-child relationships through its evocation in local commentary, in residents' attempts to locate the researcher in their system and, in the Kel Ewey case, to integrate and absorb the researcher into local structures. Thus local response to a discrepancy, rather than solely a commonality, between our experiences provided insights, offering different vantage points and suggesting ways that different kinds of involvement inform the ethnographer's own experience of the topic in portraying it. Kel Ewey values in some respects interweave with our own; in other respects, they diverge from our own. Thus field experience becomes a vehicle for understanding emotional life and learning about local efforts to interpret my own status and emotions (unfamiliar to local residents) regarding the life course in general and in one phase of it—childhood—in particular. Thus there can be recognition of multiple sources of knowledge in ethnographic analysis through divergences, as well as commonalities, of experience.

As observed, adults, as they and I grew older over my subsequent visits to the field, had difficulty "placing" me in the local structure because I was childless though married. Childlessness in itself is not a stigma, and women derive respect from other sources in addition to childbearing: for example, independent ownership and management of herds, prestigious descent, and personal attributes such as generosity, religious devotion, and musical and vocal talent. Nonetheless, children are important for security and constituted a frequent topic of conversation. Upon hearing that I was married but still childless, a woman advised me to see a marabout for treatment to induce fertility. Women frequently gave me their babies to hold, watching me intently throughout. When I appeared to respond positively, many exclaimed with approval and sometimes surprise, "Yes, she does like children, doesn't she? She knows [how to hold] babies, also."

Local children, along with smiths and former slaves, tend to be the first to approach visitors. Initially, adults, in particular elders of noble origin and marabouts, ignored me, assuming I was merely passing through as a tourist until I had remained there for several months. Small boys, in particular, came forward to guide me around villages and camps, willing to assist with taking censuses and recording folktales. This was partly due, of course, to adults' work responsibilities, but more subtle factors were at play as well. Adults of ambiguous social status such as smiths and persons from other regions (e.g., a local primary school teacher from the south) also approached me at this time. And I noticed that children, particularly schoolboys, tended to predominate as visitors in tents of lower-status or marginal local adults. For example, they were always crowding the tent of a local woman whose daughter had an illegitimate child. The technical and etiquette limitations of child guides became apparent later on; children, for example, are ashamed to ask questions of elders and are not supposed to talk about kinship or pronounce the names of deceased ancestors. Later, after I had won greater trust and convinced residents that I planned to stay longer, more local adults of higher social status began to become more sociable. On their approach, most children would scatter. But children continued to sprint after me on my walks and visits outside my residence and, until adults' reprimands, gathered around to stare at me fixedly.

The actions of children toward outsiders conveyed a mix of local adult hospitality but also ambivalence toward them, as well as local adults' ambivalence toward certain activities. Adults also observed outsiders' responses to children for the purpose of locating them within the local universe. For example, in rural areas adults often presented gifts of dates and cheese as gestures of hospitality, very rarely selling them to me. Until a few small boutiques opened in the region, vending was usually left to children, who would initiate a vendor/purchaser relationship by bringing a few sample dates to me and offering to lead me to gardens and small boutiques. Many adults were "ashamed" to sell items to a guest; this ran counter to their values of hospitality and generosity. Small children were also sent to check up on me as I lay ill, relaying the message of my condition to adults who, due to adult reserve, directly approached me only later.

Thus in many respects, Tuareg negotiations for autonomy are channeled through the medium of the adult-child relationship and beliefs and practices pertaining to childhood. Most questions that adults asked me in the field addressed age. They wished to know all about rites of passage in the United States and inquired about kinship relationships and relationships between the generations. A few adults expressed the belief that I had "few responsibilities" because I had no children. That was how, they surmised somewhat reproachfully, I could "abandon" my family at home to travel to distant places. Thus interaction between the researcher's own life situation and that of local residents undoubtedly affects the research process, but the question is the direction and purpose of this process, as defined not solely by the ethnographer but also by the "subjects," who are far from passive. Adults deploy children to restore challenged control and to explore new domains of experience.

Thus research on aging and the life course brought me face to face with the mutuality of field knowledge construction but also with resistance. Most of the time I perceived my relations with local children as pleasant, if somewhat claustrophobic. Indeed, after I was surrounded, almost mobbed "rock-star" style, by a crowd of children upon my approach to a village one afternoon, an old smith man told me not to be afraid, that they liked me. He added that most of them, now about five years old, had been babies during my previous residence there and so viewed me as a novelty. He went on to say that although I had probably attended most of these children's nameday rituals, since they had been babies at that time, they still didn't know me. But there was another side to this that made me acutely uncomfortable. One small toddler, standing at the door to her mother's compound, would shout *"Takafirt, takafirt!"* (a term denoting approximately "infidel") each time I passed by, with her mother present. It soon became apparent that many acts taken by and related to children were based upon more than idiosyncratic elements of individual personalities and rapport and involved more than differences conventionally glossed as "culture shock." On one occasion, children threw rocks at me from the Koranic school. The local council of elders and marabouts, shocked and outraged over this, were supportive of me and put a stop to it. On another occasion, during my visit to a family, a small toddler again referred to me as *"takafirt."* The parents, embarrassed, corrected him, saying "No, that's Suzanne."

Finally, one day after children followed me behind bushes and rocks where I went to bathe, I had had enough. I returned to my host household and indignantly requested some disciplinary action. Pushed to the limit, I confided in them my feelings that perhaps the children had done this because I was different. My adult hosts listened attentively and promised to speak to the parents of the children in question, who would put a stop to such acts (which they subsequently did). But they also indicated that children in all times and places "do these things all the time." A male friend present went on to relate some of his own childhood experiences in primary school on a nearby oasis. As children, he and his companions had pulled up all the vegetables in the school garden and drawn graffiti on its walls. Indeed, the present primary school located in my village of residence, a new concrete building barely four years old, was similarly riddled with crayon. Yet no other local buildings or gardens appeared damaged, and no such scribblings ever adorned local mosques or mud houses. When pressed to recall adults' responses to these incidents, he indicated that he had forgotten. He did recall, however, that adults quickly acted to reprimand children in a more recent incident, when they smashed the window of a vehicle belonging to a development agency. Such vehicles have been increasingly rare in rural Aïr recently, though due not to children's pranks but to economic crises.

These events suggest that children are the focus of older persons' efforts to keep clear boundaries of cultural autonomy and religious purity. Elders do not discourage youths from openly resisting symbols of encroachment. Until recently, most schools and clinics in the Aïr Mountain region were predominantly staffed by outside personnel, first French and later non-Tuareg teachers and health workers, many of whom local residents found intimidating (Rasmussen 1994). The terms of the April 1995 pact between separatists and government called for decentralization in the region, which included installment of more local residents in authority positions in schools and clinics. Adult concepts of personal destiny in childhood, and theories of child personality, thus become part of a political response to perceived threats to local social categories from outside forces of colonialism, secularism, and the central state. This is most strongly evident in secular schools, which many older Tuareg associate with outside authority, forced sedentization, and taxation, and which they also consider to be anti-Islamic. First under French colonialism and later with independence, for example, many nobles sent the children of slaves to school instead of sending their own children. Children thus act as buffers and points of negotiation in dealings with outsiders—central state officials, researchers, and development workers—in order to ensure survival of those local structures held most important for fulfillment of personal destiny later in life, namely, institutions of descent and religion. Secular education, as a "rite of passage" imposed by outsiders who are also often youthful (in opposition to local cultural values favoring the elderly as traditional educators), is the arena for these negotiations.

Techniques of resistance in some contexts take priority even over biological needs. This was vividly illustrated in a case of donated canned food. One season, UN canned meat was distributed in all villages with primary schools near Mount Bagzan. A local council of elders and marabouts rejected it because they suspected that this meat was pork; food distributions, of course, are normally welcome in times of duress, but as anywhere, these must consist of foods people will eat, not foods forbidden by local religion or cultural values. Unambiguously safe foods, such as grain donations, were accepted. These incidents reveal a basic underlying ambivalence on the part of many local residents, but in particular elders, Koranic scholars, and nobles, toward such "development" programs as international aid and secular education, arising from a fear that they come "with strings attached": obligations of censuses, taxation, and sedentization, or lack of sensitivity to local cultural values.

Indeed, where secular education has been established, it often has become the platform for political debates over these issues, sometimes led by elderly religious scholars or marabouts. Children and schools continue to act as a forum for dialogues with outside authorities. For example, just before a nationwide student strike in 1990, adolescent male students at the Agadez lycée (high school) wore their face-veils to classes in defiance of a rule against this act based on the perception that teachers could not recognize students' identities when they wore them. The students' action also went counter to the traditional practice of donning the veil at a slightly later age of around eighteen years. The face-veil, traditionally a symbol of an adult male gender role, signifies marriageable, and also warrior, status.

Whereas today there are both Koranic and secular schools throughout most areas of northern Niger (though only the primary school level is represented in many more rural localities), many Tuareg traditionally resisted secular schools, first established by the French and more recently by central Nigerien authorities, for two principal reasons. They feared that these schools were alienating their children from cultural and religious traditions, and they suspected that school registration records were also used as a means of surveillance for taxation and forced sedentization. Many adult friends of mine recalled being marched to school, as children, by soldiers at gunpoint. One man of about forty-five related to me how when he was a youth, he and his mother had not wanted authorities to enroll him in school. "Me, I wanted to be a marabout then . . . everyone did then. My mother told me to flee to a town north of Agadez to avoid school registration. I went there and hid there for the first semester . . . afterward, though, they [the authorities] found me and brought me back." During my Peace Corps teaching in Agadez, some children attempted to enter and leave classroom buildings through open windows and sometimes offered small contributions to beggars who passed by and placed their bowls through the windows, perhaps conveying, in avoiding the usual spatial boundaries and norms of entrance and exit, a similar political message.

Local definitions of person in children and childhood therefore evoke a more nuanced view of older persons' concerns with power, domination, subordination, autonomy, and resistance. There is a closer connection between notions of childhood—more than with any other phase of the life course—and Tuareg cultural identity. But there is contradiction and ambiguity in any ideological discourse. In Tuareg culture, persons who lack reserve—for example, former slaves and smiths—often resist through mediating between local residents and outside authorities, sometimes through play, jokes, and pranks. This points to the need to abolish the distinction between theory and ethnography (Herzfeld 1985). As Herzfeld observes, if fieldwork is seen as a form of praxis, then communication between ethnographer and local resident can produce knowledge that respects the cultural meanings of local residents about what works and also questions our own cultural and class-based assumptions. Children voice adults' true but unexpressed sentiments. In effect, older residents are able to say, "the children did it, not us," but the message of resistance remains serious. In other words, youths do what older persons would like to do but cannot do, at least not openly, due to strictures of increasing reserve as one ages.

As a result, children have become a banner in adult relations with the outside world. Elderly nobles covertly resist through their children. Keenan (1977) has described how early in this century Tuareg parents came to associate secular schools for children with two contradictory, irreconcilable roles: (1) central state authority and laxness about Islam (which they opposed) and (2) feeding children's mouths (which they needed). Niger was one of the last regions of Africa to be invaded by Europeans, who initially believed it offered no wealth. France colonized Niger for purposes of military glory and sent soldiers there to use the territory as a military buffer zone. As a consequence, children received educational and medical attention late, and local attitudes toward these programs were filtered by experiences of invasions and massacres (Keenan 1977; Salifou 1973; Dayak 1992). Traditionally, Tuareg commercial and social life had revolved around raiding, trading, and herding. After the French invasion, Tuareg were left with no choice but to concentrate their energies on herding. In intermittent droughts related to government policies, families were split up and children orphaned. Many Tuareg groups resisted the French longer than other ethnic groups within Niger.

Throughout the Sahara, governments established boarding schools. They crowded children accustomed to widely spaced nomadic residences into dormitories, and this lowered resistance to disease. For example, school uniforms were not made from the traditional blue indigo dyed cloth, which had conferred some resistance to skin infections. Attitudes toward secular schools in rural areas are gradually changing, rather predictably, along age lines: opposition tends to persist among elders, but some younger adults now appreciate, in retrospect, the secular schooling they received. A friend of mine, about twenty-five years in age, who had been one of the first local women to be educated in the primary school at the site of my research, related to me how, one day, officials had arrived in her small, nomadic camp and announced that there were not enough children in the school, especially girls:

> Our parents did not want us to go, but the officials picked me and my cousin up, placed us on the backs of camels, and took us there [to the village where the school was], where we stayed with the old grandmother of my [current] husband. At first, I was very unhappy. I did not like the teacher or the studying. But later, I began to enjoy learning. Now I am happy I went to school, but my mother still does not like the school.

As the central government abolished earlier nomadic schools and set up boarding schools in villages, their purpose was to remove children from socialization to the adult nomadic milieu at an early age. They did this by force, if necessary. For example, military vehicles went to fetch a quota of children between five and ten years of age. At first, this merely intensified nomads' general fear and resentment of central government. Traditional chiefs who cooperated with the military were seen as traitors. So initially, nomads moved further out, beyond the road. The smith population of a large oasis I visited as recently as the 1980s moved outside it to a nomadic camp, to be closer to nobles there and to avoid school registration for their children.

Later, however, there developed incentives to cooperate. These were caused by drought, meager return from the caravan trade, former slaves' taking over control of gardens, and scarce wage labor in rural areas. Some Tuareg migrated to towns. So there resulted a greater number of mouths to feed in nomadic camps and less support from the traditional livelihoods of herding and gardening. Furthermore, traditionally, the activities and education of boys centered around camel husbandry, whereas camels were now more scarce. These boys became an additional burden to adults because they were an unproductive labor force. So several things happened: nomads soon preferred to give these boys to the government boarding schools, and they came to regard the giving of children to government educators as being like the payment of taxes. They also perceived boarding schools not as educational institutions but as "hotels" where children could be fed and clothed at government expense (Keenan 1977). Authorities attempted to engineer a reorientation of values in which boarding schools became first the head and second the stomach. Government educators implemented this goal by a policy of stricter evaluation of children. They expelled some on the basis of grades. So the orientation was toward greater educational efficiency standards and selectivity and away from impressive attendance figures.

What administrators did, therefore, was to introduce local stratification into an academic setting. This gave secular education more popularity, though it did not completely divest it of the connotations of submission. The goal was to appeal to local cultural values of exclusiveness and ranking. Many rural nomads came to realize gradually that the crucial factor in obtaining employment in towns was status—achieved, rather than ascribed, through education of their children. Others, however, continued to resist this and to prefer Koranic education for their children.

In the rural Aïr communities near Mount Bagzan, there has always been a local intelligentsia of elders and marabouts, and local cultural values respecting learning and knowledge, which predate colonial and postcolonial events. A local tradition of literacy exists outside the formal, secular educational structure. In rural communities, Koranic scholarship includes religious, legal, and medical studies. Keenan (1977) and Norris (1975) have documented how Islamic education entered Tuareg regions through migrations of clans of Koranic scholars called marabouts and Sufi mystics originally from Tademekket in the Maghreb. Lettered Islamic scholars are similar in some respects to the Murabtin and Zwaya among the Moors, though among Tuareg they do not correspond to a coherent social stratum. Rather, there is correspondence to age categories in local culture. Many men wait to practice professional scholarship until after their fathers' death for reasons similar to why female herbalists wait to take up this latter profession until after their mothers' death: the belief that only older persons (whose own parents have retired or died) should practice these professions. These reasons have to do with the apprenticeship process. Koranic education extends beyond the primary level, and there is a higher education pursued after students memorize Koranic verses. This next level includes study of the Koranic verses' meaning, somewhat like Talmudic study in Judaism. There is an introduction to the religious writings, such as the Hadiths (traditions of the Prophet). The student also learns Arabic grammar, logic, jurisprudence, theology, and commentaries on the Koran. Many of my Kel Ewey friends in rural Aïr read and write in Arabic, and also in Tifinagh, a Tamacheq script. Elders told me that at one time there was a Koran written in Tamacheq with Arabic letters.

In addition to external political factors, therefore, the structure of traditional education explains why many residents resent youths being instructed by outsiders—often youthful outsiders—rather than local, respected elders. The ideal here is to learn from but not yet practice alongside elder kinspersons. The structure of traditional learning outside Islam in Tuareg society featured few specialized teachers apart from Koranic scholars, but there were other sources of learning besides Koranic scholarship. These were based on local economics and subsistence, medicine, ritual, and oral traditions. There is a continuum, an embodiment of skills, social practices, symbols, values, and attitudes that youths learn from elders in rites of passage and everyday activities, according to age, sex, and social stratum.

Thus throughout the life course, the acquisition of knowledge is conceived of as a living process linked to the daily experience of every individual: in rites of passage of birth, men's face-veil wrapping ritual, marriage, and funerals, as well as closely supervised apprenticeships with elderly persons in herbalism, smithing, and musical performance. In more nomadic conditions, women in some Tuareg groups became primary educators while men were absent on raids. Smiths and women tell tales that have a clearly didactic purpose. But Islamic scholars are the most prominent, and rural children tend to admire marabouts more than secular teachers, though they may fear these latters' officially backed powers of coercion. Thus traditional educational structures are less threatening than outside ones and are more compatible with cultural values of respect for elders. Children, closely collaborating in the transmission of cultural knowledge, voice resistance and survival in the face of perceived threats. This is how they became active subjects rather than passive objects of my study.

Children as active subjects thus revealed to me local perceptions of person and theories of development over the life course as a projection, a microcosm of a changing hierarchical social order in which cleverness, but also restraint, wins. It is a response to, defense against, and reflection of life conditions—of contact between local people, both youths and aged, and outsider visitors and intruders, these latter in some sense like children as students of local culture, in another sense like paternalistic authority figures as representatives of encroaching political institutions. Adult interpretation of childhood strengths and deficiencies, and ideas of causation and responsibility for them, reveal cumulative experiences that lead to one or another strategy in adult-child relationships. No one—adult local resident, child, outsider administrator, development worker, teacher, or researcher—is innocent or neutral, passive, or ineffectual in this scheme.

Thus although children are described as being "without sin," they are not passive. They are powerful and vulnerable at the same time, because they in effect speak for adults, revealing the latters' concepts of personal morality and destiny. In effect, this occurs in the reverse direction of causation emphasized by Fortes in his analysis of the Tallensi (1959, 1987). While noble elders in principle exert authority, this must be done ideally through allusion *(tangal)*. Children, free of these constraints, facilitate commentary on two types of outsiders who embody, respectively, metaphorical parents and children: (1) intruding authority figures (some administrators and teachers), who have tended to treat all Tuareg, including nobles and elders who in local values deserve greatest respect, paternalistically as children in order to subjugate them; and (2) outside researchers such as myself, who, while initially like children in their early residence (in efforts to learn language and make sense of and become comfortable with customs), leave as adults, in the sense of having acquired proficiency in these technical aspects of local culture, while remaining children in another sense—of never completely sharing all life experiences of Tuareg adults.

Thus in working in Aïr but standing outside local social categories of parent and child, I nonetheless participated in parent/child and elder/youth relationships on a level transcending mundane "field experience," as local residents of either sex and different classes and ages drew me into dialogues addressing paternalism in traditional local, colonial, and postcolonial structures. This angle to research on the life course cannot be dismissed or viewed as irrelevant to the data. For example, it has implications for the problem of ethnographic authority (Rosaldo 1989) as well as the problem of the aging anthropologist and the methodological problems of analyzing data many years after they were collected (Blacking 1990:121–30). But my own experience transcended problems of methodology or "pure" field data. My interpretation of past events in my field experience changed, with added insights, over time as I examined them in retrospect, in terms not solely of "pure" ethnographic data but also of my own added years and the intertextuality of local residents' response to them. Central to these responses were local cultural values that revere elders and religious authorities (and set them apart from youth), because they represent the deceased ancestors and God (Allah), authors of cultural traditions. Elderly marabouts, for example, although respected, are not supposed to seek glory but rather to reflect God's will. It is for this reason that youths, even as they are instructed by them, should not ask elders too many questions or pronounce their names, in reference or address. Likewise, the ethnographer, in signing her name to documents about Tuareg culture, is viewed ambivalently and takes on a heavy burden, in effect presuming to speak for elders, religious authorities, and ancestors.

Foods at memorial funeral/feast offering.

Idebni grave and shrine in Aïr region on road connecting villages.

Ancient sites of "People in the Past" *(Kel Nad).*

Part Three

Power and Symbolism in Concepts of Personal Destiny

Youths, Elders, and Ancestors

To sum up thus far, Kel Ewey practices surrounding age are concerned with authority and autonomy issues. As shown, age is expressed in an idiom of social stratum and crosscuts kinship and gender. Two themes pervade the power and symbolism of growing older: having children who reach marriageable age and devoting oneself increasingly to prayer. Children ensure economic security and purity of descent, both within local social boundaries and at their borders. Prayer is necessary for prevention of waning powers in senility. There are relationships between ideas about procreation and reproduction on the one hand and political power and property ownership on the other. Authority is bound up with parenthood, grounded in beliefs and practices concerning deceased ancestors.

Elders are seen as speaking for the deceased ancestors, thereby playing an important role in the shaping of collective and individual destinies within Tuareg society as well as toward the outside world. Some Kel Ewey of noble descent told me that they were "afraid" to speak into a tape recorder because they did not want their relatives to hear their voices after death. Steady progress toward religious devotion over the life course is used to explain biological and social traits of aging. Ancestors are interwoven with the Islamic God, as well as with overlapping genealogical and mythical categories of ancestors whom residents refer to collectively as "People of the Past." Tales about these peoples, called variously Kel Nad and Kel Arou, are interspersed with historic accounts of Boulkhou, a marabout hero of the region, and of the clans claiming descent from the Prophet, with their alleged powers to heal and bring rain deriving from their special relationship with these ancestors and the Prophet.

Here it is instructive to introduce key concepts in local cosmology and ritual that illustrate relations between the living and the dead. The local belief system, with its own cosmology and ritual, interweaves and overlaps with Islam rather than standing in opposition to it in several respects: belief in spirits, the Devil, and souls, and attitudes toward death. These beliefs and practices are of pre-Islamic and Islamic origin. A number of scholars (Duveyrier 1864; Rodd 1926; Lhote 1955) have argued that the Tuareg were formerly Christian. These theories are controversial, since some features may have entered Tuareg culture through contact and trade, but they find some support in evidence from material culture and language: cross-shaped pendants and sword handles, and a terminology derived from Greek (e.g., *angelous* or angels and *Messnin* or God, a term used alternatively with, albeit less frequently than, Allah).

Matrilineal clans were at one time much more jurally and ritually important; each matriclan was linked totemically to the part of an animal, over which the clan had rights, and land rights were also once connected to matrilineal descent. Nicolaisen (1963) reports that, occasionally when there is morning mist in the Aïr, Kel Ewey state that "The mother of the Kel Ewey is cold." As shown, there are vestiges of matrilineality in the present bilateral system, in origin myths and postmarital residence. In subsequent pages I show how matrilineally influenced alternative inheritance forms, which counterbalance the Islamic form, impinge upon male authority in aging and death. An ancient system of totemism occasionally surfaces. The lizard, for example, is said to be the maternal uncle of smiths. Divination is sometimes practiced with lizards; they appear in tales of heroic deeds; they are used as medicine for certain children's ailments of the stomach *(tedis)*, symbol of the matriline; and some jewelry boxes are manufactured from lizard skin. Some nobles avoid birds and reptiles as food.

Ancient matriliny therefore leaves its legacies. The establishment of Islam introduced patrilineal institutions such as Koranic inheritance and legal structures permitting polygyny. But many marriages are still monogamous, particularly those among more nomadic herders and caravanners.

Intermittently throughout Saharan history, Islamic scholars or marabouts have exerted considerable political as well as ritual power (Gellner 1969; Kennan 1977; Norris 1972, 1975). At various times the region has been closed off to nonbelievers, and some authors report that recently some Tuareg have been sympathetic toward wider movements influenced by Islamic revitalization (Casajus 1990; Bourgeot 1990). Many Kel Ewey, particularly men from the marabout clans, emphasize their devotion to Islam.

Official religion was a topic pervading my conversations and relationships in the field more intensively on my successive visits over the years. Marabouts and other elders questioned me more and more closely about my religious beliefs and practices. One marabout, whom I will call Moussa, during my earlier research had explained many intricacies of Islamic belief and ritual to me and received me with warm hospitality—offering me dates, goat cheese, honey, and tea. Marabouts' charisma, alleged mystic power of *al baraka,* and respect derive from their generosity and their winning of followers on this basis (Rasmussen 1992). Moussa, conscious of our religious difference, asked me about Christian theology: "Is it true that some Christians believe Issa [Jesus] was God, whereas others believe that he was a prophet?" He wished to know "which tradition" I adhered to. Some men in the area expressed mild disapproval when I indicated interest in matrilineal female-founding ancestress myths, insisting the stories about Boukhou represented the "real history" of the area. At a nameday I attended in 1991, a group of prominent elders and marabouts solemnly approached me and asked, "Did you go to the Gulf?" (referring to the Gulf War, perceived ambivalently due to distrust of Saddam Hussein but loyalty to Islam). They looked much relieved when I said no. Local residents had no objection to my photographing Islamic holiday prayers, but some elderly persons became upset and puzzled when I did not pray alongside them on the prayer ground.

Yet local Tuareg cultural and pre-Islamic, as well as Islamic, beliefs have fundamental importance in the human life course: *Iblis,* the devil; *djinn* (or *eljenan,* and the similar *Kel Essuf* and *goumaten*), spirits; and mortuary-related terminology, beliefs, and practices surrounding death and cemeteries, souls, angels, and ancestors. Iblis, or the devil, is present in everyone. In local symbolism and tales, he is often associated with the fingernails; in a tale I collected from two young noble women, the devil pulls a woman named Tarere ("the loved one") down into a well with his fingernails as her brothers attempt, but fail, to save her (Rasmussen 1991). Iblis has another aspect: he is also associated with sexuality, present at the secular evening festivals featuring youthful men and women of diverse social origins that center on the *tende* drum, disapproved of by many marabouts. He is believed to walk about on Islamic holidays, as well, in this context suspected by elders and marabouts to threaten religious devotion. All allusions to Iblis and his associated symbolic repertoire are forbidden in the presence of persons in ascending generations. Anger is also attributed to Iblis. But above all, Iblis is seen as a tempter who leads humans to sin against God, the latter usually designated by the Arabic term Allah. Allah is the subject of a large body of sacred music (Islamic praise-songs and liturgical songs, called *ezzeker* and *almodahan,* performed by men and elderly women, respectively). Youths' secular festival and spirit possession music stand in opposition to this liturgical music, for the former are said to address or "be about" the Iblis and the spirits.

In addition to the Arabic-derived *djinn, eljenan,* or sometimes, *djinoun,* one hears of Kel Essuf, denoting specifically People of Solitude or Wild, and *goumaten.* These latter refer to spirits possessing predominantly women.[1] Spirits are mostly considered evil, and when they attack adults, it is usually in the form of mental illness (Pottier 1946; Nicolaisen 1961; Casajus 1990; Rasmussen 1989, 1991a, 1995). Nicolaisen has described how some individuals are reputed to have a pact with the Kel Essuf who aid them (Nicolaisen 1961). Kel Ewey do not personalize spirits. Rather, spirits are associated with group identity, modeled upon local social structure. For example, some "hot" spirits who live in subterranean spots and work on tiny forges correspond to smiths. Others possess men inside mosques, and still others, women in the wild outside villages and camps; each requires somewhat different treatments. In general, good and bad spirits are associated with cool (water) and hot (fire) images, respectively, and the colors of blue and black (Rasmussen 1989, 1995). Spirits may compete for people and become jealous of them during life transitions. This was shown in the protective measures against malevolent spirits threatening babies, adolescent girls who are engaged to marry, groom and bride upon their marriage, pregnant women, and new mothers who have recently given birth. Small children are vulnerable as well; although residents do not phrase it in these terms, it appears that recent weaning and its hazards may play a role.

Thus many points of danger and vulnerability in the life course are metaphorically expressed in terms of spirit attacks. This is why persons at transition wear the most protective amulets and are surrounded, in so far as possible, by iron metal (knives and/or swords) to ward off spirits. Thus by examining categories of persons who wore amulets I was able to ascertain which phases in the life course were most frought with dangers. Cosmological transformations are also key, over the life course, in alluding to social tensions: for some djinn are born as humans and later transformed into nonhumans, and some humans are believed to acquire a status between human and superhuman. Pottier (1946) collected a tale portraying djinn who stole babies, claiming to have mistaken them for goatskin water bags such as those made for newly married couples by smiths and mothers-in-law. Thus humans, as well as "spirits," are implicitly acknowledged to represent competing claims on children at various points in the life course. These tensions are played out in cosmological beliefs.

Beliefs about angels derive from Islam and possibly Christian influence as well. Moussa the marabout told me that each person has angels on the right and left shoulders, who weigh the relative morality of lifetime deeds. For example, he said, it is not how much wealth one acquires throughout one's lifetime, but rather how one acquires it, that is important. Thus angels represent more explicitly theological doctrinal considerations of moral conduct, according to the Koran.

The soul *(iman)* is more personalized than spirits or angels in the Tuareg worldview. This is seen as residing within the living individual, except during sleep when it may rise and travel about. The souls of the deceased are free to roam but usually do so in the vicinity of graves. Divination and consulting the dead are practiced through such means as using cowrie shells, sleeping on tombstones, and sleeping with Koranic amulets under the pillow. A dead soul is sometimes conceptualized as a messenger. Sometimes a certain spirit demands a temporary wedding with its "client" as a fee. This theme of human-spirit marriage recurs throughout Tuareg verbal art and cosmology and is the basis of diviners' claim to legitimacy.[2]

There is no abrupt, clear-cut separation between the living and the dead. The spoken name of a deceased person is considered sufficient to invoke the deceased's soul. Hence the existence of practices to respectfully distance one-self from it: names of deceased ancestors and living elders, seen as being near death, are forbidden to be mentioned for fear of calling forth souls. Individuals rarely pronounced names of Boulkhou, the local male marabout/hero/founder, and Tagurmat, the matrilineal female ancestress of a local descent group, due to these fears, as well as to respect. Some Tuareg move camp upon the death of an individual. Semisedentized Kel Ewey do this on children's death. In Kel Ewey settlements where tents are interspersed with mud houses, upon a woman's death, her tent (by advanced age, usually a conical grass *tettrem* rather than the nuptial *ehan* of younger married women) is destroyed. Its mats are distributed as alms to people who need them. Its land is left vacant for a year and then is used for other structures, sometimes the nuptial tent of a marry-ing younger female relative. This pattern has the dual purpose of expressing respect for the deceased and also reinforcing the gradual, protracted jural state of early marriage and its obligations. By contrast, mud houses are not destroyed on death but are inherited. This is not due to less respect for the deceased who owned them (usually, though not always, men) but to practical reasons: houses are more permanent structures than tents. Similarly, if a young woman divorces before bridewealth is completed, her tent is destroyed and she returns to her parents; if she divorces later, she retains the tent.

Tuareg do not have as highly elaborate mortuary rituals as some other peo-ples. Burial *(asatar alezanazat)* takes place soon after death and is quickly con-cluded. Men and marabouts predominate at burials. In contrast to their prominent roles at other rites of passage, smiths are less visible in ritual roles as a social stratum in all phases of mortuary rites.

Before the burial, elderly persons stretch out the body of the deceased so that it is not bent. Then the marabout measures the deceased person's height with a cord. He gives this cord to the male kinspersons, who prepare to dig the grave. They place the cord on the ground and begin to dig. Others bring stones. If the deceased was a man, men bathe the body; if she was a woman, women bathe it. Kel Ewey compare the washing of the body to the ablutions of prayer. After this, the body is wrapped in a white cotton cloth called *mas-sare*. The marabouts take the deceased and place the body on a bed of three wooden branches, saying, "*Allahou Akoubar*," which denotes "God is great." This funerary bed is called *tadguira*. As marabouts and male relatives carry the body to the grave, they sing *ezzeker*, liturgical songs in praise of God. After the grave digging is completed, and after mourners and marabouts accompany the body on this bed, they align themselves as they do on the prayer ground at Muslim holidays, standing in a circle. Again they proclaim "*Allahou Akoubar*," and the marabout leads a prayer for the deceased while everyone remains standing. Then the deceased is placed into the grave, the head always facing south but the face turned so that it is facing east (in the direction of Mecca). The grave is normally along a north-south axis. The body is buried, and verses are pronounced ensuring that "the earth on the body will be light."

Then the marabout and other mourners return to the household of the deceased's family for condolences *(iwichken)* and a memorial offering feast *(takote)* presided over by older women. Food and *eghale* normally served at other rites of passage are given to the marabouts and other mourners. The marabouts then silently read verses from the Koran and allow several small drops of saliva to fall into a goblet containing water, which is given to the relatives of the deceased to drink "in order to give them patience and to calm them." This is also part of the mystical force *al baraka* of marabouts, believed conducted through physical contact such as water, saliva, and clothing.

Funerals are held for suicides, despite official Islamic disapproval and the insistence that suicides do not go to paradise. But there is nonetheless a stigma, and of course great sorrow also is felt about suicides. In local memory, there had been two suicides in the region. One man had hung himself from a tree by his face-veil, and a woman had drunk the liquid of the *terza* plant, a large, milkweedlike vine whose acidic pulp is said to cause blindness as well as death.

More important than burials, therefore, are the condolences offered to living relatives at funerals just following it and memorial feasts held at intervals (usually after ten and forty days, but also sometimes when a living relative dreams of the deceased). Significantly, the latter are called by the same term *(takote)* used at the baby's nameday and denoting more generally alms, and by extension, good fortune. In other words, through almsgiving, there is conducted blessing. Many more people attend condolences and memorial feasts. In these, women and smiths predominate. Memorials also feature marabouts reading from the Koran and the singing of *ezzeker* liturgical songs. Sometimes, elderly women also sing liturgical songs praising God called *almodahan*. At memorials, *eghale (eghajira)* and other special foods, identical to those served at namedays and weddings, are served. But guests do not dress up or wear jewelry, and there are no secular musical festivals held afterward.

There is a forty-day period of mourning for spouses. There are Islamic and pre-Islamic beliefs surrounding this, and these may explain contradictions between men's and women's accounts of mourning obligations. Individuals volunteered information about this piecemeal, usually on the breaking of norms. For example, a woman friend cautioned me not to put my shoes facedown on the ground, because "this means a woman has a deceased husband." *El ladat* specifically refers to the waiting period before a woman who is no longer married can remarry; she is supposed to wear a cord around her neck to signify her status as widowed or divorced during this time. If she and her husband divorced, the time is three months; if he died, four months. The latter is known as *elkhukum,* which also denotes deceased husband. Dress conventions are also important. The widow refrains from wearing jewelry and must cover her arms down to the fingertips. During the mourning period, she cannot remarry. At the memorial, the widowed spouse sacrifices an animal whose meat, like the balls of *eghale* representing the joints of the deceased and linkages of kinship, is distributed to mourners. For several weeks, secular music is banned, in particular drumming, throughout the vicinity of the village or camp. Any weddings or other festivals are postponed.

Following deaths, older male marabouts rule on inheritance, applying Islamic law but also recognizing alternatives to this in local traditional law. They leave alms in a storehouse for the entire community, from a portion of the property of a deceased prominent elder.

The proximity of death is always recognized, and there is the general idea of submission to God's will in death. As shown, there are libations given in public rituals to deceased relatives. But Kel Ewey do not have altars devoted to ancestors, and individuals give memorial alms and offerings for somewhat different reasons than other peoples with highly elaborated cults, such as the Tallensi (Fortes 1959, 1987). Most Kel Ewey do not believe that there are personalized, deceased ancestors who continue to participate actively in all aspects of the lives of living descendants, or that they retaliate if neglected. The memorial meals accompanied by Koranic readings called *takote* are, it is true, explained as a kind of almsgiving. But the foods offered at these events are primarily offered to the related guests, albeit in the name of the deceased for whom the *takote* is held. Hence the problem with rigid distinctions between "ancestor cults" and other memorial rites, from the highly formalized cults of the Tallensi to less formalized Day of the Dead rituals in Latin American countries (Fortes 1959; Goody 1962; Brain 1973; Kopytoff 1970). In my own view, these differences are in degree rather than in kind.

Many Kel Ewey also occasionally, spontaneously, and in private give offerings of water, sugar, dates, or stones to a roadside tomb, especially one of a prominent marabout or saint. But there are fewer communal pilgrimages to graves on saints' holidays than in Morocco or other parts of North Africa (Crapanzano 1992). Kel Ewey also sometimes sacrifice an animal on Tabaski, the Islamic holiday, for a deceased relative. Nicolaisen (1961, 1963) and Spittler (1993) mention beliefs concerning dead souls, divination on cemetery tombs, and prehistoric stone mounds. But my own findings are largely in agreement with those of Spittler (1993:311) that there is not great preoccupation with individual graves.

In the Aïr, cemeteries consist of tombs and different configurations of stones, clustered together but not enclosed, on the outskirts of villages and camps or along the sides of roads connecting communities. As we walked home along an unpaved road between two caravanning villages where I worked, a smith woman friend indicated to me that the stone mounds alongside this road were built by the Kel Nad, remote ancestors who Kel Ewey say were previous inhabitants in the region. A noble man from a maraboutique family explained the diversity of graves or *idebni* as due to people walking by who add a stone or two as offerings. He advised me to do the same, or to offer a date or two when I took walks by these graves, to express respect for the deceased and also to protect myself from the spirits believed to haunt these graves, as well as prehistoric mound ruins, after sundown.

Sometimes, graves are believed to greet people on the road or even ask for belongings, especially children. At night, spirits associated with some tombs of famous marabouts emerge to threaten people walking too near them. One man, leaving a festival late at night, passed by such a tomb without his usual sword. It was said that due to lack of protection from its metal, the spirit attack left him "crazy" for some time.

Through libations, therefore, some graves become larger than others and vary in shape over time. The largest graves are the oldest, of the Kel Nad, called *ibedni*. The next largest are those of the grand marabout, founder of the Kel Igurmaden, an important descent group locally. Then come other graves, which together form contemporary and recent cemeteries (*yissimssa* or *chiteksa*). *Esekset* or *asemso* denotes an individual grave. The cord marabouts use to measure the body length upon death is left on top of recent gravestones; these cords constitute the sole marker of the deceased individual and are allowed to be swept away by the wind. Thus recent graves are more individually marked, and the effect is that the long-deceased tend to merge with ancestors of the more remote past, except for relative size and the varying numbers of stones added to the more important graves. For example, *idebni* refers to the large tombs of a saint or marabout, whereas *ibedni* denotes the ruins of Kel Nad homes.

Elders relate verbal art about the ancestors to elaborate on moral points in conversation, usually during evening tea drinking and visiting. An elderly noble woman from a maraboutique family told a series of brief narratives portraying ancestors and dead souls to illustrate Kel Ewey views on proper conduct toward, and treatment of, different social categories: in particular, elders, ancestors, and slaves. She emphasized the importance of generosity, almsgiving, and restraint in treatment of others. One of her tales concerned the Tomb of the People of the Past or Night:

Kel Nad

When one passes by (such) a tomb, one sees a bull who has no neck. It walks backwards. Arrived in this place, the bull becomes tall, as if touching the sky from the earth. He becomes very, very white. There were some women once before who were passing the *ibedni*. They were afraid. It is the *ibedni* that frightened them. They saw some cattle. They ran, the cattle also ran. The houses of

stones *[ibednan]*, tombs or ruins of the Kel Nad or Kel Arou [People of the Past],
they had objects underneath the stones. The people of the past had a lot of silver. They had rings, they had all that is in silver, bracelets, headbands, small jewelry, pendants, a necklace. These items are found where they had wars.
Sometimes because of that, they hid objects in the ground. The Kel Arou [con-
temporaries of the Kel Nad who waged war against the Kel Nad, both lived
before the Kel Geres in the Bagzan region], it is they who waged war.[3] Boulkhou
[first chief of the Kel Igurmaden descent group or section] and his group, the
ones who invaded, they chased them where they lived, the Kel Arou. Boulkhou
remained inside a well for 40 days, for 40 days suspended by a cotton thread on
the interior of a well in order to obtain his magic. He had an amulet for magi-
cal protection *[safitan]*, supernatural magic, divination. If the enemies saw them,
they were afraid, he became [transformed into] a dog or sometimes a goat, or
maybe disappeared completely. When the enemies left, Boulkhou came out of
the well. Then sometime [later], they attacked him behind a crevice, the women
hid their baggage inside the crevice. He told the women, "You must tie up the
ones who made the noise of rams and donkeys, in order that the enemies not
find the camp."

Here, Boulkhou is presented as an imposing figure, toward whom reverence
is due. Youths are supposed to humbly distance themselves from ruins associated with these early events in Aïr history. Conduct toward other deceased of
more immediate, traced ancestry should also be respectful. Indeed, the
purpose of libations at tombs is to seek protection or some other favor from
the deceased. But living descendants often feel "afraid" of them, in particular
the spirits haunting large tombs of important marabouts or saints and ruins of
the Kel Nad. For this reason, young people refuse to walk home from festivals
at night on roads lined with them. They prefer to walk through the oeuds
instead. By contrast, I found oeuds more difficult to navigate, and I preferred
to take the road connecting the two villages where I conducted most of my
research. One evening, I stayed with friends in a village about a mile down the
unpaved road much later than I had planned, and contrary to my usual practice of spending the night in such circumstances decided to return to my home
in the neighboring village. The rainy-season sky was unusually dark, devoid of
stars. My hosts asked if I was not afraid: *"Wur tehe tessa?"* (literally denoting
"have a liver inside," liver being the seat of emotions such as love, anger, and
fear). They were referring to the dark and the tombs on the road, and they
asked me to stay until morning. But I had not brought provisions, and there
was a quarter-moon out, so I convinced myself that visibility would be sufficient. So I thanked them but declined their invitation and left. Less than ten
minutes into my walk, to my dismay, the moon slipped behind the clouds and
the wind began to scatter the sand, smoothing out the road's truck tire tracks
normally visible, that I customarily used to guide my feet. Thus I was left in

total darkness except for the very small beam of my flashlight, inadequate in this situation. I proceeded cautiously but fearfully, trying not to panic. Finally, I reached home. Much relieved not to have gotten off track and lost in the desert at night, I collapsed into a tent that was filled with visitors in the smith neighborhood at the edge of the village. When I related my experience to them, they insisted that the tombs alongside this road had caused the moon to recede and the wind to erase the tire tracks. They cautioned me never to walk past tombs after dark again.

Other tales about the past, souls, and spirits portray dead souls of past slaves and refer to real life experiences of suffering, causing the slaves to return to haunt or cause misfortune in some other way in order to punish the perpetrators of crimes against them. The following tale was related to me by the same elderly woman in the noble and marabout family:

> *Head of Cheese* (Also the name of a small mountain in the vicinity)
>
> Like a head of cheese a slave had, that slave he was accompanied by someone [nonservile or a noble]. A thorn pricked the slave. He told his companion, "The thorn pricked me." The other person answered, "The thorn is nothing, it is not serious. You would think it was a lance, the way you complain." They fought on the spot, and the companion of the slave pierced him with the lance. When he pierced him with the lance, he died. When he died, the companion left. That is the reason why the mountain, Cheese Head, frightens people. The slave became a white ghost (the color of goat cheese) that frightens, called *tchissirmagh*. One time he took a child and put him inside the mountain. The child who was carrying a gourd somewhere, the ghost lifted him up and put him down again. The gourd broke. Now always he frightens people. Cheese Head. Everything that happens in the night frightens; sometimes you see a goat in the night and sometimes you hear camels who cry like that.

Another tale was related by the same woman:

> *Takawat* (Name of a village near a large oasis and holy center between Mount Bagzan and the Tenere, a vast desert plain in eastern Niger)
>
> In the past, there were people, some people gave the groom [in marriage], some gave the bride [i.e., to exchange in marriage, different groups gave either men or women]. The woman one married came from Takawat. The event was complicated. On the side of the groom, people came on the first day of the wedding. When they came, people became angry and criticized; the two sides disputed. When they came to the nuptial tent, there was millet placed all around like sand [in order to show their wealth in rivalry with each other]. The millet represented the sand, and when the side of the groom who arrived saw that, they left. In the morning, the people on the groom's side mounted their camels and a slave was in front of the rider, as a bull is today. They were trying to outdo the bride's side of the family [in wealth]. They chased the slave, who was crying out,

like the bull that is chased and slaughtered today at the elaborate bull weddings. He cried, cried, until he arrived at the nuptial tent. They cut him twice with swords like they do the bull today. At Takawat. The next day, in the morning, the people there, there was a strong wind that carried away the people and all their livestock. They were dispersed, all lost, and the earth swallowed them up. A lone person was carried off alive and put down by this wind in Hausa country to the south. It was he who related this news of the whole event. He gave them news, he said to them, "Our village was Takawat. The thing that made us disappear was the chasing of the slave by the cameliers. That is the reason the wind carried us away."

Ado, wind, is sometimes also associated with spirits, albeit less explicitly so than the *iska* wind and spirits in Hausa cosmology. These tales arose spontaneously, in conversations between residents and myself during evening visits. They were interspersed with discussions about moral conduct in general, specifically toward persons of different ages and social origins. For example, when we discussed long-term illness and death, parents told me that in principle they believe their children should care for disabled elderly parents, but they admitted that some children neglect them. When the subject of caretaking came up, or some other aspect of dependency—between parents and children, elders and youth—residents often alluded indirectly to past slave-noble relationships, thereby making analogies between age and social status relationships. They said, for example, that some people used to mistreat and insult formerly servile peoples, but that "true nobles" should not do this. They went on to say that mistreatment of slaves "is not a noble trait," not the conduct of Bagzan region nobles. One person was criticized for insulting descendants of slaves. Another was criticized for not caring for a debilitated parent by refusing to bring him water when needed, but this person was said to have improved their conduct following local gossip and pressure from other kinspersons. Children who do not care for elderly parents are said to "have no *al baraka*" or "have no head" *(eghef),* as slaves formerly were regarded. This imagery pervades morally interconnected themes—of youths respecting and later caring for elderly parents upon the latters' decrepitude—and their complement: as shown in Adoum's story, of nobles caring for former slaves in fictive kinship relationships. Social stratum and age are used to reinforce one another in situations of liminality or ambiguity. The life course becomes a discourse communicating and commenting upon social boundaries within Kel Ewey society, as well as between Kel Ewey society and outside forces.

Throughout mortuary rituals and myths addressing death and souls, there reverberate issues of authority. Elders, but most prominently older male marabouts who have reached the "prime" of professional practice, attempt to preserve official history, Islamic written dogma, through prayer, writing, reading, religious practices, and pilgrimages; by observing rules of silence on pilgrimages and purity/pollution rule in prayer; and by ruling on property transfers at marriage, divorce, death, and inheritance. But elderly women on the paternal side also enjoy respect. Informants respectfully wrote these women's names in the sand rather than pronouncing them in genealogies. Old women sing songs in each other's company on gathering expeditions and beside mosques on Islamic holidays, in particular, upon Ramadan, celebration of the end of the month-long fast, and sometimes they sing along with marabouts at mortuary rites. But elderly women depart from some aspects of the religious role of elderly men, in that, along with smiths, they are much more frequent tellers of non-Islamic tales. Elderly men assert they no longer tell such tales but prefer to read and recite the Koran.

Religion and age-related values are therefore the primary standards against which local residents evaluate authoritativeness of knowledge claims (e.g., oral traditions; inheritance and descent rules; historic, legal, and aesthetic judgments), but underlying this idiom are class distinctions. Citation of sources of information concerning origins and legal practices is locally identified with the Koran. Marabouts voice these values, giving an Islamic overlay to history and myth. For example, they explained the difference between spirit terminologies, *kel essuf* and *eljenan,* as "due to Tuareg ignorance, before Islam, about the forces in the wild, so that they called them the Kel Essuf, or People of Solitude; whereas, later, upon Islamic conversion, the new Arabic-derived term, *eljenan,* came into use." But they nonetheless admitted that they considered these the same. They explained the custom of bridewealth as deriving from a local variant of the Adam and Eve myth: "Adam gave the first bridewealth for Eve by reciting the Islamic *ezzeker,* praises of God." One man described to me his experiences teaching literacy in French in his rural community. Despite his respected status as married man and father, jural adult, apprenticing marabout, and agricultural extension agent, he encountered difficulty in representing the state-sponsored educational literacy program, *Alphebetisation,* locally, due to his relative youth (about thirty-five years of age), compared to those targeted by the program for him to instruct, a group of men mostly older than he. He said that this made it impossible for him to teach these men, all senior to him in age, on his oasis.

Since youths "feel embarrassed" about acts that reverse roles of the usual student-teacher relationship, many youths felt more comfortable interviewing their joking-partners, cousins, or younger brothers- or sisters-in-law without reserve. Other persons, for example, mothers, affines, and ascending generations, were more shameful to interview. A schoolboy who assisted me early in my residence with collecting folktales and devising a few structured interviews could not ask these questions of his father, paternal grandmother, or paternal grandfather. He could, on the other hand, freely ask questions of a female herbalist and her daughter, unrelated to him and also marginal to the community because the daughter had an illegitimate child. Many elders insist "young people don't know anything." This belief is used to justify older persons' monopolization of herbalism and maraboutism, while their children only practice these skills in apprenticeships until the death of their parents.

As individuals become "older" (specifically, as locally defined, when their children are married), there is greater specialization in knowledge acquisition and monopolization of professional practices. The emphasis is upon dependency, for both males and females, in youth. One female herbalist I knew who was apprenticing with her mother refused to treat patients who came to her home while her mother, an elderly, renowned herbalist, was away on travel. She felt obliged to refrain from professional practice except in the presence and under the supervision of her mother.

Children and young women stop all performance of tales and riddles when elderly men and women approach because, in their own words, they are "ashamed" or "respectful." Only very old persons should tell origin tales considered "factual" history, as opposed to those considered "folktales," the latter being told by young women, adolescents, and smiths. One man told me that once he became old and practiced maraboutism, he stopped telling folktales (*imayen*, used to designate animal tales of mythical events associated with women and smith tellers and not validated by the Koran) and only told "true history" now. The former are dismissed by elderly persons and marabouts as "not Moslem and not true stories" or "children's tales," such as the myths attributing local origins to the woman named Tagurmat and her twin daughters.

Furthermore, rather than seeking credit for "originality" themselves in oral traditions, young people often deny that they know the type of "history" elders and marabouts tell. Here, they are eager to transfer credit to other tellers for fear of taking away the "voice" of elders and deceased ancestors. Friends of mine, youthful residents of either sex and diverse social segments, insisted that they did not know the tale about Tagurmat, a mythical female ancestress who led a battle on Mount Bagzan in the distant past. Young women say they are all descended from "the same grandmother" but hesitate to pronounce specific names or place them in tale texts, due to reserve and respect for the elders and the deceased. In effect, the deceased ancestors are authors of legends and songs, and the Koran is the word of God to the Prophet. These authors are set apart and revered. This explains the hesitation of youth, young women, and nobles to repeat them, except in measured words and by allusion, called *tangal,* a term also translated to me as a kind of "symbol" or "metaphor." Women may not tell stories in the presence of their mother-in-law. A man may only tell stories before his father-in-law provided the latter has asked him to do this. One does not initiate talk at all in front of parent, parent-in-law of either sex, or elder sibling or elders on the paternal side, without having been invited to do so.

These oral traditions reveal aging expressed in idioms of patriliny and social stratum, in order to emphasize authority: the ideal is to give to and care for others who are dependent, and for as long as possible to avoid dependency oneself.

But there is another face to this. In local founder/ancestor and other etio-logical myths, heroes are not exclusively patriarchal figures. Competing with parent-child or filial relationships as a model for identity is also an idiom of matrilineality, which conveys a different ideal of aging. The origin myth of a local descent group, the Kel Igurmaden, portrays twin daughters of Tagurmat, the female culture heroine/ancestress. An elderly female herbalist on Mount Bagzan related one version of this tale to me as follows:

> Once there was a woman whose husband killed her from jealousy when she watched some cameliers. He killed her when she was pregnant with two daugh-ters in her. He cut open the dead wife's stomach and removed the two daugh-ters. The relatives of the husband went to see him to kill him [in revenge]. They arrived and saw the two twin girls. They gave them water and left the husband [without killing him]. They said, "If we kill him (now) it will be a sin. We must first of all find someone to raise these twin girls." So they left him. When the twins grew older, one held medicines and the other touched people [to heal them]. One was called Tanike, the other Tachida. Tachida was the older girl, and Tanike emerged after her. They stayed on the Bagzan.

In another version, these girls each emerged from their mother's stomach hold-ing a medicine: one held charcoal used by marabouts, the other held tree barks used by herbalists.

The two daughters who emerged from Tagurmat's stomach became Kel Igurmaden and also founded herbal and Koranic healing professions practiced by elderly women and men, respectively, today. Recall that since Tagurmat is said to have defended her people in battle, this oral tradition figure competes in local ideology with the tale about Boulkhou.

Although elderly male marabouts often disdained the matrilineal mythol-ogy as "women's and children's tales" and not "true history," and emphasized origin tales with Islamic themes in their conversations with me, the matrilin-eal themes are nonetheless salient and have a social counterpart over the life course. Elderly female herbalists emphasized their complementary, rather than competing, relationship to male marabouts and their versions of history and Koranic healing. In other words, upon advanced age, persons of either sex practice professions that tend to break down the opposition between patrilin-eal and matrilineal versions of history. This suggests that upon increasing devotion to ritual roles of elder status, male-female gender opposition is sub-ordinated to the common, increasingly more salient category of age. Yet for aging men and women, patriliny and matriliny, Islam and pre-Islam are not so much inverted in importance or gender association, and gender roles are not so much reversed (Myerhoff 1978, 1992; Gutmann 1987) as they are complementary to each other. Upon aging, these bases of identity converge in common interests and are directed at similar goals of preserving cultural autonomy and the continuity of the social roles of youths. These themes are played out in the intensified participation of both men and women in rites of passage. For example, during rites of passage, elders work with key symbols that convey both hierarchy and complementarity: elderly women carry millet and dates in a procession promoting good luck for the child at unofficial namedays, and elderly smiths carry them to promote fertility of the marrying couple at weddings. Millet and dates also constitute tribute in traditional relationships between different social categories. Formerly, sedentized gardening peoples called *eghawalen* (a category of slaves who were not, in contrast to the *iklan,* owned but nonetheless stood in a relation of tribute and dependency to nobles) gave a proportion of their dates to noble patrons. Until the early 1990s, on certain oases, nomadic nobles who owned the date palms within the cereal gardens of oasis gardeners came in and collected them. (This practice, residents told me on my most recent field trip, has now ceased.) Dates have additional significance: they are frequently offered to tombs of deceased ancestors and marabouts and are sometimes worn by small children as amulets. Thus rites of passage and origin myths protect threatened boundaries. In microcosmic form, and with key symbols drawn from kinship, gender, and class referents, they address relations between household members that become hierarchical but also complementary and negotiable over the life course. The purpose of elders' roles is to maintain a balance between these cultural tendencies.

Accounts of life/death transitions and boundaries voice these concerns of cultural continuity, autonomy, purity of descent, and religion. Elders are narrators, verbally and nonverbally, in these dialogues. Kel Ewey notions of the life course direction, and their elaborations in myth, sociability, performance, and ritual derive from these concerns of symbolism and power rather than from biological or literal notions of age, or from linear, chronological senses of time. The poetics of aging and the life course are culturally constructed within larger contexts of social stratum, kinship, and religion. As a trope, this process contributes to texts for discourse about personal and collective destiny.

Yet other verbal art references to aging reveal contradictions and ambivalence, conveying an awareness of the politics of transitions, in particular over the developmental cycle of domestic groups. As Aihwa Ong (1987:116) points out, for too long anthropologists have tended to assume that the developmental cycle of the domestic group is a process that unfolds inevitably according to prescribed cultural norms. While I agree with Ong that cultural values and processes are not uncontested, nonetheless some individuals' resistance takes the form not solely of a "hidden transcript" in Scott's and Ong's sense but also of manipulation to suit diverse ends. Portrayals of age relations and their associated conflicts in much Tuareg verbal art express ideals of dependency and respect but also suggest tensions surrounding them and manipulations and resistance to them. Riddles contain jokes insulting elders whom youths purport to respect; for example, "What is this, a pillow of mortar? The faces of your father and mother." Significantly, riddles are told by young people. Some animal tales also indicate resentment of such ideals as reserve toward the mother-in-law, through violation of these affinal rules, thereby suggesting active manipulation of structurally based relationships and transitions. For example:

The Man and His Mother-in-Law

A man married the daughter of a woman. These two women always pounded *eghajira* for the husband. The man made some traps. Always, the wife prepared this for him. The husband asked his mother-in-law, "How do you gather the tree herb [ingredient] to make this?" He left. He arranged his traps and left to see how his mother-in-law got the ingredient.

While he was watching her, she gathered the herb and put it into her calabash. He left to try to do this himself. She then asked, "How is it that this man is obtaining the herb now [usually gathered solely by elderly women]?" And she left to watch him do this. While he was filling his basket, she said to him, "Your ostrich has been caught in the trap." They ran toward the ostrich. He took off the trap. He said to his mother-in-law, "Climb, climb the ostrich!" The ostrich ran. The woman fell little by little, until she fell off the ostrich. The ostrich stampeded the woman. The ostrich ran off. He was content.

This tale, of a genre called *imayen* that refers to a type of folktale told most often by young people and smiths, rather than the origin tales told by elders, portrays an unlikely outcome of a son-in-law's disrespect, suggesting a fantasy of resistance. Indeed, it would be unlikely to be told by an elderly woman, and I collected the tale from an adolescent male. The tale is not purely idiosyncratic; my transcriber-assistant identified it as part of the local repertoire of animal tales. Furthermore, it merits attention, whether "authentic" or not, as commentary similar to contemporary American soap operas. A man asks his mother-in-law, of whom he should never ask any question due to his reserve toward her, how she prepares the *eghale* drink. Later, the tale ends in gloating irony as an ostrich runs off with the mother-in-law on its back.

Another tale portraying an undercurrent of conflict is called "The Hyena and the Jackel":

The hyena and the jackal were very hungry. The jackal said to the hyena, "Let's assemble our old mothers and sell them at the market." When they assembled their old women, they left for the market. They got to a place and the jackal said: "Wait, I am going to urinate." When he urinated, he hid his old mother.

He left to follow the hyena. He followed. When he arrived, he said, "Hyena, my old mother is lost. We will sell yours now." Hyena said "All right, I agree." They bought seven donkeys and seven sacks of millet (with the money from selling hyena's old mother). They walked a distance, to a place. The hyena followed behind and the jackal walked beside the donkeys. He drove the donkeys to the place where he had hidden his old mother. When the hyena arrived, he told him, "The sand ate our donkeys with the millet. It left us the ears only." He told him, "Come, you'll see, they won't come out." When they pulled the ears, the jackal said, "They're broken," one by one. The hyena said, "I've lost my old mother and my millet."

In this mockingly irreverent reversal of the required respect toward the older woman as mother, there is also symbolic inversion of the process of marriage and bridewealth. The number seven corresponds to the seven-day intervals that are of ritual significance in the nameday and wedding rituals. They both involve a lull in identity, before attributes and behavior associated with a changed definition of person and social status are taken up. Women ride gaily colored donkeys to the festive "bull wedding" *(aduban n ezger)*, where a bull is given by the groom to the family of the bride, a special event. This is sometimes demanded by the bride's parents, in cases where the groom has sufficient resources to provide it, and is considered a higher-status wedding. Millet is among the gifts given by the groom to his new mother-in-law, generally called an "old woman" *(tamghart)* in Key Ewey conceptualization regardless of her age in chronological years. Here, underlying hostility and ambivalence are expressed toward the older woman, including the mother as well as the mother-in-law, thus targeting "mothers" on both sides of the family as focal points of bridewealth transaction and weddings. In contrast to the tale above, this tale also contains a warning: that alienation from respectful relationships and obligations toward older persons, particularly older women, ultimately results in deprivation for children.

The *tineseslem* or "greeting the tent" ceremony features verbal art with frequent satirical references to different age groups and social commentary on elderly persons, revealing conflicts between the generations in jural transitions on marriage. Its songs are performed by a standing chorus of young women, accompanied by the *tende* drum and the *asakalabo,* a calabash floating in water beat with a wooden stick. In principle, the songs are supposed to praise both sides of the recently married couple's family: relatives of the bride (also usually neighbors in the host village) who help greet and the visitors from the groom's side of the family. In principle, their purpose is also to "protect" the visiting in-laws from evil spirits. As shown, Tuareg believe spirits are particularly menacing at times of transition, and the "greeting the tent" ritual is one such event. Tuareg also consider sung words to work like amulets against evil forces.[4] The following verses convey this:

My soul has left [thinking about someone or something good]
My soul has left
The young girls who belong to me [i.e., who are on my side of the family]
Applaud, cry, my soul has left
Applaud, cry. Those who help the soloist
I cannot swear to this [i.e., a song is not supposed to necessarily be true
   or honest; it can flatter or exaggerate]
The women from the east, all are discouraged [i.e., they want more than
   that in singing]
He just passed me, a youth named Alhassan, a youth with a
   medium-toned complexion
You must clap loudly, to the west
The young girls on my side for the sake of God applaud
You must animate and help me out with the song
Young people who belong to me [i.e., those on my side of the family]

(Repeated refrain; vocables)

The elder, his place; [whereas] the youth in bed [i.e., she says to the elder,
   "You stay there in your residence where there is no bed, because you
   have no value as a husband; a woman prefers to marry a young man]
That's false, I cannot swear to it [i.e., you must not take me seriously;
   joking ambiguously]
My soul has left
I do not want an elder.
The women from the east [the guests] who are here.

And in another song:

I thank the three youths
(vocables)

Death, you must have patience with youths [she prays that youths do
   not die soon]

(vocables)

This song is for whom? It is for two youths
Where is Harouna? Where is Egur? [singer wants these men to dance]
My young people where are they, those who are of the smith quarter?
We have done greetings, greetings, for the youth
Greetings from the young man who is in Niamey
He greeted me on the radio [on a program]

(vocables)

The radio that he brought me with eight batteries
The price was 5,000 CFA [this is a joke]
A youth with his first face-veil, he must beat the *tende* drum
Greetings to the young people
Where is Jambo [a famous dancer]?

Where is my young husband?
You Samaghil, greetings for my Houche [in Niamey] and Ahoulou from
　　the young people
(vocables)
Greetings to the young people from my village
The travelers toward the north (Libya), greetings to my Mila [in Libya]
(vocables)
Thanks to God.

And further:

How my soul hurts me
Young people, youths, you must dance [for a song to be complete, it
　　requires dancers]
Song of Azori [man who had many camels, now deceased, a guide to
　　the Tenere and sweetheart of a woman who composed this song]
Which Azori
There are two different Azoris
My soul is hurt; who has my soul
There is an Igurmaden Azori [chief of the local descent group,
　　Kel Igurmaden]
And Azori of the Kel Awzanguef [her lover]
The word of Azori under the mountain in Tewar, it equals a camel
　　in value
Oh, my soul
There was an old senile one [reference to Azori's father] called Tchigo
He prevented him from returning [to me], the caravan to Bilma left
　　[i.e., Azori's father wanted him to go on the caravan]
He left with the caravan up to Youglou and Tablale [the last water points
　　before entering the Tenere]
My soul who has my soul
The word Azori said to the woman
Oh my soul
Who has my soul
Young women of my village
I am an orphan
Who has my soul
My friends, you must speak the word
Those who say my love, who cry from evening until dawn
Oh, my soul
How my soul is hurt
I am wounded, the wound is in my soul
Oh, my soul
Wound that it gave me, love that killed me

Oh my soul
In the name of God you understand me
Those women who do not want that [i.e., who are jealous]
Can go to the Upper Bagzan and dig a well
Oh, how my soul is wounded

Important themes emerge in these songs. First, there are two contrasts evoked, between youths and elders and between cognates and affines. The necessity to protect, as well as praise, the affine-guests through song is recognized; this implies some potential danger emanating from social tensions, and also some underlying awareness of reluctance to praise, that is, a tendency to insult or at least feel resentment toward them. Tuareg articulate danger in the metaphor of evil spirits, and songs performed with the *tende* are seen as warding off, or alternatively, "pleasing" them.[5] Second, the fact that these are held preferably at night, since affines are not ashamed to see each other then, and feature musical events with the *tende* drum, suggests an underlying recognition of potential confrontation as well as sociability and courtship here. In other words, congeniality might turn conflictual in tensions surrounding the couple during early marriage: bridewealth payments, groomservice and gifts, and disengagement of herds and kitchen.

The affine-cognate relationship in Kel Ewey Tuareg culture therefore brings to the surface contradictory aspects of intergenerational relationships. On the one hand, there is, on the surface, reverence shown toward "older" persons, that is, those having children of marriageable age: their names are forbidden to pronounce, ideally they should not be questioned, and younger persons generally try to avoid speaking about them at all. Older affines, in particular, are treated with the more extreme reserve. Parents are the object of ambivalent sentiments. Youths may apprentice under their parents but should refrain from fully practicing ritual and healing professions too independently before parents' death. Youths cannot, furthermore, pronounce the names of two popular musical instruments used in courtship, the *tende* mortar drum and the *anzad,* a bowed, one-stringed lute, before elders of the adjacent generation. Men and women, and members of all social segments, in principle deserve respect in later years. In practice, however, there is some variation on this, according to social stratum and context. Noble youths tend to feel free to tease old smiths and former slaves, as was evident in Adoum's case. Smiths display less reserve toward their parents-in-law than nobles do.

On several occasions in ordinary everyday sociability, I noticed new brides stop their conversations and adjust their headscarves upon the approach of their parents-in-law, exclaiming "Takarakit [reserve]," but exaggerating this gesture and smiling in a suggestion of mockery. But these ideals are nonetheless given lip service, albeit often by allusion or *tangal* rather than openly, by individuals from all social segments. Differences in practicing these ideals tend to occur in terms of degree rather than outright resistance. Thus the ideals are salient in Kel Ewey culture. But the issue here is, what do such contradictions imply about jural-political relationships and the status of individuals as they age? Exploring this question requires a closer examination of household and property dynamics.

Tuareg Aging and Economic/Jural Authority

Authority, dignity, reticence, allusion, reserve, and reverence upon aging are conve yed in the local "aesthetic" or "poetics" of aging, manifested affectively, and are expressed in emotion, ritual, and symbolism. These have a basis in jural and economic aspects of aging (inheritance, property, power, work). I now discuss how these alternately affect different persons from diverse vantage points. Here I continue the two interwoven strands of analysis in this book: how age is used as a commentary on boundaries, both internal and external to Kel Ewey society, on the one hand; and how life course field research articulates with anthropological concerns of ethnographic authority, offering additional insights into it, on the other hand. This leads into conclusions drawn from this dual focus.

Most inheritance is called *takachit* and refers to Koranic inheritance. In this form, one man receives what two women receive. All other forms (for example, a type called *akhu ihuderan,* meant to compensate for Koranic inheritance and protect women, and various types of preinheritance and gifts) are alternatives, if specified by the person before death, to counterbalance it. Koranic inheritance is considered automatic by marabouts unless otherwise specified in writing and with a witness. Much property from parents consists of preinheritance gifts (called *alkhalal*) bequeathed by parents before death. There is also a storehouse in semisedentized villages containing alms left from a portion of the property of prominent deceased elders, mostly chiefs and marabouts. Gardens usually are inherited from father to son or sometimes are simply started on empty, unused land. Examples illustrate these processes.

Atakor, father of a living chief, left as gifts to his children (of both sexes) a number of camels. He left a single camel to bring goods from caravanning trade. His children sold this one and divided the money obtained according to Koranic inheritance rules. He also left some donkeys to his children. One female donkey was sold, and the money was divided up in Koranic inheritance. A storehouse of his other belongings, grain and household items, is presided over by a daughter, who lives next door to it. Two of his gardens were sold and the money divided up Koranically. His thirty-two date palms also were inherited Koranically (that is, each son received four date palms to each daughter's two). He also gave one sword to each of his sons as a preinheritance gift before he died.

Another man, Almorada, left three gardens and several date palms. He made a gift of them divided among all his children before his death. He gave nine camels and a few date palms to three daughters as *akhu huderan* (literally denoting "living milk") property. This is a form of inheritance that must remain among women and must not be divided or sold without replacing it. Women describe it as a kind of long-term security for women; men speak of it as "alms" *(takote),* preferring to emphasize it as subordinate to Koranic inheritance. Two of Almorada's storehouses (presumably empty when he died) were not inherited, have not been purchased, and are currently used for storing goods by his family.

Akhmed on his death left one female camel, which he had inherited from his mother. All the family divided rights to the camel in her reproduction (articulated by Tuareg as "paws" of an animal). His personal effects were sold and the money divided according to Koranic inheritance rules.

A deceased woman, Ramatou, left her pots and jewelry to her daughters; these are not usually Koranically inherited but go from mother to daughters. Since she had owned the land beneath her residence, after her conical grass building was destroyed and its mats distributed as alms, the land was left empty for a year in respect for the deceased and then went to a married daughter, who rebuilt a nomadic *ehan* tent on it and now resides there.

Amina had a number of donkeys when she died. She had gradually sold them in her later years of life, in order to support herself, but she left no other herds. The remaining donkeys went to her surviving daughter.

Another woman, Mana, left a herd of twenty-one camels. A female camel from it, her bridewealth, was inherited along wth the others according to Koranic rules among her five daughters and one son (each daughter received three camels and her son received six camels). She had given her jewelry to her daughters before her death. One house and the land beneath it were given to her oldest daughter; this is an exception to the usual Koranic rule, and all members of the family agreed to it in this case. This oldest daughter is now a very old woman, about seventy, and a widow herself. Two goats were sold by the family for about 9,000 CFA (about $32); her son received twice as much money as each daughter from this sale, according to Koranic inheritance.

For Kel Ewey, different forms of property transfer offer alternatives and also points of dispute. A primary factor in this is the interplay between nomadism and sedentism, and how households vary along the continuum of this scheme. Another important factor is postmarital residence. As observed, throughout marriage, there is a struggle concerning where to live, since the terrain beneath the residence structures is as important in ownership as the structures on it. In the semisedentized caravanning villages where I worked most intensively, both men and women, in about equal numbers, owned the land beneath their residences. Rather than resulting from a fixed rule, however, this depends upon where the married couple decides to settle down after two to three years of marriage and, specifically, whether they remain near the bride's parents (in which case women own the land beneath the tent, regardless of later house additions to the property), or whether they leave and reside near the groom's parents (in which case the man owns the land). In more nomadic households, for example, cases where the husband is a caravanner and the wife active in nomadism with large herds, many people state that "it makes practical sense" to remain near the wife's parents, since the husband is gone for about five to seven months of the year.

Residents of either sex, even men, admit that most women should not give up their nomadic tent, at least before advanced age, acknowledging that this is a disadvantage for women jurally. Women say such women are "lazy," not wanting to bother weaving palm-fiber mats, and so forth. However, this is in part compensated by livestock ownership by both sexes. Women may have security in herds that offers as much security as ownership of the tent, if not more. But in order for this to be effective, the married woman must acquire sufficiently large herds to support her, and thus more nomadic women are more protected over time by livestock ownership than sedentized women. Furthermore, the tent, as shown earlier, occupies a very central symbolic as well as jural significance in the life course of the married couple, and men really do defer more to married women on the basis of their respected status as tent-owner.

In less sedentized, nomadic camps I studied in the same region, unlike the privately owned land system in the oases and semisedentized communities, land does not belong to anyone if left vacant, unless they have built a mud house on it, which is as yet rare in such camps. For example, at one nomadic camp about seven miles from my base of research, there were in 1991 no mud houses yet, only a small mosque and a storehouse. Many nomadic peoples use the camp as a base only. They are most often in pastures surrounding it, where the women build another nomadic *ehan* tent; the grass *tettrem* structure is rare in the pastures outside semisedentized villages and camps. But full-time nomadism is increasingly difficult as a sole means of livelihood. Most Kel Ewey admit that they must combine subsistence methods, for unless they own large herds, there is constant pressure toward sedentization throughout life. This lends great complexity to Kel Ewey subsistence and residence over the life course. For example, there is individual variation within many communities. In the seminomadic village where I resided the longest, for example, there were about ten fully nomadic men and women in the 1990s. They had land in the village but no houses, and these women took down their tents periodically during transhumence. They were usually in the pastures with herds, coming into the village only to see relatives. Most of this population, however, were more seminomadic, and some fully sedentized, practicing full-time gardening, maraboutism, or smithing.

Therefore, because residence structures and land beneath them are subject to a degree of dispute, manipulation, and uncertainty, many men and women attempt to participate as long as possible in nomadism—both sexes in livestock herding, men in caravanning trade—until, as they term it, they are "too tired" to continue in advanced age. At such a point, their pattern is to settle down in more sedentized clusters of homes, by preference with matrilineal relatives, while their children support them. They depend upon children and herds for support and often perform less demanding but still important tasks: women weaving mats for tents and making goat cheese, and men making ropes for camel trappings and caravan gear. This was apparent in the story of Chigdouane. Another woman, Amina (whose inheritance of donkeys was described above), was a neighbor of mine with whom I often visited in 1983–84, before she died in 1985. A noble woman of about seventy, she resided with her daughter, who was married to a caravanner whose relatives had gardens in the vicinity. Amina gave me this account of how she perceived her situation:

Well, now I have become old. The children do the herding. Now children do the herding, and I am at home. I (sometimes) go to [my relatives'] gardens and help with harvesting.[1] I receive my measure [of cereal]. I harvest wheat and corn. Then I bring it back home. I used to go to the well. We used to have to do the household work: pound grain, prepare meals. We did this only for the [immediate] household. After that, I took palm fibers, wet them, went together with women and chatted [while weaving mats]. When we finished, we returned and slept.

A long time ago, I was more alert. But now I am less so, because I am old. Now I haven't any "head" [eghef]. Now my work is here at home. I used to make many mats, go out and cut palm fibers, and return. I separated the fibers, cleaned them, and dried them. Then I took millet and pounded it. I fed the family. I did housework. When the children came in from pasture, I took the goats and watered them. I came back, and then the children left with their goats again. I prepared their meals. I did tasks, work around the house. If men were there, I pounded eghajira as well as the regular meal [millet, corn paste, or porridge, or wheat dishes].

Now I am old, and my strength is gone. I just do small tasks. I prepare palm fibers for mats and other things. I look for something to live on. I save little things. I make small purchases. I look for things to "put in my teapot." My work is here; it isn't something outside the home. I don't have much that takes me from my place. Also I am not strong. I can't, but I must try to move. I must find some purpose and not do nothing. So you make useful items, you sell them, you find your money. You put something "in your teapot." You don't do very difficult work. You make mats, tent ropes, caravan date containers. You do a little work; you must not exist for nothing.

Well, today, ill health has arrived, and I only watch. So today I must know God and contribute something useful. I can't do anything, only watch. I get up, walk a little, look for something to pick up. This is better when you don't have any more strength. Today with no more strength, what are you going to pick up? You get up, you thank God. There isn't much you can do, but you mustn't lead an empty life. Now something is causing my health to fail. This bothers me, now I have become poor. I must be capable. I see things going on that I don't like, but I keep my silence. I see things tolerated that I don't like, but I keep my silence. I see things tolerated, I just keep my mouth shut. You welcome something good, but it is always better to keep quiet. You have no influence on anyone. You look at God. When I am in bad health, I must stay calm until God alleviates it. I must not talk too much for nothing. At this time, people must all accept for the sake of God. If the work is pounding or crushing grain, well, all these things must be done. Today I can't do anything, and we are seated here now. One moment you can go see someone, and the next you aren't feeling well. You are here, you don't want to move. The people of God [i.e., marabouts] want you to come see them, but you can't. Staying in the same place is necessary.

Amina was born on Mount Bagzan. She had three children, all daughters, one of whom died. She was once widowed, once divorced. Her deceased husband had been a cousin of her mother; the divorced husband was of no kin relation. She divorced her husband because he became involved with another woman, who currently still resided in the same village as Amina but was now also widowed from that husband. Both husbands had been caravanners. Most elderly persons do not place so great an emphasis upon physical decline, weakness, and "not having a head," as a child would not. But Amina had a long history of physical illnesses: yellow fever during her youth and additional illnesses, including some diagnosed as possession by spirits. I noticed she and her daughter, though not herbalists, often treated each other for various ailments.

During her youth, Amina went south to Hausaland along with other families from near Mount Bagzan following the Tuareg revolt against the French. She spoke Hausa as well as Tamacheq, an ability found among many elderly women in Aïr—who, due to historical circumstances, had spent their youth in the Zinder region—but less common among young rural Tuareg women, who tend to be monolingual. From the first day of my arrival in her village, she visited me almost daily. This was contrary to the custom of many other elderly noble woman, who remained dignified and reserved in their conduct toward me until much later in my residence. I am not certain about the reason for her relative openness; others attributed it to her travels, but many elderly women had been to the south. Perhaps her relationship to me was an extension of her joking relationship with Ibro (pseudonym), her maternal nephew, and my hostess's brother-in-law.

The reminiscences of a noble caravanner whom I will call Alhosseini, an elderly man of about seventy-five from the village of my long-term residence, also offer an interesting perspective on economic and material life over time.

When I asked him to tell me a story about his life, he chose to concentrate upon his caravanning experiences; I did not phrase the question in terms of this particular topic. In his account, Alhosseini talks about his caravanning travel on the route south to Zinder and Kano.[2] Prominent themes here are his efforts to continue to participate in this as long as possible, even into advanced age. This is a source of continuing pride in male gender role identity, particularly among those who claim noble descent.[3] He also emphasizes gender, class, and ethnic/cultural distinctions through discourse on caravanning work:

> Women don't go to Hausa country. Not today. During the time of Kaousan, leader of the Tuareg revolt against the French, slave women went. It is necessary to have young men go bring the millet to Damargou [Zinder]. We never took women along then, only slave women at that time, long ago. Now there aren't any slave women [so no women go nowadays]. Our elders, they had slaves with whom they went on caravans. The slave women pounded *eghale* for their masters, while we stayed in Kano [with sedentized clients].[4] Now it is the children [boys] or "Buzu" men [descendants of slaves] who prepare the meal on caravans. Me, I [still go on caravans now], but I don't go to the wells. I only keep watch over our merchandise.
>
> When people begin travel to Hausa country, they begin preparations at home. In the beginning, when we left with our animals, we led them to where we slept and always hobbled them. When we continued the trip all day, we walked, walked [the camels were loaded with merchandise]. We made camp only in the evening. We let our camels circulate a little. We led them. [Then] we hobbled them for the night in the desert. If you let them spend the night in the desert unhobbled, thieves will take them. As you go south, there are a lot of thieves. When we start the trip again, we always keep water in water bags. There are certain spots where you gather wood. At the well you water your camels, but you need one camel to pull the bucket up to get water, pouring water into the basin [for all of them].
>
> There are times that we travel even in the night on a long trip, and later we make camp, let the camels browse a little and then hobble them beside camp. A well is 25 meters deep. The well at Takdofat in the Azawak [a region in central Niger, between Aïr and Damergou] is the only one that is not deep. That is a bad place. You cannot let your animals wander at all there, there is risk of their being stolen. Even before arriving at Tagdofat, you must always watch the camels, keep them under your eye. If you neglect this, they will be stolen by Kel Afela *imghad* [a tributary people of the Kel Afela division of Tuareg]. Even in Damargou we hobble and watch them and also the merchandise. If you leave on camelback, you cannot leave the baggage alone; there is a risk of its being stolen. The person who stays in camp watches the baggage and covers it if it rains. For sometimes, at the moment it rains, thieves will steal everything while you are inside a tent.
>
> Once we arrive in Nigeria, camels are freer because the people there are afraid of them, but we must still guard them and lead them. Upon arrival in Damargou

[Hausa country] when we lead the camels, we sell our merchandise there and also make purchases. On the way [down there], we do not load up the animals, but we stock up merchandise with our clients [living along the route in the region, who in traditional client-patron relationships, store it temporarily], . . . we pick it up only upon our return [back toward Aïr].[5] We are there, trading little by little, until arriving in Kano. In Kano, there are exchanges and profits, for example, saltpeter for tobacco, and palm mats, to meet our needs and our families'. . . it's in Kano where we find all that. After about three to four months in Kano, we return to Aïr.

The return trip is slow. We follow the pastures to feed the camels, stopping for two-to-three–day rests while we water and graze them, until [reaching] Aïr. We have by then bought clothing, shoes, small and large goods, perfume called Bint al Sudan, indigo cloth, robes, calabashes, jewelry, and candy for children. We also used to bring back clay pots from Hausaland but no longer [do so] now.

Noteworthy in Alhosseini's account is the way he imbues his life occupation—caravan trade—with typifications of gender, social stratum, and cultural autonomy. While noble Tuareg women enjoy high social status in the eyes of noble men, there is nonetheless a strict division of labor in caravanning. Women simply do not go on caravans; this is a male domain. Men say caravanning is "too exhausting" for women, except, notably, for slave women in the past, whom Alhosseini implicitly excludes from the category of "noble women." Noble men take pride in physical toughness and endurance, and caravan travel provides a showcase for these qualities. There is, in his opinion at least, still a danger of livestock theft, especially as one proceeds into the Azawak and Damargou regions of central and southern Niger. He perceives regions in the desert-savannah borderlands as theft danger zones. Significantly, this region, the border between agricultural sedentarism and more intensive pastoral nomadism, is the region of greatest political tensions in Niger (Bourgeot 1990) due to rivalries over farming and grazing. Recently the region was the focal point of contestation for Tuareg separatist groups against the central government and was also the scene of a massacre of Tuareg at Tchintabaradan in 1990.

Some older persons of noble descent perceive tributary *imghad* peoples to the west and south of Agadez as "impure," as less devout Moslems, and as prone to theft and other antisocial actions. The totally sedentized Hausa of urban centers in Nigeria are not as feared. They are believed to be "afraid of camels," thereby underlining the nomadic/sedentized distinction. Yet traditionally, there have also been elements of cooperation: for example, in client-patron relationships between Aïr nobles and semisedentized *ighawalen* clients in the south who have obligations of hospitality to caravanners and, in return, keep a portion of their merchandise (Baier and Lovejoy 1977). Yet Alhosseini regarded Kano, rather than Agadez, as the important center of trade goods for Kel Ewey despite its geographic distance from the Bagzan region, suggesting Kano's long-standing importance in Kel Ewey subsistence.

Throughout Alhosseini's narrative, therefore, are highlighted elements of boundary marking, within Kel Ewey society itself and between Kel Ewey and outsiders. Caravanning for many noble men remains a central symbol throughout the life course. Indeed, continuing his participation in caravanning is as crucial for maintaining Alhosseini's identity, based on descent and gender roles, as it is for his physical survival.

9

Aging, Ethnographic Authority, and "Objectivity"

Conclusions

The jural and economic bases of authority and autonomy through the life course became "data," not solely through structured interviews, genealogies, census results, and standard one-directional "participant-observation" going from myself as anthropologist to local residents as "subjects" of "observation"; but also, these data emerged from visits and conversations with friends who did not hesitate to question me for "news of my own life," as they termed it, as actively as I did of theirs. The most recurrent questions asked of me concerned religion, property, and marital and intergenerational roles and relationships. For example, women and men friends asked whether I had goats, where my mother and sisters resided, why I did not have children, and whether I "knew the duty of prayer." For my protection and good fortune in these matters, concerned friends urged me to see marabouts for amulets and to offer dates and stones to tombs as I passed by cemeteries in the desert. These questions as commentary reveal residents' focal concerns over the life course, but they reveal more as well. They also suggest the inherently incomplete nature of ethnographic knowledge over the long term and the double bind that researchers face in successive visits to the field over many years, during which their lives become alternately enmeshed with and estranged from those of the local residents. These two levels of analysis, interwoven as they are, need to be made explicit for they are dependent upon and influence each other in the construction of knowledge about age.

In terms of standard "data," Kel Ewey responses to my queries and their questions to me over the long term address social and jural relations with significant kinspersons and persons of diverse social origins, who specialize in rituals facilitating property transfer and the validation as well as the manipulation of preexisting property and power relationships. Having children changes one's status and the expectations about one's role. These processes are manifested in the numerous externals of personal expression: for example, only the very old tell origin myths, pronounce names of (and in effect speak for) deceased ancestors, and sing Islamic liturgical music, while they refrain from more secular pursuits seen as opposed to the concerns of Islam, official descent, and marriage. I have argued that Kel Ewey emphasize spiritual development in later stages of life, not solely because the old are intermediary between life and death, as would be tempting to conclude in the West's linear, chronological conception of time, but rather because of the need to concentrate powers that have been heretofore dispersed—physical, material, property, and abstract/esoteric—upon the marriage of children. Cultural identity and autonomy are dependent upon this. This ideology, while not a unitary characteristic equally shared by individuals of all social strata, is nonetheless salient in Tuareg culture and is not so much disputed as it is manipulated to advantage by diverse individuals in different ways. However, this ideology is most keenly felt by persons of noble origin, who are losing the socioeconomic bases of their prestige, both because of ecological disasters such as drought and diminishing pastures and because of political conflicts with the central government.

Religion is also an important source of identity and control as one's powers decline with aging. Generosity, almsgiving, and restraint toward persons in both literal and fictive kinship relationships also provide sources of support. Increasing powers of healing also protect older persons' status.

Once individuals become too frail to work, and in many cases also become bereaved upon a spouse's death, the role of children, specifically married children, becomes central to their survival. I collected a sample of twenty-two men and women who were beyond the economically active stage of their life: widows and widowers, divorced persons, and a few never-married persons of advanced age. Most persons within this sample, both men and women, were living adjacent to married daughters. The women had given up their nomadic tent and resided in a small conical grass building, either within the relatives' compound or off to one side but next door to it. Very elderly women no longer prepared meals but were fed either by a daughter or a daughter-in-law, or an adopted grandchild or niece. Where children had gardens, produce was obtained for them. Elderly women attempt to do a little harvesting as long as possible, and they are given 10 percent of the garden produce. In cases where children went on caravans and the elder owned one or more camels, they took the elderly relative's camel(s) with them, and goods were brought back to them. Some women made mats, which are taken to towns by their children and sold. Most personal effects were gradually given away to children as preinheritance.

Individuals of diverse backgrounds use restrictions in sociability, performance, and festival/ritual contexts to smooth over tensions surrounding transitions, as well as conflicts between different interest groups, both within the household and between classes outside it. Age imagery therefore constitutes an idiom for organizing other social categories. Kel Ewey invoke it to consolidate, and sometimes also to dispute and manipulate, authority. But they also invoke age for resistance purposes, for protection when facing outside, perceived dangers.

In terms of local responses toward my own quest for such "data," the limits of empirical understanding of such data become apparent, but in a way different from the sense conventionally discussed in ethnographies in general as well as studies of the life course. Much of residents' and my discussion of the ethnographic authority of such data involved local residents' analysis and judgments of my own life course. Since with each visit, friends, assistants, and acquaintances repositioned me according to local notions of personal destiny over the life course, the exegencies of extended field research required continuous work toward establishing a common ground between researcher and "subjects." The irony of this deserves comment in anthropological theory as well as that vast body of literature called "aging" and "the life course."

Thus while I grew closer to the community in one sense, as a result of frequent and long-term residence in it, with cumulative knowledge and closer friendships, in another sense I grew more estranged because my own life course was not taking the same direction as that of my "age cohorts." Superficially, this was manifested in the more obvious external material features of my personal situation, such as relative ritual devotion and different access to medical care, which had the results of reduced mortality and enhanced health (some of my own age cohorts would be deceased upon my returns or struck by catastrophic illnesses and disabilities; a few friends commented about my own seemingly "young" appearance, for instance my not losing teeth, and were aware of the existence of certain vitamins that aided health). Friends asked me if women in my own society could bear children later "because of certain vitamins they took." Although packages of medicines and other first aid I gave to friends partially relieved these problems, everyone knew these packages were short-term relief rather than permanent solutions, and that we had, over the long term, very different access to medical care in our respective communities. I could escape to the relative comfort of home, whereas they were vulnerable to the vagaries of regional droughts, famines, and political violence.

Efforts to make me similar to, rather than different from, them in dress, hairstyle, and make-up perhaps constituted unconscious efforts to minimize other, more profound differences between us. On each successive visit, many women encouraged me to resemble them closely in appearance. For example, many women urged me to wear the same ocher make-up and hairstyles they did at festivals. On one occasion, as I walked past the outskirts of the village toward the mountains, I wore a pair of loose black pants, approximately in the style of Tuareg men's pants, which some female researchers in Niger have found comfortable and also modest by local standards. This was, I hoped, an acceptable compromise when I went on a stroll. This was late in my field residence, and I felt emboldened to explore the terrain I was more familiar with. But most of the time I wore dress that conformed more closely, with slight modifications, to Kel Ewey women's standards: either a long skirt or a more traditional wrapper made of local indigo-dyed cotton. The pants did not provoke much reaction from young men who had traveled extensively, or some other residents who were more cosmopolitan or closer to me in some other respect (transcribing assistants, for example). But other residents were ambivalent about them. An elderly noble woman I often visited, named Fatima, caught sight of me and gently but reprovingly exclaimed: "Now you're like a man . . . not a woman, but a man. You've decided to become a man!" Small children chorused this disapproval less subtly, following me for a stretch of the route and giggling.

Over long-term, repeated visits, another focal issue arose: that of which household I would board with. Upon residing with a more sedentized family on a later field trip, for purposes of comparison with the more nomadic one where I had resided earlier, I was obliged to be very careful not to hurt my previous hosts' feelings. Research projects requiring slight variation of my travel over the region also caused some need to reassure friends that I was still happy in their community, but my research project required me to spend time in neighboring communities as well. Other local responses to me over time consisted of efforts to position me according to local concepts of duration and distance. When I returned in 1991 after a long absence, many women friends at first were puzzled that I had not returned sooner, for in their notion of geography they equated the United States with Niamey, the capital of Niger. I explained to them how much farther my own country was from the Aïr than Niamey by enumerating how many "nights" it took me to fly, in a plane, over a vast ocean, and then they understood more clearly the distance I had traveled and the duration of my absence.

On other levels, more subtly yet equally powerfully felt by local residents, were the different family situations—their having children, my not having them—and the discrepancies between outward religious practice—prayer versus lack of prayer—and all their implications for personal conduct, both in everyday life and in ritual and performance contexts. On still more subtle levels, even the implications of my casual visits to households were subject to local interpretation according to changing demographics and the developmental cycle of domestic groups. Postmarital residence patterns, in particular, affected mutual repositioning in the field. While earlier I could visit all four sisters in a family of close friends since they all were new brides still in their mother's household, and bring gifts of food and other items to them collectively as well as to their mother, later these sisters became dispersed into separate (though nearby) households. Henceforth, my visiting and gift bearing became an object of competition among them, and I had to visit them equally; otherwise they would interpret my individual visits as "preferring" to see one sister over another. Earlier this issue had not arisen, since they had all been in a central household. Even in interviewing, while the assumption among anthropologists is that "getting to know the people" better facilitates conducting interviews, sometimes, to the contrary, once one has crossed that boundary from friendly acquaintance to long-term friendship one encounters greater difficulty in conducting a structured interview, for this demands a more impersonal stance that my closer friends and I found awkward.

All of these differences became more, rather than less, apparent the longer I conducted research in the same region and the more often I approached the same individuals at different points in time. The irony is that a bridge, but also a gulf, is created in long-term research, in particular work on the life course. On the level of sheer quantity and detail, this provided very rich data by conventional ethnographic standards. On the more subtle level—of mutual repositioning and common ground—it created problematic dilemmas and relationships, and it also raised issues: for example, of the anthropologist's obligations to local residents, not solely during immediate visits but over the long term, both in the field and away from it, and of the limits, and also the direction, of so-called participant observation.

In anthropological theory and ethnographic analysis (Clifford 1988; Clifford and Marcus 1986; Rosaldo 1989; Crapanzano 1992), there has been considerable concern with the problematics of these principles applied by the anthropologist, and a number of works in aging studies (Myerhoff 1978, 1992; Blacking 1990:121–30) also make pioneering contributions in this area. But scant attention has been devoted to the practice of participant observation, in reflexive and dialogical terms, on the subject of age by local residents, in the life course of local residents' as well as the researcher's lives. Several critical ethnographic works have emphasized local residents as active subjects rather than passive objects, in their conducting of a kind of research in response to the outside ethnographer, in works emphasizing the mutuality of field encounters (Stoller and Olkes 1987; Gottlieb and Graham 1993). Despite reflexive intentions, and sensitivity to power imbalances and material poverty-based differences between researcher and researched, there is still the need to focus more intently on the construction of knowledge about the life course in the condition of separation between anthropologists' and local residents' life experiences over the long term. This gulf has implications for the process of long-term association and knowledge acquisition about aging as a topic, which need to be explored further in and of themselves and incorporated into life course data more explicitly.

Long-term field research provides insights, but the "depth" of knowledge and the kinds of relationships it presupposes are themselves problematic. It is tempting to suppose that this is one reason why many anthropologists eventually abandon conducting field research in their "original" site, moving in subsequent trips to a more urban one or changing culture areas and topics altogether. The physical demands of a small, rural community in nations where the material conditions of living are considered "rough," compared to those that the aging middle-class professional is accustomed to at home, may play a role in this. Yet researchers seldom openly admit that this influences their long-term field research in later years.

More significant here, however, are the emotional demands of contrasting life conditions and diverging life experiences, which become increasingly visible to both parties over time. These cannot go unnoticed. Simply stated, studying the life course raises the following question: if I were to remain permanently in this community where I work, living exactly like its people, where would I be, both in terms of my personal life condition and in terms of anthropological knowledge? And further, if I were not to remain (as is usually the case), what directions would my relationships with local residents take, and why? It is the interface between the researcher's own changing life situation and that of local residents, and the discrepancies between them, that affects ethnographic findings more and more over time as a mediating force. Life course research brings (or should bring) these issues into sharper focus, and these issues in turn illuminate the life course.

What insights do the issues yield? Throughout my field visits, key "informants" and their narratives contributed to multivocal constructions of knowledge. I have presented these narratives approximately in order of their openness and familiarity to me, on the basis of when we established mutual trust. I have shown that life history narratives and the exegesis of beliefs and practices are largely influenced by local categories of social stratum, kinship, and gender as well as age, but also by my own relationships to friends and assistants, which were shaped through local lenses of interpretation. Tuareg cultural values such as reserve or respect, restraint, generosity, and speech by allusion were prominent in many of these roles and relationships. In terms of data and the construction of knowledge about aging, this produced a multi-nuanced and emergent portrait. It was ironic and illuminating, yet not too surprising, that individuals who were somewhat atypical elders—less constrained by reserve in expression of their sentiments—became key informants early on precisely because of their greater freedom to comment on norms surrounding age. Yet these persons did not always practice these norms themselves, nor did they always receive the customary rewards. Individuals more representative of normative statements about growing older tended to respond more openly to my own questions later in my research. These contrasting personalities do not so much contest one another as act as "foils" to each other, illuminating multiple voices and also common themes in the Tuareg life course.

Relevant here are not solely the position and roles of persons of different ages as they are affected by other crosscutting social relationships and statuses but also the experience of age and the construction of knowledge about age. Hopefully, what has emerged here is what different Tuareg individuals define as their own major concerns regarding their past, present, and future. The issue here is the production of knowledge of oneself and others over the life course, both within Tuareg society and outside by researchers who begin with an idea of "the Tuareg life course" and "the Tuareg" more generally. This book, I hope, contributes to the question of whose ideas the idea of the Tuareg life course has been, from diverse points of view—who created it and for what purposes. Outside visitors and researchers have tended to describe Tuareg in terms of isolated, watertight categories of gender, social stratum, kinship, and political organization. They have also tended to overemphasize the viewpoint of one or another social stratum. For example, many generalizations about Tuareg women's social status are based on the experience of noble women and neglect the experience of women of different ages and social strata who stand in different kinship roles and relationships (Rasmussen 1995). Persons in chiefly and marabout clans tend to emphasize Islam, the maternal tent, and purity of descent as concerns of increasing importance over the life course. As shown, persons of noble origin tend to observe values of reserve and allusion more strictly as they age. Individuals of diverse social origins who have children in officially preferred marriages and have affines living nearby, fulfilling the idealized obligations, view the life course from yet another special angle, drawing on alternative resources. Persons of servile descent, as well as persons of diverse origins without kinship and economic resources, on the other hand, do not always participate fully in these official structures of age. They still assert a voice of their own, however, and exert power over ethnographic representation. They can comment critically on social events and benefit from alternative forms of support.

Thus despite a cluster of key values surrounding the Tuareg life course, different participants in Tuareg society drew myself as long-term visitor and researcher into their dialogues and narratives in different ways. They thereby expressed contrasting notions of the life course and enacted or created the life course continually in interaction with myself and with each other. This process presents age in a different light. In age, certain borders are redrawn according to imagined and real purposes. In culture, aging is part of a series of stories that addresses the question of who one is, where one comes from, and where one is going. Yet aging study must not be analyzed in linear terms. Rather, it must be analyzed in terms that capture, as completely as possible, many possibilities.

Notes

1. Droughts have struck the Saharan and Sahelian regions of Africa, the most serious occurring in 1913, 1969–1974, and 1984. For documentation and analysis of ecological conditions in Aïr, see Bernus (1981) and Spittler (1993). For discussion of historical background to current economic and political conditions in Niger, see Charlick (1991). See Dayak (1992) for discussion of recent Tuareg nationalist/separatist movements and rebellions in Mali and Niger. There is a paucity of data on demographic trends among the Tuareg. In Niger, rural infant mortality rates, often reported at 60 percent, can be deceptive since they represent a mean, subject to distortions. Likewise, while the average age at death in Niger is officially stated to be 44.5 years (Background Notes, U.S. Department of State Bureau of Public Affairs: Niger, June 1987), this figure may be influenced by extremes: a significant number of deaths occur at weaning age, but many who survive past this critical phase live well into postchildbearing years. Infertility rates are difficult to establish; for Tuareg, these do not appear unusually high. Most Tuareg women in the rural region of my research bore between six and eight children in their reproductive years; only a few women were childless. STD's, while present in Niger as elsewhere, are difficult to document as a causal agent in infertility. HIV infection, while not yet as widespread as in some other African regions, has entered Niger and is spreading through exposure to migrant labor and other traveling persons (*New York Times*, February 8, 1996). But the significance of these trends is difficult to interpret, and they are beyond the scope of the present study. Rather, here I am interested in subjective local experiences and interpretations of childhood, adulthood, parenthood, childlessness, and other aspects of the life course.

2. Within these theories, I refer to such concepts as Myerhoff's expressive/instrumental opposition, which she applies to gender roles over time, and I also refer to debates in gerontology such as that between disengagement and activity theory.

3. Here I am concerned, not solely with methodological problems, but rather with the intertextuality of ethnographic data, construction of knowledge, and mutuality of field experience, in an interpretive but also dialogical sense. My own concern approaches what Rosaldo (1989:3–5) and Blacking in Spencer (1990:123) mean when each author discusses, respectively, the interpretation of Ilongot responses to death and roles of Venda elderly women and young girls in infancy rituals.

4. I taught English as a Peace Corps volunteer from 1974 to 1977, and under contract for the Ministry of Education from 1977 to 1979, in Niamey (the capital) and Agadez. I conducted research in the rural Aïr Mountains near Mount Bagzan in 1977, 1978, 1983, 1991, and 1995. In my early visits I focused upon general culture and

language study; more recently, I studied female spirit possession, aging and the life course, and female healing specialists.

5. While these works provide valuable insights into Tuareg ethnography, none of them focuses specifically or in depth upon aging and the life course. Nicolaisen (1961, 1963) mentions older persons briefly in his analysis of Air Tuareg religion and also refers to them in general terms in his discussion of kinship and descent. Keenan (1977) only implicitly mentions relationships between the generations in his material on socioeconomic change and education among the Tuareg of the Algerian Hoggar Mountains. Casajus (1987) concentrates upon matrilineality and marriage, and includes some references to death, in his primarily structural analysis. Dayak (1992) refers very briefly to elders in his documentation of cases of military atrocities. Claudot-Hawad (1993) offers a general ethnohistorical and ethnographic study, with sections addressing such age-related practices as tent construction and men's face-veiling, but does not analyze these in terms of life course issues. Spittler (1993) provides a useful section on mortuary rites and beliefs concerning death but only those aspects that are relevant to his study of Kel Ewey subsistence and responses to drought and famine.

Introduction

1. There has been uneven economic development in Niger since French colonialism and independence (Charlick 1991). Famines, unemployment, and ethnic conflicts have resulted in labor migration, predominantly by young men, to towns in Niger and countries beyond such as Libya, Ivory Coast, and Nigeria. As of this writing, there are Tuareg refugee camps in Mauritania. There are also political exiles in France. The political details of the Tuareg Rebellion, from 1991 to 1995, are beyond the scope of this book, and moreover, their documentation is scanty as of this writing. Bourgeot (1990 and verbal information, 1995) discusses political conflict in the late 1980s between Tuareg migrants returning from Libya and the government of Niger. Dayak (1992) presents an argument and evidence in support of recent separatism, including documentation of regional development discrepancies and military atrocities.

2. See Rasmussen (1992) for discussion of rural Tuareg smiths' ritual roles, and Nicolaisen (1963), Baier and Lovejoy (1977), and Bernus (1981) for more general discussion of precolonial Tuareg social organization. Smiths among Tuareg are sometimes described by nobles as "next to slaves," although smiths themselves deny this and until recently did not intermarry with former slaves. Like other peoples in Niger (the Hausa and Zarma-Songhai), Tuareg society is characterized by stratified, hereditary occupational groups who have traditionally practiced client-patron relationships and, also in the past, slavery (slaves usually being captives taken in war). In rural areas, descent remains significant. In its precolonial form, African servitude was in many respects very different from slavery in the Western Hemisphere. I am fully aware of problems of translation in terminology; therefore, I provide brief exegesis of local terminology reflecting finer distinctions, but due to space constraints, I use the English term throughout this text. Slaves were manumitted early in the twentieth century.

In many other West African societies, such as the Wolof and the Songhai, griots or oral historians have a status apart from smiths. For discussion of smiths and griots in other African cultures, see Wright in Arens and Karp (1989) and Herbert (1993).

Among the Aïr Tuareg, smiths play a very important role approximating that of griots in these other stratified societies. Aïr Tuareg smiths recite genealogies, historical legends, and folktales, sing praise-songs, and also manufacture jewelry and household items for noble patrons. They officiate at many rituals alongside Islamic scholars or marabouts. Thus Aïr Tuareg smiths combine oral historian and artisan roles. In the towns, many Tuareg smiths are becoming more specialized as jewelers for tourists and functionaries. In my view, discussion of Tuareg social stratification and reference to individuals' social origins is relevant, indeed essential, to any multi-nuanced analysis in order to represent the diverse "voices" and to avoid totalizing generalizations in ethnographic representation.

3. See Nicolaisen (1961, 1963) and Murphy (1964, 1967).

4. See Rasmussen (1994, 1995). Women in more nomadic communities tend to retain the tent and keep more numerous livestock. In addition, there are other, more subtle differences: for example, animal sacrifice in more sedentized communities is done by men and, in principle, forbidden to women. Yet when women are out at pastures, friends indicated to me that they often sacrifice animals, though the implication here is that men are absent at such times. Islamic scholars in some respects challenge traditional Tuareg legal measures protecting women: for example, many marabouts tend to rule in favor of men in divorce property disputes and minimize the importance of non-Koranic inheritance. Yet in other respects, residents of either sex seem to regard certain Islamic and pre-Islamic Tuareg beliefs and practices as complementary: female herbalists, for example, insisted that their cures and those of marabouts are related, "like husband and wife," and performed many prayers and ablutions similar to those of marabouts in their healing.

5. See Salifou (1973).

6. *Imghad,* or tributary peoples, are believed to have been former Tuareg nobles who were subjugated by other nobles in battle. Tributary peoples raided and traded for nobles. Keenan (1977) discusses how gradually they accumulated arms and livestock through usufruct and other client-patron arrangements. Kel Ewey social organization is distinct from that of some other Aïr Tuareg groups in that *imghad* are not found among this confederation. See also Nicolaisen (1963) and Bernus (1981).

7. The traditional leader of most Aïr Tuareg groups is the Sultan of Aïr in Agadez; whereas the Kel Ewey leader, also in Agadez, is the Anastafidet. Both these leaders traditionally had the status of the *amenokal,* somewhat similar to Hausa *emirs,* in other Tuareg confederations; they did not exert absolute authority, but rather mediated between the warring descent groups and supervised economic activities, for example, caravan trade. Today these leaders still exist, but their traditional powers have been curtailed. They are primarily in charge of tax collection and school registration. For detailed discussion of their precolonial and recent roles, see Rodd (1926), Salifou (1973), and Nicolaisen (1963).

8. There are many variants of matrilineal origin myths, within and between the different confederations and clans. For details see also Rodd (1926), Casajus (1987), and subsequent sections of the present study.

9. For example, *akh huderan* or "living milk" herds are passed to sisters and nieces and cannot be sold. In addition, there are many preinheritance gifts. See subsequent sections of the present study, and see also Casajus (1987) and Rasmussen (1991a, 1995).

Chapter 1: Phases of the Life Course and Household Cycles

1. There have been a number of explanations for the Tuareg men's face-veil, ranging from social (Murphy 1964, 1967), to religious (Nicolaisen 1963; Casajus 1987), to symbolic/aesthetic (Rasmussen 1991b).

2. Many slaves were manumitted by the French after the 1917 Tuareg Senoussi Revolt led by Kaousan, although domestic slave labor continued in a few areas until mid-century. Traditional social distinctions persist more in ideology than actual practice among rural peoples, except in the case of smiths, whose roles, while modified, are still specialized. But this ideology is expressed in oral art (current as well as traditional songs, tales, and poetry) and informal conversation. On these subjects, see Rodd (1926), Baier and Lovejoy (1977), Keenan (1977), and Bourgeot (1990).

3. Damagerem is the term for the southern region of Niger where the Hausa predominate. Hausa are also numerous in the Aïr town of Agadez, which has recently been becoming more multiethnic.

4. Among the Kel Ewey, most communities are semisedentized. Men build and own mud houses, women build and own tents. But there is some variation in ownership of land beneath the residence structures, according to the degree of nomadism and the location of the postmarital residence.

5. For complex reasons, some Tuareg of servile origins have become prosperous. In rural areas, many could inherit from former owners. In settled oases and towns, servile peoples were exposed to more secular schools. This factor, along with initial ambivalence among nobles toward secular schools, resulted in a greater representation of persons of servile origins in jobs in the infrastructure of the towns. In addition, former slaves (as well as smiths) in some Tuareg groups were more willing than nobles, initially, to take up manual labor. Kel Ewey, however, tend to display less reluctance toward manual labor than some other groups, particularly today. Although gardening is still slightly stigmatized by some Kel Ewey nobles, many have taken it up. Yet nomadic stockbreeding and caravanning remain more prestigious, idealized, and romanticized in the culture. Many individuals indicated that they would prefer full-time herding or caravanning but could not subsist on these activities alone in current conditions. Gardens are easier to replace than herds after a drought, and one needs large herds to support oneself solely from nomadic stockbreeding. Kel Ewey combine subsistence more extensively than some other Tuareg. But recently, Tuareg of diverse social origins have suffered upheavals in subsistence conditions.

Chapter 2: Aging, Gender, and Social Stratum

1. Formerly, nobles monopolized most resources (arms, camels, caravan trade). A slave was sometimes included in a marriage dowry. Yet not all nobles owned slaves, and there were fine distinctions among the different servile peoples—most notably, between the recently captured, owned persons *(iklan)* often from outside groups, who performed domestic and herding labor, and persons more closely approaching "client" status *(eghawalen),* sedentized gardening populations who gave a proportion of their produce to noble overlords who came in from the desert to collect it and who often also owned date palms within client gardens. During my residence in Aïr in the 1970s and

1980s, I noticed some vestiges of former client-patron relationships. For example, nobles collected dates within clients' cereal gardens on some oases, and formerly servile women in one clan assisted noble women with mat and tent construction. In exchange the latter received sugar, tea, and millet. But by the early 1990s, local residents told me that these practices had been discontinued.

2. See Rasmussen (1991a).

3. *Al baraka,* which may approximately be translated as a mystic blessing force, is believed to emanate from Islamic scholars and to be connected to their charisma. Kel Ewey often also use this term to convey happiness, prosperity, and good luck in general. See Nicolaisen (1961, 1963) and Rasmussen (1991a) for a more complete discussion of this force.

4. The *agar* tree is believed to have medicinal properties and also to be haunted by spirits.

5. *Eghajira* (or *eghale,* as it is more commonly called around Mount Bagzan) is, along with tea, perhaps the most important beverage in Tuareg society. The grain infusion is pervasive in Tuareg rituals, in particular rites of passage, and Islamic holidays. It is also consumed when traveling, for example, on caravans. It is made of pounded millet, goat cheese, and dates, and is dried into doughlike balls until ready for consumption, when it is occasionally eaten, but more commonly mixed with water and drunk with large, ornately carved wooden ladles. It resembles the gruel drinks in other parts of Africa, but unlike brewed beers of non-Islamic peoples, it is not fermented.

6. *Aborak,* or *Balanites aegyptiaca,* is often used by smiths to make wooden spoons and ladles.

7. *Essuf* denotes "wild" and "solitude," conveying a state as well as a location outside villages and camps, a sense of desolate loneliness and remoteness from civilization. Spirits of the wild or solitude *(kel essuf)* are believed to possess humans, most often women (Rasmussen 1995). In this context, the term is used to refer to marriage with an outsider (i.e., a man not from the maternal tent, distantly related or unrelated to the bride's family). Among Kel Ewey, official preference as voiced by older women is for marriage among close cousins on the maternal side, especially children of sisters; many youths, however, prefer more distant matches, and my own census material is in accordance with Murphy's observations (1964, 1967) that in practice most marriages are to distantly related or unrelated persons.

8. Bridewealth among Kel Ewey consists of one camel and various gifts. The advantage of close cousin marriage is that it keeps resources within the family.

9. Although polygyny is permitted by Islam, many Tuareg women resist it. See Rasmussen (1991a).

10. Nowadays there are two caravan routes still followed: to the East, to Bilma, near salt mines, where caravanners pick up salt and dates; and to the South, toward the Hausa towns of Zinder and Kano, where caravanners trade salt, dates, millet, and household and luxury items. For a more complete analysis of caravanning trade see Baier and Lovejoy (1977) and Bernus (1981).

11. These forces are variously translated as "evil eye" and "evil mouth," that is, they are based upon jealousy of property or good fortune. *Tezma, tehot,* or *tégaré* (varying regional terms) refer to specialized mystic powers believed activated by smiths upon nobles' refusal to give them presents. For the social dynamics of these forces, see Rasmussen (1992).

Chapter 3: Life Course Rituals

1. Specifically, see Crapanzano on "Rites of Return" (1992).

Chapter 4: Intergenerational Relationships and Intercultural Encounters

1. In particular, see Bernus (1981).
2. The history of Aïr includes a series of wars. These include the war between the Kel Geres and the Kel Ewey, Tubu raids, the Tuareg Rebellion against the French in 1917, and most recently, the separatist rebellion. See Bernus (1981) and Dayak (1992).
3. For extensive analysis of initial resistance by nobles in Algeria, see Keenan (1977).
4. See, for example, remarks on the subject of relationships with children by Stoller and Olkes (1987) and by Mead in the film *Taking Note*. Rabinow (1977) also alludes to this briefly. But none of these authors frames discussion of relationships with children explicitly, as I do here, in terms of intergenerational roles, resistance over the life course, and ethnographic authority and repositioning issues.

Chapter 5: Parents and Children, Anthropologist and Residents

1. Male caravanners usually leave the Bagzan region in October and return in April, being absent on these expeditions for about half a year, during the cold, dry season. During this time, wives of caravanners support themselves on herds and on produce from relatives' gardens, as well as grain and other produce stocked in storehouses from the caravanning trade of the preceding year. Households tend to be more matrifocal during this time. Sisters and mothers pool food and share cooking more closely than they do during men's presence at home.
2. Many nobles, especially men, have traditionally attributed to themselves the most reserve. This is connected, albeit not equivalent to, other factors such as intelligence and proximity to spirits. Children, women, and smiths, stereotypically having less reserve and intelligence, also stand closer to the spirit world. Yet these qualities are subject to manipulation and transformation through time. For example, as individuals grow older, regardless of social origins, they tend to view themselves and to be viewed by others as increasing in reserve. But nonetheless noble male elders are said to possess more reserve than female, smith, and former slave elders. Thus reserve is possessed in varying degrees.

Chapter 7: Youths, Elders, and Ancestors

1. The *tende n goumaten* possession exorcism ritual is usually staged for women for the purpose of curing them of spirits called the "spirits of the wild or solitude" that are believed incurable according to Koranic verses. Women say they are often struck by these spirits upon hearing beautiful music. In contrast, men are believed most often possessed by spirits curable by Koranic verses called "illnesses of God," which often strike them in mosques while they are reciting the *ezzeker* that praises God. What is sig-

nificant here is that both sexes may become possessed; it is the respective cures that are distinct. The former are considered "effeminate," featuring music of the *tende* and a special trance dance involving primarily the head of the possessed. The latter are considered masculine. See Rasmussen (1989, 1995).

2. See Nicolaisen (1961). Diviners indicated to me that this skill requires "pleasing" the spirits by making offerings of animals, perfumes, etc.

3. Kel Nad appears to be a term that Kel Ewey use to refer to non-genealogical or vaguely genealogical ancestors who are not precisely traced.

4. Amulets (generally called *ciraw*) are of several types. Many are visual, manufactured by smiths and marabouts. The smith makes a leather or silver case, and the marabout inserts Koranic verses believed to ward off illnesses and other misfortunes on papers inside. Another type, however, is aural. This consists of the alleged power of words on their subject; for example, many songs sung at female spirit possession rituals are said to have this effect, as are the songs of the "greeting the tent" ritual. The mouth *(imi)* is also associated with dangerous forces, in particular, "evil eye" and "sorcery"; it is considered particularly vulnerable to spirits. This is in fact one explanation of the men's face-veil (Casajus 1987; Rasmussen 1991b).

5. The *tende* instrument is identified with the ground, the spirits, women, and smiths and lower social strata. It is the centerpiece of most youthful evening festivals and is also a generic term for musical events where the instrument is featured.

Chapter 8: Tuareg Aging and Economic/Jural Authority

1. Menstruating, childbearing women do not harvest, whereas elderly, postchildbearing women do. These restrictions are part of the complex of "menstrual pollution beliefs," as these are conventionally termed in the literature. See Rasmussen (1991a).

2. The Bilma route is considered more dangerous and exhausting; thus Alhosseini no longer travels on that route.

3. The relationship between social stratum and caravanning trade is complex. On the one hand, many older noble men tend to idealize this occupation and attempt to participate as long as possible; but often, they manage it from a distance, sending either younger male relatives or descendants of slaves on the actual expedition.

4. See Baier and Lovejoy (1977) for a description of degrees of servitude and clientage as well as hospitality obligations toward nobles in the southlands. Many such clients are sedentized, long-freed slaves who practice specialized trades and have to varying degrees become integrated into Hausa culture.

5. On these expeditions, caravanners sometimes lodge with clients or former slaves in southern Niger and northern Nigeria and sometimes camp outside population centers. Baier and Lovejoy (1977:391-411) describe how some clients were once slaves but now reside in areas beyond direct control and today owe only hospitality to their former owners.

Works Cited

Abu-Lughod, Lila
  1990   The Romance of Resistance: Tracing Transformations of Power through
            Bedouin Women. *American Ethnologist* 17(1):41–55.
Arens, William, and Ivan Karp, eds.
  1989   *The Creativity of Power.* Washington, D.C.: Smithsonian Institute Press.
Aries, Phillipe
  1962   *Centuries of Childhood.* New York: Vintage.
Bachelard, Gaston
  1964   *The Poetics of Space.* Boston: Beacon.
Baier, Steven, and F. Lovejoy
  1977   The Desert-Side Economy of the Central Sudan. In *The Politics of
            Natural Disaster: The Case of the Sahel Drought,* edited by M. H. Glantz,
            pp. 144–75. New York: Praeger.
Barth, Heinrich
  1857   *Travels and Discoveries in North and Central Africa, Being a Journal of an
            Expedition Undertaken under the Auspices of H.B.M.'s Government in the
            Years 1849–1855.* London: F. Cass.
Batoutah, Ibn
  1843   Voyage dans le Soudan (traduction sur les manuscripts de la biblioteque
            du Roi par M. MacGuckin de Slane). *Journal asiatique,* Paris.
Bernus, Edmond
  1981   *Touaregs nigeriens: Unité d'un people pasteur.* Paris: Editions de l'Office de
            la Recherche Scientifique et Technique de'Outre-Mer.
Bird, Charles, and Ivan Karp, eds.
  1897   *Explorations in African Systems of Thought.* Bloomington: Indiana
            University Press.
Blacking, John
  1990   Growing Old Gracefully: Physical, Social, and Spiritual Transformations
            in Venda Society, 1956–1966. In *Anthropology and the Riddle of the
            Sphinx,* edited by Paul Spencer, pp. 121–30. London and New York:
            Routledge.
Bohannan, Laura
  1964   *Return To Laughter.* New York: Anchor Books.
Bourdieu, Pierre
  1977   *Outline of a Theory of Practice.* Translated by Richard Nice. Cambridge:
            Cambridge University Press.

Bourgeot, André
1990   Identité touarègue: de l'aristocratie à la revolution. *Etudes Rurales,*
            120(Oct.–Dec.):129–62.
Brain, James L.
1973   Ancestors as Elders in Africa: Further Thoughts. *Africa* 43:122–33.
Briggs, Jean
1970   *Never in Anger.* Cambridge: Harvard University Press.
Buckley, Thomas, and Alma Gottlieb, eds.
1988   *Blood Magic: The Anthropology of Menstruation.* Berkeley: University of
            California Press.
Cartry, Christiane
1978   Jeux d'enfants Gourmanche. In *Systèmes de signes. Textes réunis en hom-
            mage à Germaine Dieterlen,* pp. 73–78. Paris: Hermann.
Casajus, Dominique
1987   *La Tente dans l'Essuf.* London: Cambridge University Press.
1990   Islam et noblesse chez les Touaregs. *L'Homme* 115, juillet–septembre,
            XXX(3):7–30.
Charlick, Robert
1991   *Niger: Personal Rule and Survival in the Sahel.* Boulder, Colo.: Westview
            Press.
Claudot-Hawad, Hélène
1993   *Touareg: Portrait en fragments.* Aix-en-Provence: Edisud.
Clifford, James
1988   *The Predicament of Culture.* Cambridge: Harvard University Press.
Clifford, James, and George Marcus
1986   *Writing Culture: The Poetics and Politics of Ethnography.* Berkeley:
            University of California Press.
Cole, Thomas
1992   *The Journey of Life.* Cambridge: Cambridge University Press.
Cowan, Jane
1990   *Dance and the Body Politic in Northern Greece.* Princeton: Princeton
            University Press.
Crapanzano, Vincente
1992   *Hermes' Dilemma and Hamlet's Desire: On the Epistemology of
            Interpretation.* Cambridge: Harvard University Press.
Croll, Elizabeth
1990   The Social Construction of Parenthood in the People's Republic of
            China. In *Anthropology and the Riddle of the Sphinx: Paradoxes of Change
            in the Life Course,* edited by Paul Spencer, pp. 147–56. London and New
            York: Routledge.
Cumming, E., and W. E. Henry
1961   *Growing Old: The Process of Disengagement.* New York: Basic Books.
Dayak, Mano
1992   *Touareg, La Tragédie.* Avec la collaboration de Michael Stuhrenberg et de
            Jerome Strazzula, sous la direction de Jacques Lanzmann. Paris: Editions
            Jean-Claude Lattes.

De Certeau, Michel
1984   *The Practice of Everyday Life.* Translated by Steven Randall. Berkeley: University of California Press.
Devereux, George
1956   Normal and Abnormal: The Key Problem of Psychiatric Anthropology. In *Some Uses of Anthropology: Theoretical and Applied.* Washington, D.C.: The Anthropological Society of Washington.
Di Leonardo, Michaela
1990   *Gender at the Crossroads of Knowledge.* Berkeley: University of California Press.
Duveyrier, Henri
1864   *Exploration du Sahara: Les Touareg du Nord.* Paris: Challamel, Ainé.
Foner, Nancy, ed.
1984   *Ages in Conflict.* New York: Columbia University Press.
Fortes, Meyer
1959   *Oedipus and Job in West African Religion.* Cambridge: Cambridge University Press.
1987   *Religion, Morality and the Person.* Edited and with an introduction by Jack Goody. Cambridge: Cambridge University Press.
Foucault, Michel
1972   *Archaeology of Knowledge and the Discourse on Language.* New York: Pantheon.
1980   *Power/Knowledge: Selected Interviews and Other Writings.* Edited by Colin Gordon. New York: Pantheon.
Fry, Christine L., ed.
1981   *Dimensions: Aging, Culture, and Health.* New York: Praeger.
Geertz, Clifford
1973   *The Interpretation of Cultures.* New York: Basic Books.
Gellner, Ernest
1969   *Saints of the Atlas.* London: Weidenfeld and Nicolson.
Gluckman, Max
1965   *Politics, Ritual, and Law in Tribal Society.* Oxford: Basil Blackwell.
Goody, Jack
1958   *The Developmental Cycle of Domestic Groups.* Cambridge: Cambridge University Press.
1962   *Death, Property, and the Ancestors: A Study of the Mortuary Customs of the Lodagaa of West Africa.* Stanford: Stanford University Press.
Gottlieb, Alma, and Philip Graham
1993   *Parallel Worlds.* New York: Crown Publishers.
Gutmann, David
1987   *Reclaimed Powers: Men and Women in Later Life.* Evanston: Northwestern University Press.
Herbert, Eugenia
1993   *Iron, Gender, and Power: Rituals of Transformation in African Societies.* Bloomington: Indiana University Press.
Herzfeld, Michael
1985   *The Poetics of Manhood: Contest and Identity in a Cretan Mountain Village.* Cambridge: Cambridge University Press.

Huizinga, Johan
1950   *Homo Ludens: A Study of the Play Element in Culture.* Translated by R. F.
          C. Hull. New York: Roy.
Jackson, Michael, and Ivan Karp, eds.
1987   *Personhood and Agency: The Experience of Self and Other in African
          Cultures.* Washington, D.C.: Smithsonian Institute Press.
Jean, C.
1909   *Les Touareg du Sud-est: L'Air.* Paris: Emile Larose Librairie-Editeur.
Katz, Cindi, and Janice Monk, eds.
1993   *Full Circles: Geographies of Women over the Life Course.* London and New
          York: Routledge.
Keenan, Jeremy
1977   *Tuareg: People of Ahaggar.* New York: St. Martin's Press.
Keith, Jennie
1980   The Best Is Yet to Be: Toward an Anthropology of Age. In *Annual Review
          of Anthropology,* vol. 9, edited by Bernard Siegal, Alan R. Beals, and
          Stephen A. Tyler.
1985   Age in Anthropological Research. In *Handbook of Aging and the Social
          Sciences,* edited by Robert Binstock and Ethel Shanas, pp. 231–64. New
          York: Von Nostrand Reinhold Co.
Keith, Jennie, and David Kertzer, eds.
1984   *Age and Anthropological Theory.* Ithaca: Cornell University Press.
Kopytoff, Igor
1970   Pietas in Ancestor Worship. In *Time and Social Structure and Other
          Essays,* edited by Meyer Fortes. London: Athlone Press.
Le Moal, Guy
1973   Quelques aperçues sur la notion de personne chez les Bobo, pp.
          193–203. In *Colloques Internationaux de Centre National de la Recherche
          Scientifique* No. 544.
Lévi-Strauss, Claude
1963   *Structual Anthropology.* New York: Basic Books.
LeVine, Robert
1978   Adulthood and Aging in Cross-Cultural Perspective. *Items* 31/32:1–5.
1980a   A Cross-Cultural Perspective on Parenting. In *Parenting in a Multi-
          Cultural Society,* edited by M. Fantini and R. Cardenas, pp. 17–27. New
          York: Longman.
1980b   Adulthood among the Gusii of Kenya. In *Themes of Work and Love in
          Adulthood,* edited by Neil Smerser and Erik Erikson, pp. 77–105.
          Cambridge: Harvard University Press.
LeVine, Robert, and Richard Schweder, eds.
1984   *Cultural Theory: Essays on Mind, Self, and Emotion.* Cambridge:
          Cambridge University Press.
Lhote, Henri
1955   *Touaregs du Hoggar.* Paris: Payot.
Lukes, D. W., ed.
1968   *Aristotle.* Oxford: Clarendon Press.

Manheimer, Ronald
1989   The Narrative Quest in Humanistic Gerontology. *Journal of Aging Studies* 3(3):231–52.
Maybury-Lewis, Davis
1984   Age and Kinship. In *Age and Anthropological Theory*, edited by J. Keith and D. Kertzer. Ithaca: Cornell University Press.
Mull, Dorothy S., and J. Dennis Mull
1987   Infanticide among the Tarahumara. In *Child Survival: Anthropological Perspectives on the Treatment and Maltreatment of Children*, edited by Nancy Scheper-Hughes, pp. 113–32. Boston: D. Reidel Publishing Company.
Murphy, Robert
1964   Tuareg Kinship. *American Anthropologist* 69:163–70.
1967   Social Distance and the Veil. *American Anthropologist* 66:1257–74.
Myerhoff, Barbara
1978   Bobbes and Zeydes: Old and New Roles for Elderly Jews. In *Women in Ritual and Symbolic Roles*, edited by Judith Hoch-Smith and Anita Spring, pp. 207–45. New York: Plenum.
1979   *Number Our Days*. New York: Simon and Schuster.
1992   *Remembered Lives*. Ann Arbor: University of Michigan Press.
Nicolaisen, Johannes
1961   Essai sur la Religion et la Magie touarègues. *Folk* 3:113–60.
1963   *Ecology and Culture of the Pastoral Tuareg*. Copenhagen: Royal Copenhagen Museum.
Norris, H. T.
1972   *Saharan Myth and Saga*. Oxford: Clarendon Press.
1975   *The Tuareg: Their Islamic Legacy and its Diffusion in the Sahel*. Wilts, England: Aris and Phillips, Ltd.
Ong, Aihwa
1987   *Spirits of Resistance and Capitalist Discipline*. Albany: State University of New York Press.
Ottenberg, Simon
1982   Boys' Secret Societies at Afikpo. In *African Religious Groups and Beliefs*, edited by Simon Ottenberg, pp. 170–84. Cupertino, Calif.: Folklore Institute.
Parkin, David
1991   *The Sacred Void: Spatial Images of Work and Ritual among the Giriama of Kenya*. Cambridge: Cambridge University Press.
Pottier, Jeanne
1946   *Légendes Touaregs*. Paris: Nouvelles Editions Latines.
Rabain, Jacqueline
1979   *L'Enfant du Lignage. Du sevrage à la classe d'âge chez les Wolof du Senegal*. Paris: Payot.
Rabinow, Paul
1977   *Reflections on Fieldwork in Morocco*. Berkeley: University of California Press.

Rasmussen, Susan
　1987　　Interpreting Androgynous Woman. *Ethnology* 26:17–30.
　1989　　Accounting For Belief. *Man* (n.s.) 24:124–44.
　1991a　Lack of Prayer. *American Ethnologist* 18(4):751–69.
　1991b　Veiled Self, Transparent Meanings. *Ethnology* 29:101–17.
　1992　　Ritual Specialists, Ambiguity, and Power in Tuareg Society. *Man: Journal of the Royal Anthropological Institute* 27(1):105–28.
　1993　　Speech by Allusion: Voice and Authority in Tuareg Verbal Art. *Journal of Folklore Research* 29(2):155–77.
　1994　　Female Sexuality, Social Reproduction, and the Politics of Medical Intervention in Niger: Kel Ewey Tuareg Perspectives. *Culture, Medicine, and Psychiatry* 18:433–62.
　1995　　*Spirit Possession and Personhood among the Kel Ewey Tuareg.* Cambridge: Cambridge University Press.
　1996　　The Tent as Cultural Symbol and Field Site: Social and Symbolic Space, "Topos," and Authority in a Tuareg Community. *Anthropological Quarterly* 69(1):14–27.
Read, Margaret
　1960　　*Children of Their Fathers: Growing Up among the Ngoni of Nyasaland.* New Haven: Yale University Press.
Richards, Audrey
　1956　　*Chisungu: A Girl's Initiation Ceremony among the Bemba of Northern Rhodesia.* London: Faber and Faber.
Riesman, Paul
　1986　　The Person and the Life Cycle in African Social Life and Thought. *The African Studies Review* 29(2):71–138.
Rodd, Francis Rennell
　1926　　*People of the Veil.* London: Anthropological Publications.
Rosaldo, Renato
　1989　　*Culture and Truth.* Boston: Beacon Press.
Rowland, Jacky
　1992　　The Tuareg Rebellion. *Africa Report* 37(4)(July):43–45.
Rubinstein, Robert L.
　1990　　*Anthropology and Aging: Comprehensive Reviews.* Boston and Dordrecht: Kluwer Academic Publishers.
Said, Edward
　1979a　*Orientalism.* New York: Pantheon Books.
　1979b　Representing the Colonized: Anthropology's Interlocutors. *Critical Inquiry* 15(Winter):205–25.
Salifou, A.
　1973　　Kaousan ou la révolte senoussiste. *Etudes Nigeriennes,* no. 33. Niamey: IRSH.
Scheper-Hughes, Nancy, ed.
　1987　　*Child Survival: Anthropological Perspectives on the Treatment and Maltreatment of Children.* Boston: Reidel.
Scott, James
　1990　　*Domination and the Arts of Resistance.* New Haven: Yale University Press.

Smelser, Neil, and Erik Erikson, eds.
1980   *Themes of Work and Love in Adulthood.* Cambridge: Harvard University Press.
Sokolovsky, Jay, ed.
1989   *The Cultural Context of Aging: Worldwide Perspectives.* Grandy, Mass.: Bergin and Garvey Publishers, Inc.
Spencer, Paul, ed.
1990   *Anthropology and the Riddle of the Sphinx: Paradoxes of Change in the Life Course.* London and New York: Routledge. ASA Monographs 28.
Spittler, Gerd
1993   *Les Touaregs face aux sécheresses et aux famines: Les Kel Ewey de l'Aïr (Niger).* Paris: Karthala.
State Department
1987   *Niger: Background Notes.* Washington, D.C.: United States Department of State, Bureau of Public Affairs, June.
Stenning, Derrick
1958   Household Viability among the Pastoral Fulani. In *The Developmental Cycle of Domestic Groups,* edited by Jack Goody. Cambridge: Cambridge University Press.
Stoller, Paul, and Cheryl Olkes
1987   *In Sorcery's Shadow.* Chicago: University of Chicago Press.
Turner, Victor
1967   *The Forest of Symbols.* Ithaca: Cornell University Press.
Van Gennep, Arnold
1905   *The Rites of Passage.* [1960 rpt.] Chicago: Chicago University Press.
Wright, Bonita
1989   The Power of Articulation. In *The Creativity of Power,* edited by William Arens and Ivan Karp, pp. 39–57. Washington, D.C.: Smithsonian Institution Press.

Index